Sport in Scandinavia and the Nordic Countries

The Scandinavian and Nordic countries have some of the highest participation rates in sport and physical activity in the world and are therefore important case studies across a range of subjects, from sport policy to physical activity and health.

This is the first book to bring together studies of all those countries in one volume, examining sport, physical activity and exercise, and exploring the factors behind such high levels of participation. Rich in empirical data, the book examines trends in sports participation, organisation and policy in each of the constituent countries, highlighting common themes and outcomes.

This is a valuable resource for students, researchers and academics working in the fields of sport, physical education, leisure, sport policy, sport development, the sociology of sport and physical activity and health.

Ken Green is Professor of Sociology of Physical Education and Youth Sport and Head of Sport and Exercise Sciences at the University of Chester, UK. He is also Visiting Professor at Innland University of Applied Sciences, Norway and Editor-in-Chief of the *European Physical Education Review*. Ken's main research interests revolve around physical education and youth sport in the UK and Norway.

Thorsteinn Sigurjónsson is Associate Professor of Sport at Innland University of Applied Sciences, Norway, and a former Head of Sport and teacher of school physical education. His main research interests include children and orienteering.

Eivind Åsrum Skille is Professor of Sports Sociology at Innland University of Applied Sciences, Norway and a Visiting Professor at UIT, The Arctic University of Norway, Norway and the Russian International Olympic University, Russia. His research interests revolve around sports policy and politics, sports organisations and youth sport.

Routledge Research in Sport, Culture and Society
Knowledges, Practices, Structures
Edited by Thomas F. Carter, Daniel Burdsey and Mark Doidge

99 The Aesthetics, Poetics, and Rhetoric of Soccer
Edited by Ridvan Askin, Catherine Diederich and Aline Bieri

100 Politics and Identity in Chinese Martial Arts
Lu Zhouxiang

101 Corruption, Mafia Power and Italian Soccer
Alberto Testa and Anna Sergi

102 Researching Difference in Sport and Physical Activity
Edited by Richard Medcalf and Chris Mackintosh

103 Surfing and Sustainability
Gregory Borne

104 Women, Sport and Exercise in the Asia-Pacific Region
Domination, Resistance, Accommodation
Gyozo Molnar, Sara N. Amin and Yoko Kanemasu

105 Gender Diversity in European Sport Governance
Edited by Agnes Elling, Jorid Hovden and Annelies Knoppers

106 Figurational Research in Sport, Leisure and Health
Edited by Dominic Malcolm and Philippa Velija

107 The Historical Sociology of Japanese Martial Arts
Raúl Sánchez García

108 Sport in Scandinavia and the Nordic Countries
Edited by Ken Green, Thorsteinn Sigurjónsson and Eivind Åsrum Skille

https://www.routledge.com/sport/series/RRSCS

Sport in Scandinavia and the Nordic Countries

Edited by Ken Green,
Thorsteinn Sigurjónsson and
Eivind Åsrum Skille

LONDON AND NEW YORK

First published 2019 by Routledge

2 Park Square, Milton Park, Abingdon, Oxfordshire OX14 4RN
52 Vanderbilt Avenue, New York, NY 10017

Routledge is an imprint of the Taylor & Francis Group, an informa business

First issued in paperback 2020

British Library Cataloguing-in-Publication Data
A catalogue record for this book is available from the British Library

Library of Congress Cataloging-in-Publication Data
A catalog record has been requested for this book

ISBN: 978-1-138-05215-4 (hbk)
ISBN: 978-0-367-52027-4 (pbk)

Typeset in Goudy
by Deanta Global Publishing Services, Chennai, India

Contents

Figures

Tables

Contributors

Trygve Laub Asserhøj is Consultant at the Sports Confederation of Denmark, Denmark and recently worked as an Analyst at the Danish Institute for Sports Studies, Denmark. As an Analyst at the Danish Institute for Sports Studies, Trygve's main research areas were sports participation in Denmark and Greenland (in cooperation with the Sports Federation of Greenland).

Josef Fahlén is Associate Professor in Education and works as Senior Lecturer at the Department of Education, Umeå University, Sweden, as well as Visiting Professor at the Norwegian School of Sport Sciences, Norway. He currently serves on the editorial boards of *The International Journal of Sport Policy and Politics*, *European Sport Management Quarterly* and *European Journal for Sport and Society*. Josef's research is concerned with the intersection between sport policy and sport organisation and, more specifically, with the political use of sports clubs as vehicles for social change. His recent work includes an exploration of national structures for building and managing sports facilities in the Nordic countries and the role of voluntary sports organisations in the implementation of physical activity policy, as well as state sports policy towards indigenous sport.

Magnus Ferry is Senior Lecturer at the Department of Education, Umeå University, Sweden where he teaches on the Sport Science and Physical Education Teacher Education programmes. His research is concerned with the development of the Swedish school sports system, beginner physical education teachers' backgrounds and beliefs, and sport participation patterns among children and youth.

Viðar Halldórsson is Associate Professor of Sociology at the University of Iceland, Iceland. His main research interests revolve around the positive development of youth sport and the cultural production of sports achievement. Viðar also serves as a Sports Consultant for Icelandic youth and high-performance sports.

Pasi Koski is Professor of Physical Education at the University of Turku, Finland. Having previously lectured at the University of Jyväskylä, Finland, for the past 20 years he has taught under- and postgraduate students at the University of

Turku, Finland, and supervised PhD students in the field of sociology of sport and physical education. He has been Editor-in-Chief of *Liikunta & Tiede [Sport & Science]*. His main research interests revolve around physical education, sport management and youth sport.

Kati Lehtonen is Researcher at the LIKES Research Centre for Physical Activity and Health in Jyväskylä, Finland. Her main research interests focus upon on sports civic activities, sport organisations (from sport clubs to business-oriented firms) and sport policy. She has also conducted evaluation studies related to government subsidies and sports development projects.

Maja Pilgaard is Acting Director at the Danish Institute for Sports Studies and has worked as Head of Research in the Department of 'Sport for All' at the Danish Institute for Sports Studies, Denmark. The department conducts research in various areas concerning sports participation, facilities, voluntarism, municipal sports policy, commercial sport and exercise as well as non-formal adult education. Maja has worked with changes in the ways of organising sport and exercise in different population groups (i.e. age, gender, education, geography), and how such changes affect and challenge existing structures in the sporting landscape.

Ørnulf Seippel is Professor of Sociology of Sports at the Norwegian University of Sports Sciences, Norway. Ørnulf's main research interests are sport and organisations, sport politics, social inequality, social capital/integration and social networks.

Hanna Vehmas is Senior Lecturer on the International Master's Degree Programme in Sport Management and Health Promotion at the Faculty of Sport and Health Sciences at the University of Jyväskylä, Finland. Her research interests and activities focus on sport participation, the societal role of sport and physical activity, sport and health-related tourism, sociology of sport and leisure, and, most recently, on the private sport sector and the correspondence between sport education and employment. She has been an active member in the Finnish and European academic sport management, sport sociology and tourism organisations. Since 2016, Hanna has served as Secretary General of the European Association for Sociology of Sport.

Chapter 1

Introduction

Ken Green, Thorsteinn Sigurjónsson and Eivind Åsrum Skille

The case for studying sport in Scandinavia and the Nordic region

At a time when governments across the developed world are showing growing interest in sport and physical activity (PA) as vehicles for combatting a range of so-called 'lifestyle diseases' (e.g. cardio-vascular disease, stroke, type-2 diabetes and cancer), increasing attention is being paid to the Nordic countries (where sports participation is high and health-related PA relatively commonplace) as models of 'good practice'. Nowadays, governments of all political persuasions promote sport as a vehicle for public health gains but nowhere more so than in the Nordic region. Sports participation and PA have become important public health issues in all Nordic countries, especially in relation to young people (Støckel, 2010).

As Bairner (2010) has noted, the relative dearth of interest in Scandinavian and Nordic[1] sport (beyond the region itself) is, therefore, somewhat surprising given the seemingly high levels of participation and the particular features of Nordic sport – vis-a-vis Nordic societies – which may or may not be transferable. This collection seeks to address that omission.

As well as the prominence of health in PA and sports discourses, the propensity of young people and adults to take part is also an expression of the social significance of sport and physical recreation in the region: Bairner (2010, 736) talks of "the overwhelming sense that sport matters in those countries". Nowhere, perhaps, better epitomises Crum's (1991, 15) depiction of the 'sportisation of society' since the 1970s than the Nordic countries, where sport has gained enormous cultural traction (Roberts, 2016a). Cultural traction refers to the rootedness of sport in what sociologists might call the 'group habitus' or 'natural attitude'; in other words, those aspects of physical culture deeply embedded in the everyday attitudes (or 'second nature') and practices of individuals and groups in particular societies and nations – the habits acquired (via socialisation) by Nordic peoples as a consequence of growing up and living in cultures within which sport and physical exercise are so common-place and so highly valued.

Nordic countries make a particularly interesting case-study of the cultural traction of sport, not least because their (sporting) cultures contain within them – in the form of *friluftsliv* – what, historically, has amounted to an almost ideal type or archetypal example of PA as a style of life. Literally translated as 'free or open-air living', but more generally and colloquially taken to mean outdoor life and activities, *friluftsliv* has been described not only as the Nordic way of outdoor recreation but also as a chief characteristic of the Nordic cultural legacy; as Meinander (2006, 6) has observed, "it is almost as if our national and Nordic existence is confirmed and embodied only through a physical pilgrimage back to nature". In reality, rather than being a singular activity, *friluftsliv* has long been constituted of a relatively broad spectrum of outdoor pursuits, ranging from simply living or 'being' in the outdoors (camping, fishing, horse-riding, 'berry and mushroom trips' and so forth – the 'pilgrimage' activities), through what are often referred to as 'adventure' activities (skiing, climbing and mountaineering and kayaking, for example) to more-or-less common-place recreational activities (such as walking, cross-country skiing and cycling).

The social significance (or cultural traction) of sport and outdoor physical recreation in the Nordic region is, as one might expect, reflected in the sheer volume of participation. The highest proportion of regular sports participation (among young and old alike) in Europe, and probably across the developed world, is to be found in the northern countries of Europe, followed by the western and central European countries (European Commission, 2014; van Tuyckom, 2016).

The social significance of sport and the pervasiveness of sports participation in the region point to a further reason for a collection such as this – what Bairner (2010, 734) referred to as "evidence of a specifically Nordic and/or Scandinavian *approach* to sport" (our emphasis) that "continues to offer salutary lessons" (p. 734) not only about how to play but also, and crucially, how to organise and facilitate sport. This ostensibly Nordic and/or Scandinavian approach to sport points to the relationship between politics and sport in the region. In particular, it raises questions about the potential significance of welfare states in social democracies. Social democracy is the name given to those societies that have transformed free markets into social markets (i.e. economic systems that are more or less regulated by the state and underpinned by a universal welfare system that guarantees the welfare of its citizens). In the second half of the twentieth century, the Nordic countries built and retained the world's strongest state welfare regimes (Roberts, 2012). Consequently, such social democracies, and their welfare states, "have been stronger and more comprehensive in Northern Europe than in most other countries" (Roberts, 2009, 315). In Esping-Andersen's (1990a, 1990b) widely used (but also widely criticised)[2] classificatory system of welfare states, the Nordic countries are assigned to the category 'social democratic' wherein welfare services are almost entirely publicly funded (partly through relatively high personal taxes) and provide universal benefits across a wide range of areas while paying higher wages to workers (Roberts, 2012). In keeping with their standing as the foremost social welfare democracies, the Nordic countries tend to be proud of their welfare systems and Nordic governments have long viewed their welfare responsibilities as extending to leisure, including sport. It is interesting to reflect, therefore, on whether we can continue to talk, meaningfully, of a distinctly Nordic approach to sport – in, for example, participatory or policy terms – and, if so, what the common and distinctive features of such an approach might be, given that much has changed in the region in recent years in both socio-economic and political terms. What, if anything, we might ask, is Scandinavian or Nordic about Scandinavian and Nordic sport?

One noteworthy aspect of Nordic social democracies is the manner in which deliberate government intervention appears to have played a part in the creation of favourable conditions for sports participation. Combinations of equal opportunity legislation and policies alongside quota schemes have improved the socio-economic position of females, in particular, and influenced, among other things, attitudes towards equal opportunities in sports organisations (Ottesan, Skirstad, Pfister & Habermann, 2010). The Nordic countries of Iceland, Finland, Norway and Sweden, for example, regularly occupy the top four positions in the *Global Gender Gap Index* (Hausmann, Tyson & Zahidi, 2012).

Increased social mobility is particularly significant for girls' and women's participation in sport. All countries recording high levels of sports participation, by definition, also record high levels of female participation (Coalter, 2013) and convergence between the sexes has been a feature of participation trends. Few countries can boast the levels of sports participation among women (young and old) of the Nordic countries and it is unlikely to be a coincidence that nowhere is women's social status (as indicated by the percentage of women in legislatures and senior positions in business, the proximity of male/female incomes and the percentage of women completing higher education (Coalter, 2013)) of a similar standing to that of their male counterparts than in the Nordic countries. Gender has been re-shaped and is less significant for sports participation in the region than it was as recently as the 1990s. All-in-all, the significance of ascribed statuses has diminished in the Nordic countries as that of achieved statuses has increased markedly.

A commitment to gender equality is one manifestation of the strong egalitarian values common to the Nordic region (Skille, 2011). A particularly striking feature of Nordic policies towards sport has been their commitment to 'sport for all'. The 1975 *European Sport for All Charter* (Council of Europe, 1975) – which posited a right to sport participation for every European citizen – reflected the growing prominence of sport in governmental policies across the Western world; nowhere more so than in Nordic countries, where universalist strategies and programmes have provided citizens with the kinds of economic and social security (Raphael, 2014) that serve to enable and facilitate sports participation.

All-in-all, the links between sport and politics have tended to be consistently closer in the Nordic countries than elsewhere. Fahlén and Stenling (2015, 1), for example, talk of the "century-long relationship between national and local governments and voluntary, non-profit and membership-based club sport [in Sweden]" as an 'implicit contract' in which the government decides not only the extent of the funding but also its purpose(s), while the recipients, the national sports confederations, determine the details of its distribution – towards, among other beneficiaries, the well-established voluntary sports club sector.

Here again, however, we need to be mindful of difference as well as similarity. Bairner (2010) reminds us that similarities between the Scandinavian countries of Denmark, Norway and Sweden notwithstanding, "it would be misleading to ignore differences between these countries in terms of their approach to issues such as respective levels of state involvement, sources of funding and the role of the private sector" (p. 736). National differences notwithstanding, it is clear that across the Nordic region the sports movements in general and sports clubs in particular have benefitted greatly from state support, not least in terms of funding for the sports facilities that local government provide and voluntary sports clubs utilise.

Voluntary sports clubs are central to understanding Nordic sport. Bairner (2010) views the multi-sport community-based clubs in Scandinavia as having "contributed to the inclusive character of sport" (p. 736). He contrasts this with "most western societies ... [where] there is no real sense of an overarching sports movement and clubs themselves tend to concentrate on single sports" and many sports clubs and associations are, as Roberts (2016b, 47) puts it, "aggressively independent". For Fahlén and Stenling (2015), however, the 'wider social role' (Coalter, 2007) often assumed for sport in Nordic countries – and that has gathered momentum with various Nordic governments' adoption of quasi-neo-liberal policies in recent years – is testing the 'implicit contract' between the state and voluntary sport, as well as the sovereignty of the latter. Despite the quasi-autonomous position of the sports associations and their member clubs, governments in the Nordic lands are increasingly expecting clubs and associations to deliver on 'performance outputs' (usually in the form of 'key performance indicators'), such as the previously highlighted public health goals.

The role of the voluntary sector in sport matters and not merely because, historically, sports participation has its roots in the voluntary sector – "Voluntary associations predate the development of welfare states in Western countries" (Roberts, 2016b, 42). Voluntary associations created and then ran most of the modern sports played in Scandinavia, as well as elsewhere. Sport not only developed from a voluntary base, but for the most part continues to be run by volunteers, acting as members of voluntary bodies. Until relatively recently, it has been the voluntary sector – aided by the public sector in the second half of the twentieth century – that has enabled sports participation in the Western world. Welfare states have not replaced the voluntary sector. Rather, they have provided improved outdoor and indoor sports facilities and amenities and made these available to voluntary groups. This is important because indoor sports provision increased markedly from the 1970s, becoming strongly associated with increases in participation in general and among females especially, such that girls and women now play indoor sports to a greater extent than boys and men.

Thus, the place of the voluntary sector in sport has not declined with the advent of provision, first by the state and more latterly by commerce, in the latter decades of the twentieth century. Overall, volunteering is flourishing rather than shrinking. The membership rates of voluntary associations in general are especially high in Scandinavian countries, at four out of every five adults (Roberts, 2016b). In the Nordic region this tends, more than anywhere else, to include sports clubs. Thus, people in Nordic countries are more likely to be involved in sport, not only as participants but also, and very often, as volunteers, than in other western countries. This is another reason for studying sports participation in the region. The vast majority of the work in Norwegian sports clubs, for example, is undertaken by volunteers (Skille & Säfvenbom, 2011) and the volunteers themselves often take on a variety of different roles, as carers, coaches, club management, supporters and many other positions.

All told, the close links between sport and politics and the inevitably volatile nature of the relationship should not blind us to the continued and persistent vibrancy of the voluntary sector in the Nordic region. Nor should the fact that a good deal of academic as well as practitioner concern has been focused, latterly, upon the 'state' of the voluntary sector in the Nordic countries surprise us. It is in the nature of voluntary associations that they are always inclined to want more by way of memberships, volunteers, funds, financial support, policy prioritisation and so forth. We must also keep in mind the heterogeneity of voluntary sport; not least because the voluntary sector as a whole "is notoriously untidy" (Roberts, 2016b, 47).

The high sports club membership and associated strength and cultural centrality of sports clubs in Nordic cultures make them powerful players in sports policy-making and implementation. Here again, however, there are differences as well as similarities between countries. Eurobarometer 2014 confirms that the proportion of young people and adults who are members of a club tends to vary quite substantially across countries. The highest proportions of youth memberships at sports clubs in the European Union (EU) are to be found in Sweden. Counter-intuitively, however, Finland is among the countries with the lowest youth memberships at sports clubs, according to Eurobarometer (European Commission, 2014). Differences in relation to the centrality of sports clubs to sports participation notwithstanding, one obvious similarity across the region is the downwards trend in sports club membership among youth and adults.

The shift away from sports club membership among youth, in particular, has been matched by a movement towards commercial provision (particularly in the form of commercial health and fitness gyms). An additional reason for studying the Nordic region, therefore, is the growth of commercial provision. Although the majority of sports participation among children in the Nordic region occurs in voluntary sports clubs, as they approach youth and adulthood it increasingly shifts towards commercial sport settings (Toftegaard Støckel, Strandbu, Solenes, Jørgensen & Fransson, 2010). Despite this, in terms of overall sporting provision, commerce adds to rather than eliminates the existing 'offer' from the voluntary and public sectors. Indeed, in Nordic countries, the co-existence of the voluntary sector and the commercial and public sectors is widely viewed as beneficial.

The rapid development of commercial gyms has not, for example, impacted on the provision of opportunities to play team games.

A relatively novel feature of the organisation and commercial/public provision of sport in the Nordic region is so-called 'Company Sports' – especially popular in Scandinavian countries. Company Sport in countries such as Denmark and Norway, is said to have emanated from a desire for a counter-offer to the 'bourgeois sports' undertaken by upper- and middle-class participants in these countries (Eichberg, 2009). Nonetheless, the class-related rationale for the Company Sport system has diminished markedly in recent decades as the Nordic countries have become wealthier and the classes converged, such that the recent political focus on public health in Denmark, for instance, has led Company Sport towards a focus on PA in the service of health and wellness (Eichberg, 2009).

It is, as Bairner (2010, 736) puts it,

> a moot point ... whether Scandinavian sport has been heavily influenced by social democratic ideals because of the direct influence of social democratic parties or if social democracy itself was facilitated by specifically Nordic values which have also been largely instrumental in propagating particular attitudes towards sport.

That, perhaps insoluble, question notwithstanding, recent political developments suggest that the Nordic countries may be viewing strong welfare states as less necessary and less desirable as their citizens have become more able and inclined to provide for themselves. They may, in other words, be in the process of moving towards Esping-Andersen's corporatist–statist category, wherein the redistributive role of the welfare state is reduced and markets, by degrees, freed up. Some of the Nordic countries are becoming increasingly pragmatic regarding public services, incorporating increasing amounts of market provision. At the time of writing, Denmark and Norway, for example, have allowed the private sector into the provision of public hospitals. Similarly, Sweden allows private for-profit schools to compete with public schools. Nor has sport and leisure remained beyond, and ring-fenced from, the kinds of cutbacks in consumer and public (government) spending on leisure associated with post-2008 austerity Norden (Leader, 2013). Participation in an age of austerity, when government spending on all areas of leisure, including sport, has been cut back heavily, has resulted in closures or reduced opening hours for libraries and cultural and sport facilities. All told, and in tandem with the increasing influence of neo-liberal ideologies in the Western world as a whole, the private sector is assuming a more substantial share of the economic mix in the Nordic region – even in the provision of welfare – albeit alongside a relatively large state (that still employs around one-third of the workforce in these countries). It is interesting to explore the relationship between politics, policy and sports participation, particularly in the context of the shift towards quasi-neo-liberal political ideologies, manifest in the election of relatively 'right-wing' governments in countries such as Norway and Sweden in recent years.

A further reason for studying sport in Scandinavia and the Nordic region is the significance of the *physical* environment. All of the Nordic lands rely heavily on their natural resources in recreational as well as economic terms. Some of the Nordic countries are especially fortunate when it comes to the kinds of natural resources likely to facilitate outdoor life (*friluftsliv*) and outdoor sports. Thus, the physical environment of the Nordic countries is conducive to outdoor pursuits and sports (such as fishing, canoeing, sailing, surfing, skiing, orienteering, walking and hiking, winter mountaineering, climbing and mountain-biking), in particular. Finland, Norway and Sweden are semi-arctic countries (part of the country is located within the Arctic Circle). Norway and Sweden, for instance, have an abundance of mountains, forests, rivers, lakes and coastline and, being semi-arctic, experience snowy winters and warm summers. While Finland rarely gets as cold as Norway and Sweden, its winters can be conducive to cross-country skiing, particularly in the north. Denmark is the most southerly of the Nordic countries and, as a consequence, receives comparatively little snow in winter. It, however, has plenty of open countryside. All of the Nordic countries have long coastlines (ranging from over 6,000 kilometres in Finland through around 7,000 kilometres in Denmark and 11,000 in Sweden to 29,000 in Iceland and 44,000 in Greenland). Some Nordic countries have very many lakes (Finland) and archipelago islands (Sweden). Finland, indeed, is known as 'the land of the thousand lakes': lakes and rivers make up 10% of the country – the same amount of land mass covered by lakes and large rivers in Sweden. Denmark is, itself, a large group of islands. Some countries have high mountains (Greenland and Norway) or smaller mountains or hills (Finland and Sweden) while others are relatively flat (Denmark). Finland, Norway and Sweden are renowned for their large coniferous forests. Almost two-thirds of the land mass of Finland is covered by forest. Greenland, on the other hand, has no forests to speak of.

Another feature of the Nordic countries conducive to outdoor sports provision is the relatively low population density. With around 10 million inhabitants, Sweden has the largest population while Greenland[3] has the smallest at 56,000 people. The population density ranges from less than one person per kilometre in the ice-free areas of Greenland and around four people per kilometre in Iceland, through 17, 18 and 24 in Norway, Finland and Sweden respectively, to around 131 per kilometre in Denmark. With almost 6 million people, Denmark is the most densely populated country in the region. However, none of the Nordic countries or autonomous regions[4] are population-dense in the manner of western European countries such as England (413 per kilometre) and Belgium (371 per kilometre).

Having outlined a number of salient reasons for studying *Sport in Scandinavia and the Nordic Countries* – including the high levels of participation, the social significance of sport, the supposedly Nordic or at least Scandinavian approach to sport, the close relationship between sport and politics and the socio-economic and physical facilitators of sports participation – the next sections will say something about terminology and the structure of the collection, respectively.

Terminology

Scandinavia or Nordic?

The title of this edited collection – *Sport in Scandinavia and the Nordic Countries* – is something of a misnomer. Strictly speaking, all of the countries included in the collection belong to the over-arching collective noun, the Nordic countries (or Norden, as they are referred to in the region itself). In other words, although the Scandinavian countries of Denmark, Norway and Sweden make a significant contribution to the text, the coverage extends beyond these to the Nordic lands – i.e. the Scandinavian countries plus Finland, Iceland and the autonomous region of Greenland; all of which have political ties with one or other Scandinavian country. This is because the Nordic countries, as a whole, share not only a common (northern Germanic) history (including speaking similar languages) and political ties,[5] they also possess similar cultures (and, in the case of the Sámi[6] peoples, sub-cultures) – a long-standing feature of which has been sport. Nonetheless, although only one (albeit core) element of the overall picture, Scandinavia (in effect, a subset of the Nordic countries) is foregrounded in the title, partly because it has greater traction and currency in the popular imagination when it comes to sport but also because it has been the subject of the vast bulk of the extant research. The coverage, nevertheless, is Nordic.

Sport

The term 'sport' requires some initial consideration. As Coalter (2009) observes, use of the word sport often disguises more than it reveals. The various processes and practices typically labelled 'sport' tend, nevertheless, to display certain (empirically verifiable) common features; in particular, competition, physical vigour and institutionalisation (put simply, organisation, when something – such as the game of football – takes on the characteristics of a structured, well-organised and established system) as well, some would argue, as physical skills (Coakley, 2000). In this collection, however, sport will (unless indicated) be used in a more general sense – commensurate with the term's everyday usage – to incorporate not only competitive game-contests (that is to say, conventional sports such as football, handball, bandy, basketball and badminton) but also less competitive, less organised, recreational versions of these sports (e.g. 'pick up' basketball, *futsal* and 'street' football) alongside more recreationally oriented physical activities and exercise (swimming, aerobics, cycling, skateboarding, surfing, cheerleading, parkour and so forth), often referred to as 'lifestyle' or 'lifetime' sports and activities. Given their growing significance for sports participation, among the young especially, it is worth saying a little more about lifestyle as well as adventure sports.

Lifestyle and adventure sports

The terms 'lifestyle sports' or 'lifestyle activities' tend to be used in one of two (overlapping) ways. For those charting allegedly postmodern trends in youth cultures, lifestyle sports are defined as "a specific type of alternative sport, including both established activities like surfing and skateboarding through to newly emergent sports like kitesurfing" (Wheaton, 2008, 155). In this 'alternative' sense, the term lifestyle "encapsulates the cultures that surround the activities" (p. 155) as much as the activities themselves. In contrast to postmodern perspectives, Coalter's (1999) conception of lifestyle activities (rather than merely sports) is based on a more conventional use of the term 'lifestyle' – implying merely a larger element of possible choice characteristic of modern-day consumer societies (Roberts, 2009), one grounded more in empirically observable patterns and trends (extensive survey data, for example). Thus, while the term is not literally accurate, Coalter describes 'lifestyle activities' in terms of the more-or-less common features of the many and varied activities (new and old) that have become increasingly popular among young people in recent decades. These, he suggests, are characterised as being non- or, at least, less-competitive (than traditional team sports), rather than more recreational in nature, rather than flexible, individual or small group activities; sometimes with a health and fitness orientation; in other words, activities that can be undertaken *how* (more-or-less competitively, for example), *where* (commercial gyms, voluntary or public sports centre), *with whom* (singly or with friends) and *when* (in bouts of spare time, for instance) people choose.

So-called 'adventure' sports – a term nowadays used (in academia at least) to refer to activities variously labelled 'adrenaline', 'extreme' and 'buzz' sports, among others – have witnessed increases in participation over several decades. They are said to be differentiated not only from other lifestyle sports but from sport more generally by, for example, strong and intense sensations often – indeed, usually – accompanied by risk (Breivik, 2010). Nevertheless, because they share very many of the key features of lifestyle sports, adventure sports will, for present purposes, be treated as a sub-category of lifestyle sports and referred to explicitly as and when the need arises.

Exercise

Some surveys (e.g. in Denmark and Greenland) do not define terms such as 'motion'. In these surveys, 'sport/physical exercise' are conflated in their Danish and Greenlandic translations. In Danish, the equivalent of physical exercise is 'motion'. However, it is important to bear in mind that 'motion' is not understood as the same as PA – in essence, any physical movement that raises the heart rate, whether recreation, active travel or housework. Rather, 'motion' is understood as recreational health-oriented activity in itself and not active travel, such as cycling to work.

Structure

The book as a whole is structured by the individual country-based chapters. Each chapter consists, in turn, of several themes or sub-sections. The first provides coverage of participation *rates* (the numbers and proportions of people engaging in sport – i.e. the propensity to take part – usually expressed in percentage terms), as well as *trends* (patterns in rates over time), alongside *frequencies* (the number of times people take part – each week, month or year) and *types* (i.e. the form of participation in general terms – such as organised sports, games and lifestyle activities – but also more specific activities – football, skateboarding and swimming, for example). The descriptive aspect of each chapter is based on the best and most recent data from national sources (where available) supplemented by research articles and other suitable material. In effect, this section provides an over-arching portrait of the propensity of the population to participate in sport, how *often*, what *kinds/forms* (e.g. particular sports as well as general types, conventional sports versus 'lifestyle sports'), what *age*, where (*settings and venues*) and so forth.

In discussing participation, each of the chapters will explore the significance – or otherwise – of various *social divisions* (e.g. class, sex/gender, ethnicity and disability). Two aspects of the social dynamics of participation that will receive particular attention are the case of the Sámi people (see below) and the various waves of immigration to the Scandinavian countries since the late 1960s that consisted, for the most part, of Pakistani Muslims (see Walseth, 2015).

High levels of sports participation are generally assumed to correlate strongly with high levels of PA among the population. Thus, each of the chapters will also provide a commentary on studies of PA and sedentariness in their respective countries, not least in order to demonstrate how levels of sports participation and PA are typically secular trends.

In addition to sketching sports participation, the contributions will explore the cultural significance of sport in each of the countries – including the supposedly Nordic or Scandinavian approach to sport. The relationship between politics (in the form of sports policy, for example) will also be covered alongside the relative contributions of the voluntary, public or state and commercial sectors to sports provision and participation. This leads to coverage of government policies towards sport, funding, interventions and the impact of these and the socio-economic and physical facilitators of sports participation.

At this juncture, it is worth saying a little more about the source of much of the empirical dimension to each chapter, the data itself.

The data

Sports participation data is relatively plentiful for Scandinavia and, to a greater or lesser extent, the Nordic countries as a whole. Many (e.g. Finland, Norway and Sweden) have their own government-generated national survey data. In addition to these, the EU's *Eurobarometer* surveys provide useful comparative data for the three countries – Denmark, Finland and Sweden – that are members of the EU.[7] Some countries have additional data generated by independent research centres (e.g. Denmark and Greenland) and commercial sources, as well as additional commercial sources (Norsk Monitor in Norway, for example).

At this point, it is necessary to acknowledge the well-established caveat regarding surveys of participation. Studies of participation have one weakness – the tendency to rely upon self-reported data. Self-reported data is problematic for several reasons. First, there is the difficulty of recall – especially when it involves remembering relatively less-structured activities such as lifestyle activities. The second reason is the likely impact on recall of 'social desirability' (that is, the tendency for people to over-estimate involvement in activities likely to be viewed positively by wider society – such as sports participation – and to under-report behaviours that may be viewed negatively – such as smoking or 'binge-drinking'). The third problem with self-reported data is a consequence of the first two, that is, the resulting difficulties in obtaining the rich, nuanced data necessary to accurately represent the often-complex nature of participation. The upshot of all this is that measures of sports participation tend, almost inevitably, to be "somewhat conservative", providing "little evidence about the intensity and quality of the activity" (Coalter, 1999, 25). Those caveats notwithstanding, recall data remains pretty much the only game in town for anyone wanting to explore sports participation. At the very least, it enables a mapping of (perhaps slightly inflated) trends over time.

The Sámi

It is estimated that there are somewhere around 60,000 Sámi living in northern Norway and around 20,000 and 8,000 in Sweden and Finland, respectively. The Sámi are the only recognised indigenous people of Europe (Trudel, Heinämäki & Kastner, 2016). While Sámi people do not live in the kinds of poverty typically associated with other indigenous peoples in the post-colonial world, they do share a history of colonisation and discrimination in the three Nordic countries they inhabit (Trudel *et al.*, 2016).

Since their emergence as a distinct ethnic group in northern Europe around 2,000 years ago, they have relied for their livelihoods on hunting, fishing, trapping and farming and are mostly semi-nomadic reindeer herders. Over time, the Sámi have been squeezed further and further north in the Nordic region as a consequence of migration into the emerging nations of what were to become Finland, Norway and Sweden. This led not only to a progressive loss of land as well as access to natural resources but also to the undermining of traditional cultures (Trudel *et al.*, 2016). Nowadays, it is the growing extraction industries (oil, gas, mining and logging), in particular, that threaten the Sámi people's traditional lifestyles, including their physical recreation lifestyles, not least because these tend to utilise the natural environment (Trudel *et al.*, 2016).

Although the Sámi have made political and legal gains in the past decades, their situations remain precarious. Norway and Sweden, in particular, attempted to assimilate the Sámi from the late nineteenth century and the Sámi languages and cultural activities were suppressed (Trudel *et al.*, 2016). While the constitutions of Finland (in 1995) and Sweden (2010) explicitly recognise the Sámi as a people, the Norwegian constitution does not, although it does offer legal protection for Sámi. While there continue to be no comprehensive guarantees regarding cultural self-determination (Trudel *et al.*, 2016), nevertheless, and although largely symbolic, so-called Sámi parliaments have been established in Finland (1973), Norway (1989) and Sweden (1993). Although the Sámi may lack real self-determination or adequate protection of their culture and lifestyle, it has become the norm for cultural impact assessments to occur in all three countries before developments that might impact the natural environment in the Sámi homeland, in particular, their hunting and fishing rights, are allowed (Trudel *et al.*, 2016).

Concluding remarks

The undoubted similarities and continuities between the Nordic countries notwithstanding, there are some noteworthy differences from one country to another. As Bairner (2010, 741) observes, "the Nordic (or Scandinavian) way of playing and organizing sport may well be considerably less homogeneous than outsiders ... have been led to believe"; hence, Dobeson's (2010) observation that "Where insiders tend to see differences and diversity [in Scandinavia], outsiders see similarity ... the closer we get, the more diversity do we see". In this regard, it is our hope that an editorial team made up of an Englishman, an Icelander and a Norwegian will provide, if not the opening line of a stereotypical joke, then a suitable blend of involvement in and detachment from the region to provide an adequate portrayal of *Sport in Scandinavia and the Nordic Countries*.

Acknowledgements

First and foremost, we would like to thank all the contributors to this collection for giving of their time and expertise so generously. We are indebted to Simon Whitmore and his editorial team (and latterly Rebecca O'Connor, in particular) at Routledge for their unflinching support and forbearance. Ken would also like to thank Sam Humphreys for the endless photocopying alongside a constant supply of tea!

Ken would like to dedicate the book to Ejgil Jespersen, Sigmund Loland and Ivan Waddington – for providing him with the initial opportunity to work in

Norway – as well as Dag Vidar and Trine, Jakob and Jonas Hanstad for their hospitality and friendship alongside constant reminders of just how sporty Norwegians are! Thorsteinn dedicates the book to Trine, Stiven and Jeisson for their unconditional love and understanding and Eivind dedicates the collection to Rønnaug, Tarjei, Torjus and T. Madonna for love and support throughout the hard academic days.

Notes

1 See the section entitled Terminology towards the end of this introduction for an explanation of why the term 'Nordic' is used wherever possible hereafter.
2 Critics of Esping-Andersen point to the over-simplicity of his classificatory system, arguing that the ways in which welfare states have developed has resulted in many (possibly all) becoming composed of more than one typology, such that they are better conceptualised as points on a continuum rather than as rigid typologies (see Bambra, 2007).
3 Greenland is the world's largest island, and almost 80% of this self-governed area is covered by an ice cap and many glaciers. The ice-free area is still almost as large as the whole of Sweden. The country is part of the North American continent but geopolitically the island is part of Europe.
4 It is important to note that the two other autonomous regions of the Nordic region – the Åland Islands and the Faroe Islands – are not covered by this collection due to a dearth of suitable data from which to extrapolate sports participation. In the case of the Faroes, at least, this is likely to be remedied in the near future and it is our hope, therefore, that any future editions of this collection will be in a position to consider sports participation in all of the autonomous regions.
5 Iceland on account of its populations being largely descended from Scandinavians and Greenland based on its historical association with Denmark.
6 The Sámi (otherwise known as Lapps or Laplanders in English-speaking countries) are an indigenous people inhabiting the Arctic areas of northern Finland, Norway and Sweden. They have ancestral lands, their own Sámi languages and traditional cultural activities, including 'sports'. Their cultures inevitably articulate with the wider national cultures of which they are also a part.
7 *Eurobarometer 2014* is a survey of the 28 EU member states. Of the Nordic countries, only Denmark, Finland and Sweden are members of the 28. The Eurobarometer survey – Special Eurobarometer 412 report (European Commission, 2014) – reports data from nearly 28,000 respondents across the 28 member states of the EU, of which just over 10% could be broadly defined as youth (aged between 15 and 24).

References

Bairner, A. (2010). What's Scandinavian about Scandinavian sport? *Sport in Society, 13*(4), 734–743.

Bambra, C. (2007). Going beyond the three worlds of welfare capitalism, regime theory and public health research, *Journal of Epidemiology & Community Health, 61*(12), 1098–1102.

Breivik, G. (2010). Trends in adventure sports in a post-modern society, *Sport in Society, Special Issue, Directions in Contemporary and Future Sports, 13*(2), 260–273.

Coakley, J.J. (2000). *Sport in Society, Issues and Controversies*. Columbus: McGraw-Hill Education.

Coalter, F. (1999). Sport and recreation in the United Kingdom: flow with the flow or buck the trends? *Managing Leisure*, 4(1), 25.

Coalter, F. (2007). *A Wider Social Role for Sport. Who's Keeping the Score?* London: Routledge.

Coalter, F. (2013). Game plan and the spirit level, the class ceiling and the limits of sports policy? *International Journal of Sport Policy and Politics*, 5(1), 3–19.

Council of Europe (1975). *The European Sport for All Charter*. Strasbourg: Council of Europe.

Crum, B. (1991). *Over versporting van de samenleving. Reflecties over de bewegingsculturele ontwikkelingen met het oog op sportbeleid* [Sportification of society. Reflections for policy]. Rijswijk, The Netherlands: Ministerie van Welzijn, Volksgezondheid & Cultuur.

Dobeson, A. (2010). Scandinavian sociology in context. Interview with PD Doctor Patrik Aspers (Stockholm University) on 7 January 2010. Accessed on 16 February 2016 from https://f.hypotheses.org/wpcontent/blogs.dir/718/files/2012/11/11_SSM_3_Interview_Aspers_Dobeson.pdf

Eichberg, H. (2009). Organizing sports around the workplace. Some experiences from Scandinavian Company Sport. *Physical Culture and Sport*, 46(1), 130–136.

Esping-Andersen, G. (1990a). *The Three Worlds of Welfare Capitalism*. New Jersey: Princeton University Press.

Esping-Andersen, G. (1990b). The three political economies of the welfare state. *International Journal of Sociology*, 20(3), 92–123.

European Commission (2014). *Special Eurobarometer 412. Sport and PA*. Brussels: Directorate-General for Education and Culture.

Fahlén, J. and Stenling, C. (2015). Country profile: sport policy in Sweden. *International Journal of Sport Policy and Politics*, 2(1), 1–17.

Fouché, G. (2015). Why Scandinavia can teach us a thing or two about surviving a recession. Sweden, Denmark and Norway are coping better with the economic downturn than most countries, despite having an expensive welfare system. *The Guardian*. 5 August 2009.

Hausmann, R., Tyson, L.D. and Zahidi, S. (2012). *The Global Gender Gap Index 2012*. Geneva, World Economic Forum. http://bit.ly/14dI2Mv

Leader (2013). The next supermodel. Politicians from both right and left could learn from the Nordic countries, *The Economist*, 2 February 2013.

Meinander, H. (2006). Prologue, Nordic history, society and sport. In H. Meinander and J.A. Mangan (eds.) *The Nordic World. Sport in Society*. (pp. 1–10). London: Frank Cass. 1st edition, 1998.

Ottesen, L., Skirstad, B., Pfister, G. and Habermann, U. (2010). Gender relations in Scandinavian sport organizations – a comparison of the situation and the policies in Denmark, Norway and Sweden. *Sport in Society*, 13(4), 657–675.

Raphael, D. (2014). Challenges to promoting health in the modern welfare state. The case of the Nordic nations. *Scandinavian Journal of Public Health*, 42, 7–17.

Roberts, K. (2009). *Key Concepts in Sociology*. Basingstoke, UK: Palgrave MacMillan.

Roberts, K. (2012). *Sociology. An Introduction*. Cheltenham, UK: Edward Elgar.

Roberts, K. (2016a). Youth leisure as the context for youth sport. In K. Green and A. Smith (eds.) *Routledge Handbook of Youth Sport*. (pp. 18–25). London: Routledge.

Roberts, K. (2016b). *The Business of Leisure: Tourism, Sport, Events and Other Leisure Industries*. London: Palgrave.

Skille, E.Å. (2011). Sport for all in Scandinavia. Sport policy and participation in Norway, Sweden and Denmark, *International Journal of Sport Policy and Politics. Special Issue, The Governance of Sport from a Scandinavian Perspective*, 3(3), 327–339.

Skille, E.Å. and Säfvenbom, R. (2011). Country profile. Sport policy in Norway. *International Journal of Sport Policy and Politics, Special Issue, Anti-doping, Governance, Research and Policy*, 3(2), 289–299.

Toftegaard Støckel, J.T., Strandbu, Å., Solenes, O., Jørgensen, P. and Fransson, K. (2010). Sport for children and youth in the Scandinavian countries, *Sport in Society, Cultures, Commerce, Media, Politics. Special Issue, Sport in Scandinavian Societies*, 13(4), 625–642.

Trudel, E.R., Heinämäki, L. and Kastner, P. (2016). Despite gains, Europe's indigenous people still struggle for recognition, *The Conversation*, May 17 2016. Accessed 5 June 2017. https://theconversation.com/despite-gains-europes-indigenous-people-still-struggle-for-recognition-54330

van Tuyckom, C. (2016). Youth sport participation. A comparison among European member states. In K. Green and A. Smith (eds.) *Routledge Handbook of Youth Sport.* (pp. 61–71). London: Routledge.

Walseth, K. (2015). Muslim girls' experiences in physical education in Norway. What role does religiosity play? *Sport, Education & Society*, 20(3), 304–322.

Wheaton, B. (2008). Lifestyle sports. In D. Malcolm (ed.) *The Sage Dictionary of Sports Studies.* (pp. 155–157). London: Sage Publications.

Chapter 2

Sports participation in Denmark

Maja Pilgaard

Introduction

National-level surveys on sports participation in Denmark hold information about more than 50 years of involvement in sport. The first survey was conducted in 1964 and revealed sports participation as a leisure-time occupation, mainly for younger men. The most typical sports activities included gymnastics, soccer, handball, badminton and swimming, and such activities took place predominantly in voluntary sports clubs. Today the picture is almost identical when looking into children's participation patterns (until 12 years of age). However, teenagers and adults take up very different activities, with fitness and running as the most popular examples.

The past 50 years has been a growth story with an increasing proportion of Danes taking part in sport and exercise, especially adults, and women in particular. This development has strongly influenced the profile of specific popular activities and the ways they are organised. In general, there is a shift towards self-organised sports participation and increased participation in private/commercial settings. Both private and commercial forms of participation have gained ground in relation to the voluntary sports sector, which experienced stagnation among children aged 7–15 years and a slight overall decline among adults (aged 16 years and older) between 2011 and 2016.

Modernisation is presented as a popular culprit for the changes taking place within the field of sport and exercise participation (Borgers *et al.*, 2016; Guttmann, 1978; Horne *et al.*, 1999; Klostermann and Nagel, 2011). Nevertheless, there remains a dearth of evidence to explain the apparent inertia in the tendency to participate in terms of socio-demographic and socio-economic differences.

Sports participation in Denmark[1]

In Denmark, The Danish Institute for Sport Studies conducted representative surveys of leisure-time sport and exercise among Danes (children aged 7–15 years and adults aged 16 and over) in 2007, 2011 and 2016. The questions and methodology sought to create a reliable comparison with earlier surveys of cultural and leisure activities – in 1964, 1975, 1987, 1993 and 1998 – conducted by the Danish National Institute of Social Research (among adults aged 16 and over).

The surveys use two different questions in order to estimate the overall level of participation in sport and exercise. The first question is "Do you normally participate in sport/exercise?", to which the available responses are "yes", "yes, but not at the moment" and "no". The other question includes a list of specific activities and an open 'other' category asking whether the respondent has taken part in any activities on a regular basis within the last year. 'Regular' is not defined further in the questionnaire but is included in an attempt to avoid people from 'clicking' activities they only tried once or twice.

The proportion answering '"yes" to the question "Do you normally participate in sport/exercise?" is used as the most reliable estimate of participation levels among Danes since it is the only question that has been repeated with minor adjustments since 1964. The question is not framed with any predefinition of sport and exercise and depends, therefore, on the respondent's own understanding of sport and exercise. When referring to the proportion who answered "yes", we must acknowledge, therefore, that the data may not express an objective 'truth'. However, from a cultural perspective, there is valuable information to be gained from looking into the proportion of Danes who consider themselves as part of a sporting culture and how this has developed over time. This is especially true when this question is analysed in combination with the other questions about active participation in specific activities and general activity levels in everyday life. These methodological issues are discussed further in Pilgaard (2012).

In addition to the two overall questions about sport and exercise participation, the questionnaire includes a question on frequency ("How often do you participate in sport/exercise?") and amount ("How many hours per week do you spend doing sport or exercise?"). These questions can be seen as yet another way of measuring sports participation levels in Denmark. However, these questions were not included systematically in the surveys before 2007 and in the Danish reports of sport and exercise, only the proportion taking part in at least one activity within the past year was included in analyses of frequency and time use.

Current participation

The most recent survey from 2016 revealed that 61% of adults and 83% of children answered "yes" to the question "Do you normally participate in sport/exercise?" A much higher proportion had taken part in at least one activity within the past year, namely 82% of adults and 95% of children. The higher proportions generated by the question of annual participation are likely to be a function of seasonal activities and/or because of drop-out within the past year. Also, some may have participated in activities without considering them as 'sport/exercise' when first confronted with the question "Do you normally participate in sport/exercise?"[2]

Teenagers (aged 16–19 years) and younger adults (aged 20–39 years) are especially likely to drop out of sport or exercise activities and to put active leisure time on hold for a while. This results in a response of "yes, but not at the moment" rather than "yes" when people in this life-stage answer the question "Do you normally participate in sport/exercise?" (Tables 2.1 and 2.2).

On average, active children (the 95% that had taken part in at least one activity within the past year) spent 5 hours and 3 minutes per week doing leisure-time sport and exercise in 2016. Among the 82% of active adults, the average time spent per week was 4 hours and 31 minutes. A small majority of active children (69% of 95%) and adults (61% of 82%) were active at least three times per week. In terms of the percentages of children and adult 'populations' as a whole, this translates into 66% of children and 49% of adult Danes taking part in leisure-time sport and exercise at least three times per week.

Table 2.1 Participation in sport/exercise among Danish children (aged 7–15 years) according to gender and age (in %)

	Total	*Gender*		*Age*		
		Boys	*Girls*	*7–9*	*10–12*	*13–15*
Question 1: Do you normally participate in sport/exercise?						
Yes	83	83	82	85	86	76
Yes, but not at the moment	9	9	9	7	8	13
No	8	8	9	8	6	11
Total	100	100	100	100	100	100
Question 2: Have you taken part in any of the following activities on a regular basis within the past year?						
At least one activity regularly within the past year	95	95	95	95	96	94

Table 2.2 Participation in sport/exercise among Danish adults (16 years and above) according to gender and age (in %)

	Total	*Gender*		*Age*						
		Women	*Men*	*16–19*	*20–29*	*30–39*	*40–49*	*50–59*	*60–69*	*70+*
Question 1: Do you normally participate in sport/exercise?										
Yes	61	62	61	61	61	57	62	62	66	61
Yes, but not at the moment	14	16	13	22	19	17	14	14	10	8
No	25	23	27	17	20	26	24	25	25	31
Total	100	100	100	100	100	100	100	100	100	100
Question 2: Have you taken part in any of the following activities on a regular basis within the past year?										
At least one activity regularly within the past year	82	83	82	90	85	81	83	82	82	79

Forms of sports participation

Adults participated most frequently in individual fitness-like activities (or 'lifestyle activities' as they are referred to in the Introduction to this text), such as strength training, running, walking, swimming and spinning. As the tenth most popular activity overall, soccer was the largest team sport among adults. Among children, however, soccer was in first place, with 37% of all children participating in the activity within the past year. Children also clustered around activities such as swimming, gymnastics, running and trampolining, the latter being most likely to take place at home on garden trampolines (Tables 2.3 and 2.4).

Men and women tended to engage in different kinds of activities with the vast majority of women doing lifestyle activities such as yoga, gymnastics, dancing, Pilates, Nordic walking and horse-riding, and men being the main participants in cycling, mountain biking, soccer, badminton, golf, angling, hunting, tennis and bowling. Interestingly, the most popular activities – strength training, running, walking, swimming and spinning – tended to be popular among both sexes.

As with adults, Danish boys and girls engaged in different kinds of activities. More than twice as many boys had played soccer compared with girls (53% versus 20%), although soccer was the fourth largest activity among girls. Boys also outnumbered girls in street sports activities such as skateboarding, scooters (løbehjul) and parkour, as well as in mountain-biking, angling, basketball, table tennis and shooting. On the other hand, a majority of girls clustered around gymnastics, dancing, roller-blading and horse-riding.

In terms of overall categories, adults appeared most likely to take part in 'individual exercise' (running, cycling, walking), followed by 'fitness' (strength training, aerobics, spinning, CrossFit) and 'aesthetic activities' (gymnastics, dancing, horse-riding, yoga, martial arts, track and field and ice-skating). 'Water activities' also attracted a significant proportion of adult Danes, who engaged in swimming, rowing, canoe/kayaking, sailing, diving and windsurfing/surfing/stand-up paddleboarding. The last categories were 'individual ball games' (tennis, badminton, golf, bowling, petanque, billard, table tennis), 'team sports' (soccer, handball, basketball, volleyball, floorball) and 'street sports' (rollerblades, skateboard and parkour).

By contrast, team sports remained the largest group of activities among children, followed by 'aesthetics' and 'water activities'. These were followed, in terms of popularity, by 'individual exercise', which exceeded 'street sport' and 'individual ball games'. 'Fitness activities' was the least popular group of activities among children aged 7–15 years. However, 'fitness activities' was the only group of activities still gaining ground in 2016, as will be mentioned later in this chapter. In general, children tended to drop out of many of the conventional team sports activities during adolescence and change to fitness-like activities, similar to adults (Figures 2.1 and 2.2).

Settings and venues for sports participation

The preferred activities and activity patterns among children and adults determine the most popular arenas for sport and exercise. In 2016, children most often

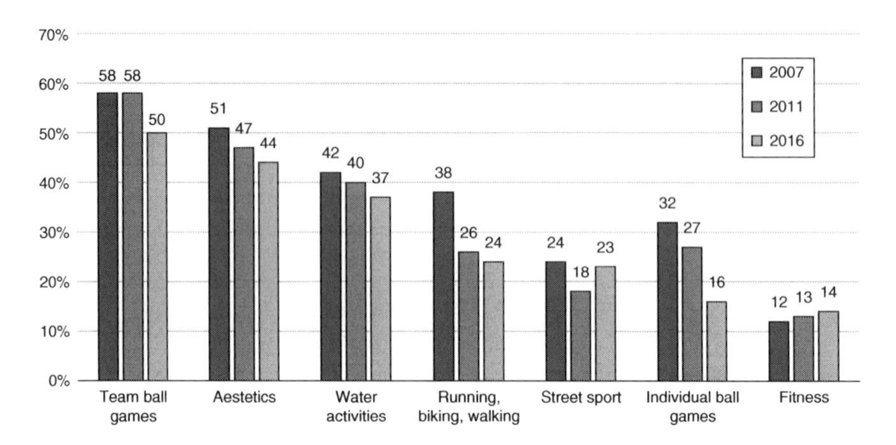

Figure 2.1 Participation in activities clustered into overall categories among Danish children (aged 7–15 years) in 2007, 2011 and 2016 (in %).

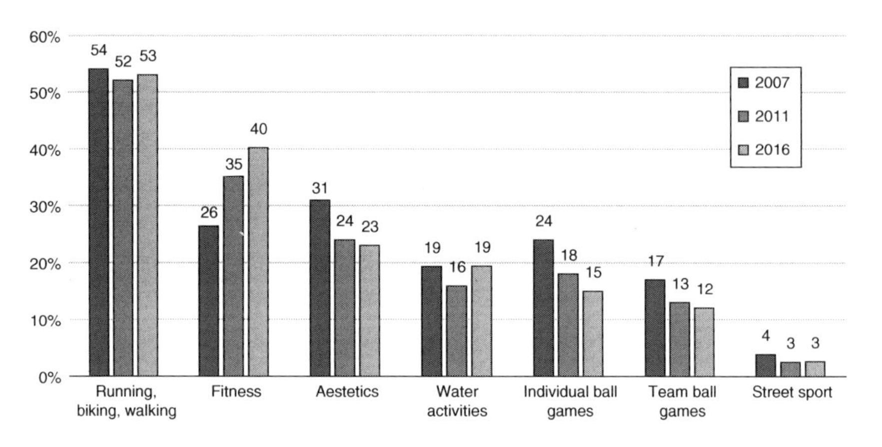

Figure 2.2 Participation in activities clustered into overall categories among adult Danes (16 years and above) in 2007, 2011 and 2016 (in %).

undertook sports in regular 20×40 metres gyms, smaller gyms and outdoor soccer fields, whereas adults mostly used the outdoors, the streets or fitness centres. Both children and adults also made use of water (both swimming pools and outdoor water, such as the ocean or lakes). Adults used outdoor water to the same extent that they used football pitches (Figures 2.3 and 2.4).

The Danish data only allowed us to look at adult's 'social relations' when participating in sport. Even though adults took part most often in 'individual' fitness or exercise activities (lifestyle activities), they tended to do so in social groupings, with 60% reporting that they exercised with friends. Just as often, though, they exercised alone, indicating that adults tend to alternate between individual and

Table 2.3 Ranking order of the most popular sports activities among Danish children (aged 7–15 years) according to gender and age (in %)

	Total	*Gender*		*Age*		
		Boys	*Girls*	*7–9 years*	*10–12 years*	*13–15 years*
Football	37	53	20	35	39	35
Swimming	35	32	38	50	38	17
Gymnastics	24	13	34	32	24	16
Running	18	19	16	11	17	27
Trampolining	17	17	17	20	20	11
Scooters (Løbehjul)	15	18	12	24	16	5
Handball	13	12	14	11	15	13
Strength training	12	12	11	1	6	29
Dancing (all forms)	12	2	22	11	14	10
Boy scouting	11	12	10	14	12	6
Badminton	9	10	8	6	11	10
Roller blades	8	5	12	11	8	6
Horseback riding	8	1	15	8	10	7
Martial arts*	7	8	5	6	6	7
Skateboard/waveboard	6	9	3	6	7	6
Walking	6	6	6	6	6	6
Other sport	5	4	6	5	5	5
Tennis	4	4	4	3	4	4
Mountain bike	3	6	1	2	4	5
Angling	3	5	1	2	2	3
Basketball	3	4	1	2	2	3
Parkour	3	5	1	2	4	3
Other team ball game	3	4	2	2	2	4
Table tennis	2	4	1	1	3	3
Shooting	2	4	1	1	3	3
Ice skating	2	2	3	3	2	2
Other forms of fitness	2	2	2	1	2	4
Volleyball/beachvolley/kidsvolley	2	1	2	1	2	2
Spinning	2	2	2	1	1	5
Track and field	2	1	3	1	2	3
Role playing (not card games)	2	3	1	1	3	1
Yoga, meditation	2	1	2	1	1	2
BMX	1	2	0.4	2	2	1
Aerobic/step†	1	0.4	2	0.4	1	3
Biking (not as transport)	1	2	1	1	0.3	2
Golf	1	2	1	1	2	1
Hockey/floorball	1	2	1	1	1	2
Canoe/kayak/rowing	1	1	1	0.2	0.2	2
Other individual ball game	1	1	1	0.4	0.7	1
Sailing/windsurfing/kite	1	1	1	1	1	1
Other water activity	1	1	1	1	1	1
Surfing/stand-up paddle	0.2	0.4	0.1	0.1	0.2	0.4
No activities	5	5	5	5	4	6
Sport for disabled	0.2	0.2	0.1	0.1	0.1	0.3

* Boxing, karate, aikido, taekwondo, judo, wrestling, fencing etc.

† Aerobic/step/HIIT/pump/Zumba, or other group fitness.

Table 2.4 Ranking order of the most popular sports activities among adult Danes (16 years and above) according to gender and age (in %)

	Total	*Gender*		*Age*						
		Women	*Men*	*16–19*	*20–29*	*30–39*	*40–49*	*50–59*	*60–69*	*70+*
Strength training	30	28	31	52	50	29	30	27	16	17
Running	29	29	30	43	43	41	39	30	13	3
Walking	25	29	22	12	18	17	19	31	40	34
Swimming	15	16	14	13	16	17	15	13	13	15
Spinning	11	11	11	7	12	11	11	15	10	7
Yoga/meditation	9	15	2	7	9	10	9	9	9	6
Biking (not as transport)	8	5	11	4	5	8	8	10	10	7
Gymnastics	8	13	4	10	3	3	2	6	15	22
Skiing/ snowboard	8	7	9	10	8	8	9	10	7	4
Football	7	1.5	13	26	14	9	6	4	1.7	0.8
Aerobic*	7	13	1.2	8	14	7	9	6	4	3
Badminton	6	4	7	9	7	4	5	6	6	6
Mountain bike	6	3	10	7	4	10	9	8	4	1.2
Other forms of fitness	5	6	4	3	5	3	4	6	7	6
Golf	4	3	6	2	1.5	1.4	3	3	10	7
Dancing (all forms)	4	7	1.4	8	5	3	3	4	5	5
Crossfit	4	4	5	8	8	6	4	3	1.2	0.3
Angling	4	0.8	8	3	4	5	3	6	5	2
Other sport	4	4	4	3	3	4	4	3	4	6
Pilates	3	6	0.5	2	1.5	4	3	4	4	3
Hunting	3	0.4	6	2	1.9	4	3	4	3	3
Other water activity	2	4	1	0	0.6	1.2	0.7	2	4	6
Handball	2	1.8	3	9	6	3	1.6	1.3	0.5	0.2
Tennis	2	1.5	3	3	1.5	0.7	2	1.9	4	3
Bowling	2	1.6	3	3	1.8	1.9	1	1	2	6
Nordic walking	2	3	0.8	0	0.6	0.2	0.9	1.6	2	8
Horseback riding	2	3	0.6	4	1.8	1.4	2	2	1.4	0.8
Canoe/kayak	2	1.4	3.3	1.7	1.5	1.2	3	4	3	1.7
Roller blades	1.7	1.8	1.5	3	3	4	0.9	0.6	0.5	0.2
Martial arts†	1.6	1.2	2	4	3	1.6	3	0.3	0.2	0.2
Billards	1.5	0.4	3	3	1.9	2	1.2	0.9	0.7	0.8
Shooting	1.5	0.4	3	1.3	1.8	3	1.2	1.9	0.9	0.7
Other individual ball game	1.4	0.9	2	0.8	2	1.1	1.5	1.3	1.2	1.7
Volleyball	1.3	1.4	1.2	5	1.5	1.4	1.8	0.9	0.7	0.2
Other team sport	1.2	0.7	1.7	3	0.3	1.4	1.3	0.9	1.2	1.3

	Total	*Gender*		*Age*						
		Women	*Men*	*16–19*	*20–29*	*30–39*	*40–49*	*50–59*	*60–69*	*70+*
Petanque	1.1	1.2	1	0.4	0.3	0	0.4	0.6	1.9	4
Table tennis	1	0.3	1.7	6	1.5	0.9	0.3	0.5	0.2	0.8
Orienteering	1	0.6	1.1	3	1.1	1.1	0.7	0.5	0.5	0.3
Diving/UV hunting	1	0.3	1.7	1.3	1.3	2	1	0.9	0.3	0
Sailing	1	0.6	1.5	0.8	0.6	0.5	1	1.3	1.7	1
Basketball	0.8	0.4	1.2	6	1.5	0.9	0.7	0	0	0
Hockey/floorball	0.8	0.3	1.4	3	0.5	1.6	1.3	0.5	0	0
Rowing	0.8	0.5	1.1	1.7	0.8	0.5	0.3	1.1	0.5	1.2
Climbing	0.8	0.5	1	1.3	1.9	0.9	0.3	0.9	0.3	0
Triathlon	0.7	0.2	1.2	1.7	1.5	1.6	0.6	0.3	0	0
Skateboard/ waveboard	0.7	0.3	1.1	3	2	0.4	0.1	0.2	0	0
Boy scouting	0.7	1	0.5	3	1	0.9	1.2	0.2	0.2	0.2
Windsurf/kite	0.5	0.4	0.6	0.8	1.5	0.4	0.6	0.3	0.2	0
Open water-swimming/life guard	0.4	0.2	0.6	0	0.5	1.2	0.1	0.5	0	0.2
Parkour	0.4	0	0.8	3	1	0	0.1	0.2	0	0
Track and field	0.3	0.3	0.3	1.7	0	0.2	0.3	0.2	0.2	0.5
Role playing (not cards)	0.3	0.3	0.3	1.3	0.6	0.5	0.1	0.2	0	0
Sport for disabled	0.3	0.3	0.3	0.4	0	0	0.1	0.5	0.3	0.5
Surfing/standup paddle	0.2	0.1	0.3	0.8	0.5	0	0	0.2	0	0
No activities	18	17	18	11	15	19	18	18	18	21

* Aerobic/step/HIIT/pump/Zumba or other group fitness.
† Boxing, karate, aikido, taekwondo, judo, wrestling, fencing etc.

social forms of participation. Furthermore, 30% of active adults did activities together with family members, while 20% were part of social groupings with people they did not know. Finally, a much smaller proportion, 8%, undertook sport or exercise with work colleagues.

Children reported the importance of seven statements when doing sports. This was the clearest indication in the data of the social relations among children. 'Having fun' and 'being with friends' were the two most important things for children, indicating how much the social aspect means in leisure-time sport and exercise (stated as very important by 93% and 81%, respectively, of children). In comparison, 59% reported 'keeping in shape' as very important, 40% found it very important to compete and 25% found it very important to win.

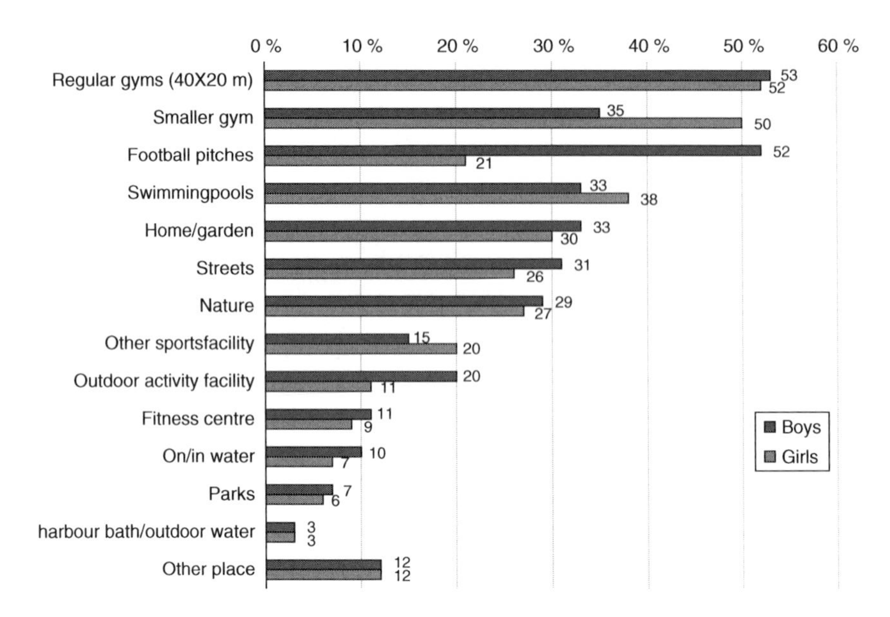

Figure 2.3 Use of facilities among Danish children (aged 7–15 years) according to gender (in %).

Trends in participation

Over time, there has been close to linear growth in the overall participation levels of children and adults in Denmark (see Table 2.5). However, the most recent survey, from 2016, was the first to show a slight decrease in participation (3% for both adults and children) compared with the 2011 survey.

The decrease was true for all age groups under 60 years, whereas the elderly still had a tendency to report higher participation levels than the same age group did in earlier surveys. Teenagers aged 16–19 years reported the lowest participation level in 2016 since 1987 (61%) (see Table 2.5). This also means that age differences have diminished over time. The first measurement in 1964 revealed much higher participation levels among young people than among older people. In 2016, by contrast, there was basically no age difference in terms of the overall proportion of Danes who answered "yes" to the question "Do you normally participate in sport/exercise"?

Trends over time also tell a story about convergence between the sexes. Women used to be rare participants in sport or exercise but during the 1980s and 1990s they caught up with their male counterparts. Indeed, in the new millennium, Danish women outnumber men when it comes to the proportion involved in leisure-time sport or exercise. Among the Danes who participate, however, men tend to devote more time to sport and exercise than women. In addition, men and women, and girls and boys, still tend to be found in gender-stereotypical

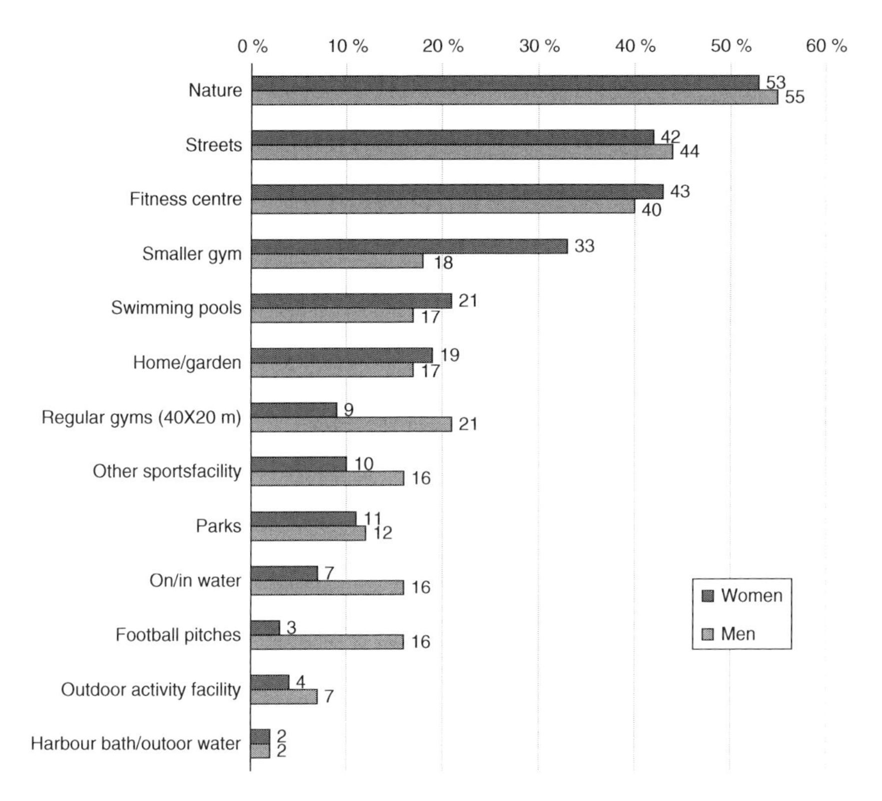

Figure 2.4 Use of facilities among adult Danes (16 years and above) according to gender (in %).

Table 2.5 Participation in sport/exercise among Danish adults (16 years and above) and children (aged 7–15 years) according to gender and age (in %)

	1964	*1975*	*1987*	*1993*	*1998*	*2007*	*2011*	*2016*
Total	15	29	43	46	50	56	64	61
Female	10	27	42	47	51	58	65	62
Male	20	32	43	47	50	53	63	61
16–19 years	53	56	61	67	67	63	67	61
20–29 years	27	42	49	56	59	58	67	61
30–39 years	17	41	46	49	52	47	63	57
40–49 years	10	27	44	48	50	54	64	62
50–59 years	5	21	31	42	46	55	63	62
60–69 years	3	13	31	33	47	63	65	66
70 years+	2	12	27	22	37	58	58	61
Total (children 7–15 years)					89	84	86	83
Boys					87	85	84	83
Girls					91	83	87	82

Source: Pilgaard & Rask, 2016; Laub, 2013; Pilgaard, 2010; Fridberg 2000.

male/female sporting domains, as indicated earlier. Furthermore, adult men were more involved than women in club-organised sport, whereas women tend to outnumber men in commercially organised sport and exercise. The corollary of organisational differences is a higher tendency among men to engage in voluntary positions in sports club settings as well as being more involved in competitive sport than women. Such gender differences beneath the surface of equal participation levels in sport and exercise in general suggest that certain gender-related cultural capitals still relate to the specific ways of engaging in exercise (Table 2.5).

The lower participation level among teenagers (16–19 years) and young adults (20–39 years) can be explained by an increased tendency over the years to answer "yes, but not at the moment" instead of "yes" when asked about their participation. This indicates that youth and young adulthood is a life-stage in which active engagement in sport and exercise is put on hold in Denmark. Simultaneously, sports-involved teenagers spend more time on sport and exercise, creating a polarisation between a growing number who have taken a 'break' and a group with increased engagement in terms of how much time they spend on sport and exercise on a weekly basis.

An important question in this regard is, of course, whether those that take a 'break' are able and likely to re-enter the sporting scene of active participation later in life. Cross-sectional data from 2016 indicated that some will manage to do so since the participation level is higher among age groups older than 40 years than among younger age groups. Furthermore, there are activities with rather low average years of participation among adults, indicating that adults take up new activities in adult life. Good examples of such activities are yoga, Pilates, mountain-biking, triathlon, CrossFit and stand-up paddleboarding (Pilgaard & Rask, 2016). Adults aged 16 years and older have taken part in such activities at an average of 3–5 years. However, it is uncertain as to what extent the pattern with higher participation rates among older age groups in 2016 is due to life-stage trends. It may be a generational effect, meaning that the new generations are establishing lower tendencies to participate in sport and exercise compared with their predecessors, causing overall participation levels to decrease in the years to come. Examples based on longitudinal data reveal that social background as a child and good experiences with sport as a child are more important for a person's participation 40 years later than their social position as an adult. The early development of social disposition and sporting habits (or habitus) is, in other words, a predominant factor in lifelong sports participation tendencies (Engström, 1999). There are also, however, examples of longitudinal data with the opposite findings, namely, that sports participation throughout life is a complex process of ongoing socialisation/de-socialisation into and out of sports activities (Vanreusel *et al.*, 1997). Another interesting question with regard to the tendency to put sport on hold is the extent to which solutions can make it more feasible to maintain sports involvement while going through young adulthood, where everyday life in general is full of changes and important transitions (e.g. in education).

The large group of adults and elderly people entering sport in the years leading up to the millennium resulted in increased participation rates in most activities. This was especially true for the most popular adult activities, such as individual exercise and fitness, which have grown so rapidly that they can be seen as megatrends that occur in most Dane's everyday lives today. Only strength training, yoga and cycling continued to gain ground in participatory terms while all other individual activities, even running, peaked in either 2007 or 2011.

Furthermore, team ball games – and individual ball games, in particular – lost popularity, with fewer Danes taking part in such activities in 2016 compared with 2011 and 2007 (see Figures 2.1 and 2.2). At the same time, new activities arose that had not previously been included in sports studies and, therefore, cannot be described in developmental terms. Examples of such recent additional activities include mountain-biking, parkour and triathlon/duathlon, which were added to the 2011 sports survey, while cross-fit, diving/underwater hunting, floorball, open water swimming/coastal life and stand-up paddleboarding are examples of new activities included in the study from 2016. Common to many of the more recent activities is the opportunity to practice them in an informal outdoor setting, in the city or in nature, individually or together with others – what have come to be known as 'lifestyle sports'.

Physical activity

The Danish study on sports participation habits primarily focuses on leisure-time physical activity but briefly touches upon people's general physical activity levels in everyday life. A series of questions asks how often the respondents walk, run, bike or rollerblade/skateboard as a means of active transportation, as well as how often the respondents do physically demanding labour at work or in the house and/or garden. Among adults, 44% reported doing at least one of the above listed physically demanding activities at least five times per week and 82% at least once a week. Among respondents who answered "no" to the question "Do you normally participate in sport/exercise?", 43% were physically active at least five times per week elsewhere in everyday life, leaving a total of 14% of adult Danes with completely sedentary lifestyles.

Another question investigated respondents' self-reported physical activity level on a four-step scale during leisure hours in everyday life. This question was included in the Danish study on sports participation from 2016. It also revealed that 14% reported leading sedentary lifestyles (reading, watching TV or other sedentary activities), whereas 50% walked, cycled or did other forms of exercise for at least 4 hours per week. Furthermore, 29% exercised and/or undertook physically demanding garden work for more than 4 hours per week. Finally, 7% reported regularly exercising hard at a competitive level, several times per week.

Social divisions

Over time, there has been a levelling-out in terms of the impact of age and gender on sports participation in Denmark. However, level of education remains a strong

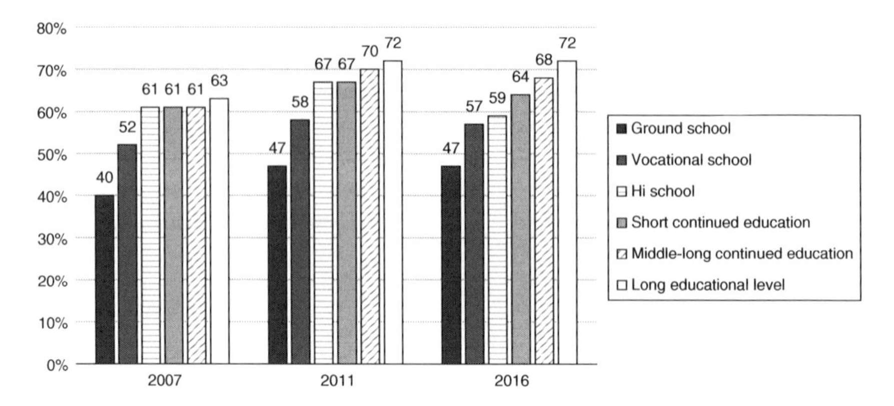

Figure 2.5 Participation in sport among adult Danes (16 years and above) according to educational level in 2007, 2011 and 2016 (in %).

indicator of the tendency to participate in sport and exercise. The longer individuals remain in education and the higher the educational level achieved, the higher the proportion reporting participation in leisure-time sport or exercise. Between 2007 and 2016, the difference between educational groups in participation level basically remained the same. The data revealed similar trends with regard to educational level prior to 2007. This was not, however, included in the figure since the educational categories have been modified over time (Pilgaard, 2012; Fridberg, 2000) (Figure 2.5).

Against this backdrop, it is worth noting that the general education level in Denmark has risen over time, with the corollary that the groups with lower educational levels are getting smaller. This means that the challenges of social division among the Danes in relation to sports participation has changed, even though the data related to differences between educational groups show close to no change over time. The inactive group is getting smaller, but possibly also more socially vulnerable. People with the minimum nine years of schooling are often outside of the labour market or have mental or physical disabilities that challenge everyday life in general and make it difficult to engage in leisure-time sports activities in particular. This becomes visible when examining sports participation levels among different occupational groups. As Figure 2.6 shows, participation levels drop remarkably among adults outside the labour market.

Ethnicity is also a strong source of social division in terms of differing activity levels in Denmark. People born in Denmark or other European/western countries are more likely to participate in sport or exercise than people born elsewhere.

The social divisions in sport and exercise among adults shine through in the patterns of children's participation, which seem to mirror their parent's leisure-time habits (see Table 2.6). This is especially true for girls. If both parents are born outside Europe, if both parents are unemployed or if no other family member is engaged in sport or exercise, girls are less likely to engage in sport. Among boys, the

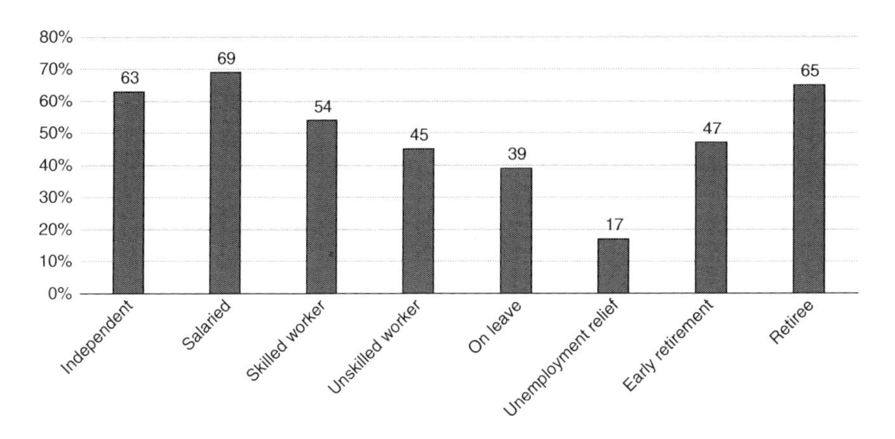

Figure 2.6 Participation in sport among adult Danes (16 years and above) according to current occupation in 2016 (in %).

Table 2.6 Participation in sport/exercise among Danish children (aged 7–15 years) according to their parents' background status (in %)

	Total	*Gender*		*Age*		
		Girls	*Boys*	*7–9 years*	*10–12 years*	*13–15 years*
Both parents born in Denmark (n=2,668)	84	84	85	87	88	78
Parents born in Denmark or elsewhere in Europe (n=249)	79	83	75	86	79	72
Parents born in Denmark/Europe and non-European country (n=154)	76	74	78	70	85	73
Both parents born outside of Europe (n=140)	61	43	73	69	57	59
Both parents employed (n=2,762)	85	85	84	87	88	78
One parent employed (n=382)	73	71	75	76	75	67
None of the parents employed (n=52)	60	53	63	60	60	61
Other family members are engaged in sport (n=2,972)	85	84	85	87	88	79
None of the family members are engaged in sport (n=248)	57	58	57	64	62	47

importance of ethnicity diminishes if their parents are in employment or participate in sport or exercise themselves. This suggests that girls appear more vulnerable to social conditions than boys when it comes to participating in sport and exercise.

The organisation of sport in Denmark

Voluntary sports associations are a cornerstone of Danish children's initial experiences with sport. Approximately nine out of ten children have been a member of the voluntary sporting sector before the age of 12. During youth, the domination of voluntary sports clubs diminishes and a growing number of youngsters find their way to commercial provision, such as private dance studios or fitness centres. In addition, self-organised activities gain ground during the teenage years and become by far the most popular organisational form of participation among Danish adults – often in combination with either private or voluntary memberships. The move towards more informal means of participation notwithstanding, the voluntary sector manages to retain a good proportion of adult members. In 2016, 39% of adult Danes reported participating in activities provided in the voluntary setting within the past year (41% of men and 36% of women). This represented a 3% decrease from 41% in 2011 but remained a solid proportion.

The private sector is growing rapidly and is no longer the preserve of young adults, as was typically the case only a decade ago (see Figure 2.7). Nowadays, the commercial sector is gaining more and more participants from both younger and older segments of the Danish population and remains slightly more popular among women than men. The private sector is most popular in the large cities and now claims more participants than the voluntary sports clubs in the capital of Denmark, Copenhagen (Rask, 2017).

Self-organised sport and exercise is the most popular organisational form of participation among adult Danes. Outdoor activities in the streets and in nature make it possible to organise activities alone or together with others in an informal manner. More and more opportunities for such outdoor activities pop up in the local neighbourhoods around the country.

Denmark is divided into 98 municipalities (in Danish, *kommuner*), and each municipality has powers and independency in the major fields of work, health, school and social affairs (including building local sports facilities). Following an administrative reform in 2007, the municipalities gained more responsibility for health leading to increased interest in inhabitants' physical and mental health. In this regard, most municipalities have acknowledged the

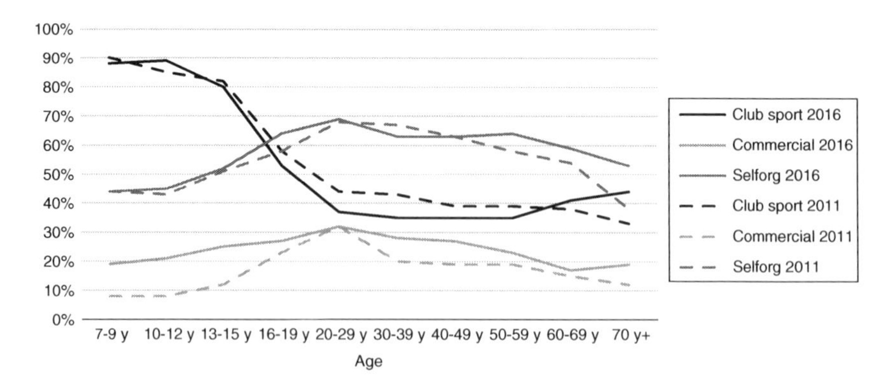

Figure 2.7 Participation in the three major organisational settings (self-organised, voluntary club organised and private/commercially organised) among Danes (7 years and above) in 2007, 2011 and 2016 (in %).

importance of self-organised sport for the overall level of active citizens and take this into account when developing sports policy and strategies. Building running paths, outdoor fitness stations, skate- and parkour ramps or public (ball) pitches are examples of the increased opportunities for making self-organised active lifestyles available in local neighbourhoods by Danish municipalities. In addition, an increased focus on access to open water has been a recent theme, with several examples of harbour remodelling projects in the cities creating harbour baths, with storage and easy access for kayaks, surfboards, stand-up paddleboards and the like.

With the growth of individual and informal activities in mind, it is noteworthy that rapidly developing social media and innovative businesses also make it easier for individuals and informal groups, as well as traditional formally organised groups, to communicate and organise activities.

It is worth noting that social stratification also occurs in the organisation of sport and exercise. Age and gender differences have already been mentioned, but educational differences are also apparent in the specific ways of engaging with sport. Self-organised and commercially organised sport and exercise are more prevalent among the population that remains in education the longest. Although club-organised sport attracts members from different educational backgrounds, once again they are mostly people who have remained longer in education.

Besides leisure, many Danes are offered sport or exercise through work or school/education. A school reform in 2015 made it obligatory for public (i.e. state) schools to include a minimum of 45 minutes of physical activity every day during school hours (including physical education (PE)). In 2016, 43% of children reported meeting this target (see Table 2.7). Most of the active children were also involved in leisure-time sport and exercise during school hours, resulting in even more active children and, possibly, a larger gap between active and non-active children. Among those children who did not participate in leisure-time sport and exercise, 31% reported fulfilling the goal of 45 minutes of physical activity during school hours, thereby minimising the proportion of Danish children with completely inactive daily lifestyles.

Among adults, 42% of those working or studying were offered exercise through work or school – often in the form of a discount at a fitness studio. Paradoxically,

Table 2.7 Participation in sport/exercise among Danish children (aged 7–15 years) according to their parent's background status (in %)

Do you normally participate in sport/exercise?	*Obtain at least 45 minutes of physical activity 5 days a week*		*Total*
	Fulfil the goal	*Does not fulfil the goal*	
Yes (83%)	45	56	100
Yes, but not at the moment (9%)	36	64	100
No (8%)	31	69	100

people in occupations requiring lengthier education were more likely to work at companies that offered their employees exercise, whereas skilled or unskilled workers were rarely employed at workplaces with such an offer. This means that population groups who are generally less likely to participate in leisure-time sport and exercise are also less likely to benefit from opportunities for exercise through the work setting. Among the total proportion of offers through work (42%), only 29% were utilised, leaving most unused. Interestingly, no differences in educational background could be found among workers who make use of the offers through work. All-in-all, work exercise offers can, to some extent, make up for educational imbalances in sports participation in general, insofar as the tendency to make offers to employees becomes more equalised.

Sports policy and politics in Denmark

Denmark does not have a formal, national strategy for sport and exercise. Voluntary sport clubs are seen as the main organisational setting and, in this respect, Denmark has a long, proud tradition of a well-developed civil sector (Ibsen, 2009). The government does, however, subsidise the sector financially, through lottery money from 'Danske Spil', and has recently re-stated the importance of maintaining the pre-eminence of the voluntary sport sector:

> The parties to the agreement [Political Agreement on Sport] agree that sport policy must build on the voluntary sport sector that has been the foundation of Danish sport for more than 100 years. The parties are backing up the common vision '25-50-75' introduced by the Danish Sports Federation (DIF) and DGI.
> (Kulturministeriet, 2014)

The common vision 25-50-75 is a cooperative strategy introduced in 2013 by the two main sports federations, namely Danmarks Idrætsforbund[3] (DIF) and DGI (the former 'Danske Gymnastik- og idrætsforeninger'[4]) in Denmark. The strategy includes the goal that, by 2025, 50% of the population should be members of sports clubs and 75% should be physically active, regardless of the organisational setting. By supporting this strategy, the Danish state is implicitly signalling its expectation that the voluntary organisations will take responsibility for the general physical activity level and health of the population. This is an interesting paradox because the government generally seeks to remain at arm's length from the work of the voluntary sector, avoiding interfering with how the governing bodies of the organisations manage and utilise financial support received from the state. One might ask what the consequences would be if the voluntary organisations fail to meet the targets of the 25-50-75 strategy? Would the state feel obliged to support the organisations even further? Or would they cut funding in order to support alternative actors working within the field of 'sport for all'?

In contrast, the state does not offer financial support to the other sporting sectors, such as commercial gyms, or leave space in the budget for innovative start-ups or alternative structures, like a recent street sport initiative named GAME, which supports self-organised street sport activities. Instead, the government supports the voluntary sector as it attempts to develop engagement with fitness activities, innovation and street sport initiatives. Support for the voluntary sector is deeply rooted in arguments about the reproduction of democratic values, such as voluntary engagement and binding communities (*forpligtende fællesskaber*).

Many municipalities support the 25-50-75 strategy and work together with the sports federations in a common attempt to meet the aforementioned targets. However, in contrast to the state, many municipalities have a broader view on the organisational ways of cooperation and support a variety of opportunities for participating in sport and exercise, not least, and as mentioned earlier, by building public facilities available to all, regardless of membership. Sporadic examples of cooperation between the public and the private sector also appear: for example, schools working together with a local fitness studio in an attempt to fulfil the goal of 45 minutes of physical activity per day.[5]

In general, there has been strong political focus on 'sport for all' in Denmark and an acknowledgement of the shift towards more informally organised and health-oriented sports participation – a so-called "silent revolution of sport" (Larsen, 2003; Pilgaard, 2012). The sports organisations were not completely ignorant of this 'silent revolution', and both DIF and DGI developed their structures during the 1990s in order to meet the growing demands for 'sport for all'. DGI had 'sport for all' as a central purpose in the first place, and a concrete change took place in DIF in 1992 with a much stronger 'sport for all' perspective emerging than ever seen before (Trangbæk *et al.*, 1995). Since then, both DIF and DGI have taken initiatives alone and in cooperation in order to remain relevant to all conceivable population groups in Denmark. The rapidly growing commercial market seems to have inspired the voluntary sector to broaden their palette of sports participation opportunities. Adults (the parent group) have been a particular target in the initiatives taken by the voluntary federations over the past two decades with the rise of 'Foreningsfitness' (Association Fitness), handball fitness, soccer fitness, attempts to recruit members to running clubs and cycling clubs and the recent common strategy 25-50-75.

Explaining sports participation in Denmark

At the macro level, the high participation rates in Denmark can be linked to generally high educational levels and high standards of living (Fridberg, 2010). Fridberg (2010) suggests that participation rates on a national level correlate with GDP (gross domestic product) in the sense that higher GDP leads to higher proportions of sports-involved inhabitants. Furthermore, the high proportion of women taking part in sport is very likely to be a result of greater gender equality in Denmark. A high proportion of Danish women have entered the labour market, resulting in both sexes experiencing similar everyday life structures and thereby similar leisure time opportunities. As previously mentioned, however, gender-specific cultures still occur *within* the field of sport. Women and men, and boys and girls, still tend to be socialised into male–female stereotypical sports-related behaviour. This is also the case in the labour market, with men and women clustering around different job types (Minister of Gender Equality, 2006). This indicates that gender socialisation remains significant in the development of economic, social and cultural capital, notwithstanding the clear changes over time in gender relations in Denmark.

The socialisation thesis is also a likely contributor to the explanation of educational differences in sport, especially with reference to the strong socialising relationship between adults and their children's tendencies to become actively involved in sport and exercise, as indicated earlier. Everyday life conditions may also explain why some population groups with limited education tend to stand outside or on the margins of leisure-time sport and exercise. This is a population group often incapable of maintaining a stable work life and, therefore, everyday and leisure lifestyles that incorporate sport and exercise (Pilgaard, 2011).

At the local level, it is generally difficult to establish a straightforward connection between local municipal sports policy and participation in sport in a specific area. Furthermore, there is no direct link between the amount and share of facilities per capita or the budget per capita in a specific municipality and the tendency to participate in sport (Pilgaard, 2017; Pilgaard & Forsberg, 2015). Participation seems to be very closely linked to the proportion of the population who remain in education longest. Urbanisation, however, seems to influence the organisational pattern, with a higher private sector share and lower voluntary club sport share in municipalities around big cities with high population densities, and vice-versa outside the big cities (Pilgaard, 2017; Pilgaard & Forsberg, 2015; Rask, 2017). A relatively high share of those population groups who remain in education longer in the big cities also influences this dynamic.

The more-educated groups are generally more involved in informal and commercially organised sport and exercise than groups with shorter educational careers. The need for informal and commercial sport and exercise can be seen as a consequence of modernisation processes in everyday life in general. Work life (and school/educational life among children) has become more flexible in recent decades with changing school schedules and more opportunities for flexible working hours. Such flexible opportunities occur most frequently in work positions that require lengthier education (Personalestyrelsen, 2006). Thus, the population groups who remain in education the longest can be said to be taking the lead. In a sport-specific context, this viewpoint is supported by Engström, who noted that sport and exercise develop under the aegis of the middle- and upper-class groups in society (Engström, 1999; Pilgaard, 2011; Pilgaard, 2012). From this macro-level perspective, development in leisure-time sports participation in Denmark seems to be closely linked to modernisation processes in other phases of everyday life. During and after the industrialisation period, physical activity moved towards the domain of leisure time as work, and everyday life in general, became less dependent on manual labour. In Denmark, the working day was already reduced to eight hours in 1919, allowing for more leisure hours to carry out such recreational activities (Elias & Dunning, 1986; Hans-Erik Olson, 2010; Kühl, 1980).

Over recent decades, a strong health discourse has also emerged and developed within the Danish population in response to increasingly physically inactive lifestyles and a corresponding occurrence of 'lifestyle diseases'. Indeed, in motivational terms, it is difficult to differentiate between physical activity for health reasons and sport for its own sake. Nevertheless, health can be seen as a major player in the marked developments in participation in sport and exercise among adult and senior populations and in the development of fitness, running and lifestyle activities more generally.

In 2002, the Danish government published a report called *Sund hele livet* (Healthy throughout life) (Regeringen, 2002). The report set out national goals and strategies for public health and encouraged the public, private and civil sectors to take responsibility, independently and together, in order to meet the goals. Today, all three sectors play important roles in adding to overall sports participation in Denmark.

Alternative sport and exercise activities (so-called 'lifestyle activities') that take place beyond the traditional organised sports club setting have developed and matured in Denmark ahead of other Nordic countries. This may be because there has been a tradition in Denmark of taking a critical approach to understanding sport and exercise in cultural terms (Eichberg, 1989; Pilgaard, 2012). In addition, the emergence of The Danish Foundation for Culture and Sports Facilities in 1994 put the issue of alternative facilities on the political and sporting map. Alternative, in this sense, refers to seeking to be innovative and developmental-oriented rather than supporting traditional sports-specific standard facilities, such as handball gyms or football pitches.

The voluntary sector in Denmark consists of the two major organisations mentioned above (DIF and DGI) along with a third, smaller, federation – The Danish Federation for Company Sport. Historically, there has been rivalry between DIF and DGI, causing them to challenge each other in order to gain recognition and, as a corollary, financial support from the state. In the context of debate about increasing tendencies among the Danish population to engage in self-organised and commercially provided sport and exercise, the voluntary sector has also perceived other organisational forms as competitors rather than sports suppliers with completely different agendas or purposes. DiMaggio and Powell (1991) use the framing of 'institutional isomorphism' to describe the dynamic whereby different actors are oriented towards each other in acknowledgement of operating within the same field (Borgers *et al.*, 2016). As a result, the organisations are often inspired by each other and eventually appeal to the same recipients. In Denmark, the voluntary sector is (still) larger than the commercial sector, even among adults, whereas in Norway, for instance, adults more often engage in commercial sport rather than with voluntary sports clubs. It seems reasonable to assume that the Danish voluntary sector has been under greater pressure from both within and outside and, therefore, still has a greater sport and exercise 'market share' of the Danish population.

It is noteworthy that the recent turning point in sports participation between 2011 and 2016 coincided with a continuous growth on the supply side. That is, all age groups under the age of 40 years reported lower participatory levels in 2016 compared with 2011, alongside increasing opportunities to participate in sport through the public, private and civil sectors (Borgers *et al.*, 2016). Among the increased opportunities have been a growing number of commercial fitness centres, yoga studios, fitness facilities in voluntary clubs, football fitness, handball fitness for adults in sports clubs, outdoor fitness, running paths, mountain-biking courses, skate ramps and so forth. In addition, technological development is making it easier for sports participants to organise their activities through social media. Facebook is an example of a general social media communication resource, but sport specific apps – such as Endomondo,[6] WannaSport[7] or Bobleberg[8] – have also emerged more recently. While it seems reasonable to assume that the development of opportunities for practising sport and exercise would lead to a continued growth in active Danes, such an effect has yet to transpire.

Future surveys on sports participation will reveal whether a generational shift is occurring among Danes. An obvious question may be to what extent the health agenda has permeated the Danish population, and the younger generation, in particular, living as they do in increasingly obesogenic societies. Evidence for growing inactivity among the young in Denmark is the growing tendency among young people to answer "yes, but not at the moment" to the question "Do you normally participate in sport/exercise?". Surveys on young people's health and wellbeing show increasing tendencies (especially among teenage girls) to report low wellbeing and high levels of stress (Rasmussen *et al.*, 2014; Sundhedsstyrelsen, 2014). In this regard, it would be interesting to further investigate the specific needs and demands among youngsters in order to make it possible to remain in sport even when going through the youth life stage and transitioning to adulthood.

Conclusion

Sports participation in Denmark has been an uninterrupted growth story in recent decades. However, the latest nationwide survey from 2016 may have revealed a preliminary saturation point in the overall level of participation among both children and adults. Distributed by age groups, trends indicate that age groups younger than 50 years indicate lower sports participation levels than among the same age groups previously, while age groups over 60 years continue to report increasing participation levels.

In organisational terms, participation has moved from traditional club-organised towards more self- and commercially organised sport and exercise. More precisely, the voluntary sector grew until the first decade of the millennium and now remains stable while supplemented by other organisational solutions, thereby creating a greater 'market' of alternative sports participation opportunities for Danish citizens of all ages and both sexes.

While democratisation in sports participation ('sport for all') has occurred over time in Denmark, particularly in relation to age and gender, social stratification in sport (still) occurs in relation to educational background and ethnicity. The proportion of Danes with only basic school education is decreasing, though, making the inactive 'target group' smaller and possibly more vulnerable. For the providers of sport seeking to reach the targets of 'sport for all', this means that it is not enough to reach out to the vast majority of children and adults. In order to overcome social division in sports participation, specific proactive initiatives targeting specific vulnerable groups appear necessary.

The Danish state has signalled its clear preference for the voluntary sector to take the lead in providing 'sport for all' and supports the two main organisation's common vision 25-50-75 with the goal that, in 2025, 50% of Danes will be members of a voluntary sports organisation and 75% actively involved in sport or exercise regardless of organisational setting. The apparent stagnation of sports participation among the younger generations in 2016 stands out as the major sporting and political challenge in the coming years. The 'easy pickings' would be to continue the focus on recruiting members among the growing number of adults and senior active citizens. The question remains, though, as to what extent voluntary sports clubs can be held responsible for engaging with the most vulnerable parts of the population, such as the homeless, the disabled, the early retired or other groups outside the labour market and their children. Alternatively, to what extent should other specialised actors working with specific vulnerable target groups have a place under the state-supported umbrella?

Notes

1 The text about sports participation in Denmark is a summary of a Danish report from 2016 (Pilgaard & Rask, 2016), from which most of the analysis and graphs originate.
2 The most frequent activities among people who participate in activities while answering "no" to the question "Do you normally participate in sport/exercise?" is walking, swimming, strength training, angling and hunting (Pilgaard & Rask, 2016).
3 NOC and Sports Confederation of Denmark
4 Danish Gymnastics and Sports Association
5 https://www.tv2ostjylland.dk/artikel/utraditionelt-samarbejde-faar-boern-til-tabe-sig
6 An app that allows the user to track running, walking or biking routes, search for routes, interact with other users, measures speed, distance, calories etc.
7 An app that allows the user to search for – and book – more than 10,000 facilities in Denmark as well as search for other participants.
8 An app that allows the user to search for other participants in the local neighborhood interested in the same activity.

References

Borgers, J., Pilgaard, M., Vanreusel, B. and Scheerder, J. (2016). Can we consider changes in sports participation as institutional change? A conceptual framework. *International Review for the Sociology of Sport*, DOI:10.1177/1012690216639598: 1–17.

DiMaggio, P.J. and Powell, W.W. (1991). *The Iron Cage Revisited: Institutional Isomorphism and Collective Rationality in Organizational Fields in the New Institutionalism in Organisational Analysis*. Chicago: The University Press.

Eichberg, H. (1989). Body culture as paradigm. The Danish sociology of sport. *International Review for the Sociology of Sport, 24*(1): 43–62.

Elias, N. and Dunning, E. (1986). *Quest for Excitement. Sport and Leisure in the Civilising Process*. Oxford: Basil Blackwell Ltd.

Engström, L.M. (1999). *Idrott som social markör [Sport as a social marker]*. Stockholm: HLS Förlag.

Fridberg, T. (2000). *Kultur- og fritidsaktiviteter 1975–1998 [Culture- and leisure time activities 1975–1998]*. Copenhagen: Socialforskningsinstituttet.

Fridberg, T. (2010). Sport and exercise in Denmark, Scandinavia and Europe. *Sport in Society, 13*(4): 83–592.

Guttmann, A. (1978). *From Ritual to Record. The Nature of Modern Sports*. New York, NY: Columbia University Press.

Horne, J., Tomlinson, A. and Whannel, G. (1999). *Understanding Sport: An Introduction to the Sociological and Cultural Analysis of Sport*. London/New York, NY: E and FN Spon.

Ibsen, B. (ed.) (2009). *Nye stier i den kommunale idrætspolitik [New paths in municipal sports policy]*. Copenhagen: The Danish Institute for Sport Studies.

Inglehart, R. (1977). *The Silent Revolution: Changing Values and Political Styles Among Western Publics*. Princeton, NJ: Princeton University Press.

Inglehart, R. (1990). *Culture Shift in Advanced Industrial Society*. Princeton, NJ: Princeton University Press.

Klostermann, C. and Nagel, S. (2014). Changes in German sports participation. Historical trends in individual sports. *International Review for the Sociology of Sport, 49*(5): 609–634.

Kühl, P.H. (1980). *Fritid 1964–75 (Udviklingstendenser i fritidsadfærd og kultur) [Leisure time 1964–75 (developing tendencies in leisure time behaviour and culture)]*. Copenhagen: Socialforskningsinstituttet i kommision hos Teknisk Forlag.

Kulturministeriet (2014). *Politisk stemmeaftale om idræt* [Political Agreement on Sport]. Copenhagen: The Danish Ministry of Culture.

Larsen, K. (2003). *Den tredje bølge – på vej mod en bevægelseskultur [The third wave – towards a new movement culture]*. Copenhagen: Lokale- og Anlægsfonden.

Laub, T.B. (2013). *Danskernes motions- og sportsvaner 2011 [Sports participation among the Danes 2011]*. Copenhagen: The Danish Institute for Sport Studies.

Ministry of Gender Equality (2006). *Kvinders og mænds uddannelser og job - Hvordan bløder vi op på det kønsopdelte uddannelses- og erhvervsvalg og det kønsopdelte arbejdsmarked? Redegørelse fra den tværministerielle arbejdsgruppe til nedbrydelse af det kønsopdelte arbejdsmarked [Women and men in education and employment – how do we overcome a gender segregated choice of education and career? Presentation from the interdepartmental work group for breaking down the gender segregated labour market]*. Copenhagen: Minister of Gender Equality.

Olson, H.E. (2010). *Fri Tid eller Fritid? Fritidens idéhistoria ur ett framtidsperspektiv [Free time or leisure time? Leisure time history of ideas from a future perspective]*. Stockholm: Fritidsvetarna.

Personalestyrelsen (2006). *Motivationsundersøgelsen 2006 – Vejen til en attraktiv arbejdsplads [The survey of motivation 2006 – towards an attractive workplace]*. Albertslund, Denmark: Personalestyrelsen, Finansministeriet.

Pilgaard, M. (2010). Når sport og motion bliver et spørgsmål om fysisk aktivitet [When sport and exercise becomes a question about physical activity]. *Forum for Idræt, Historie og Samfund*, *2*: 113–128.

Pilgaard, M. (2011). Danskernes motions- og sportsvaner [Sports participation among the Danes]. In L.F. Thing and U. Wagner (eds.) *Grundbog i idrætssociologi*. (pp. 198–2010). Copenhagen: Munksgaard.

Pilgaard, M. (2012). *Flexible sports participation in late-modern everyday life*. Unpublished PhD Thesis. Odense: University of Southern Denmark.

Pilgaard, M. (2017). *Idræt i danske kommuner. Betydningen af facilitetsdækning og kommunale udgifter til idræt for foreningsdeltagelsen [Sport in Danish Municipalities. Importance of facility coverage and municipal expenses for club sport]*. Copenhagen: The Danish Institute for Sport Studies.

Pilgaard, M. and Forsberg, P. (2015). *Analyse af idræts- og bevægelsesfaciliteter i Gladsaxe kommune. Afslutningsnotat [Analysis of sport and exercise facilities in the municipality of Gladsaxe. End report]*. Copenhagen: The Danish Institute for Sport Studies.

Pilgaard, M. and Rask, S. (2016). *Danskernes motions- og sportsvaner 2016 [Sports participation among the Danes 2016]*. Copenhagen: The Danish Institute for Sports Studies.

Rask, S. (2017). *Teenageres idrætsdeltagelse [Teenagers' participation in sport]*. Copenhagen: The Danish Institute for Sports Studies.

Rasmussen, M., Pedersen, T.P. and Due, P. (2014). *Skolebørnsundersøgelsen 2014 [The study of school children]*. Copenhagen: Statens Institut for Folkesundhed, Syddansk Universitet.

Regeringen (2002). *Sund hele livet - de nationale mål og strategier for folkesundheden 2002-10 [Healthy throughout life – national goals and strategies for public health 2002–10]*. Copenhagen: Indenrigs- og Sundhedsministeriet.

Sundhedsstyrelsen (2014). *Danskernes Sundhed – Den Nationale Sundhedsprofil 2013 [Health among the Danes – The National Health Profile 2013]*. Copenhagen: Ministry of Health.

Trangbæk, E., Hansen, J., Ibsen, B., Jørgensen, P. and Nielsen, N.K. (1995). *Dansk idrætsliv – Velfærd og fritid [Sportsparticipation in Denmark – welfare and leisure time]*. Copenhagen: Gyldendal.

Vanreusel, B., Renson, R., Beunen, G., Claessens, A.L., Lefevre, J., Lysens, R. *et al.* (1997). A longitudinal study of youth sport participation and adherence to sport in adulthood. *International Review for the Sociology of Sport*, *2*(4): 373–387.

Chapter 3

Sports participation in Finland

Pasi Koski, Kati Lehtonen and Hanna Vehmas

Introduction

Finland is a Nordic but not a Scandinavian country. This geographical and semantic point reminds us of Finland's more general cultural, as well as linguistic, distinctiveness. Although part of the Swedish kingdom for approximately 700 years and, subsequently, a Grand Duchy of Russia for more than 100 years, Finland gained full independence in 1917. As the Nordic country that lies closest to the 'East', and Russia in particular, the influence of both Western and Eastern cultures is recognisable in Finnish society, and nowhere more so, perhaps, than in sport.

As with very many Western countries in the nineteenth and early twentieth centuries, the promotion of physical activities in Finland was linked to the issue of national defence (e.g. Kokkonen, 2015). Unlike its neighbours, however, the development of sport was closely associated with the process of political independence and the creation of national identity, especially in the form of elite sport. Finland has typically been among the most successful countries, in relation to the size of its population, not only in terms of elite sporting success but also in levels of sports participation and physical activity (PA).

Sports participation in Finland

In this chapter, we look separately at the sports participation of adults and young people. This is partly because of different data sources but also because of differing patterns and trends compared with international developments.

Sports participation among adults

Sport and exercise are important leisure activities for Finns. This has been exemplified in a number of surveys over the last few decades, although it is somewhat difficult to make exact comparisons between the different data sources. A major shortcoming is the fact that no national survey of Finns' sports participation has been conducted since 2010. The most recent information needs to be gathered, therefore, from different databases that are not entirely comparable. Nevertheless, it is assumed that no major changes have occurred during the intervening years when it comes to different sports and the general ranking orders.

According to the latest *National Sport Survey*, undertaken in 2009–2010, nearly 90% of adult Finns reported participating in sport at least two or three times each week (Finnish Sports Federation, 2010a). In 2013, the study of the *Health Behaviour and Health Among the Finnish Adult Population* (15–64 years) revealed that 54% of Finnish men and 60% of women participated in leisure sport at least three times a week (Helldán & Helakorpi, 2014a). The level of regular sports participation, on the other hand, was lowest among respondents between 35 and 44 years of age (men: 48%; women: 55%).

With regard to the time spent on each bout of participation, the latest *National Sports Survey* reported men spending 41 minutes and women 36 minutes per week on sport and outdoor activities on average (Finnish Sports Federation, 2010a; Statistics Finland, 2011). Subsequently, the *Finnish Adult Population Study* indicated that, in 2014, as many as 70% of men and 76% of women participated in sport for a minimum of 30 minutes at least twice a week, while 31% of men and 36% of women participated four times each week or more. The share of those who participated at least four times a week has remained stable since the mid-1990s (European Commission, 2014).

According to the national *FINRISK 2012 Study*, Finns' leisure-sport participation increased significantly in the 1970s and 1980s. Subsequent changes have been relatively small. Between the years 2007 and 2012, men's sports participation increased slightly whereas women's decreased. In 2012, sport was undertaken by four out of every five (79.9%) 25–64-year-old Finnish men and three-quarters (76.7%) of Finnish women. Young and more-educated adults participated in sport more than older adults and those less educated (Borodulin *et al.*, 2015).

Finns have long been considered an especially physically active nation, ranking alongside other Nordic countries among the top sports participation countries in Europe for many years (see Compass, 1999; European Commission, 2010, 2014). According to Eurobarometer, 13% of Finns reported exercising at least five times each week and 53% between one and four times a week, both of which are above the European averages (European Commission, 2014; Gratton *et al.*, 2011). Although sports participation among Finnish adults increased during the 1970s and 1980s, subsequent changes have been minimal and the earlier increases have stagnated. Simultaneously, daily PA among adult Finns has decreased. Put simply, although more Finns participate in sport and exercise, the population as a whole has become more sedentary in everyday life. Indeed, every fifth Finnish adult is totally sedentary during leisure time. In addition, exercise related to commuting to work has decreased (Borodulin *et al.*, 2015).

Forms of sports participation among adults

When Finns are asked which sports and physical activities they practice, the most common answer is walking (see Table 3.1). Approximately 1.8 million

Table 3.1 The 20 most popular sports among Finnish adults (19–65 years) in 1994–2010 (%) (counted from Finnish Sports Federation, 2010a, and converted into percentages based on the population size at respective time)

	1994 (n=10,972)	*1997–1998 (n=5,520)*	*2001–2002 (n=5,505)*	*2005–2006 (n=5,500)*	*2009–2010 (n=5,588)*
Walking	63	67	61	56	54
Bicycling	21	31	28	25	26
Gym	12	11	11	16	22
Cross-country skiing	21	23	23	23	20
Running	14	15	11	15	19
Swimming	16	18	16	18	17
Gymnastics (incl. aerobics)	11	12	13	15	16
Nordic walking	–	–	9	14	14
Floorball	3	5	5	7	6
Badminton	5	5	4	4	5
Downhill skiing	6	5	5	4	4
Football (soccer)	3	3	4	5	4
Skate boarding	–	1	5	5	4
Volleyball	5	4	3	3	3
Ice hockey	2	2	2	3	3
Dancing	1	2	2	3	3
Tennis	3	3	2	2	3
Skating	2	2	2	2	2
Horse riding	1	1	2	2	3
Golf	1	2	2	2	2

adult Finns, about 54% of 19–65-year-olds, reported walking in 2009–2010. The second most popular activity was cycling (26%) and the third, gym training, in which 22% of adult Finns were engaged in 2009–2010.

The next most popular sports participated in by Finnish adults in 2012 were cross-country skiing, running, swimming and gymnastics. Cross-country skiing has maintained its position as one of the most popular sports in Finland, and running (jogging) has long been one of the most popular leisure activities among Finns. Like many other countries in Europe, there has been a 'second wave' of running popularity in recent years (Scheerder *et al.*, 2015). Finns had already become enthusiastic runners by the 1970s, around the time when Finnish athletes were particularly successful in distance running. Despite a downturn in the 1990s, the numbers of runners and related mass running events have grown significantly in Finland since the 2000s.

Other interesting developments in Finnish adults' sports participation include the growing popularity of Nordic walking, floorball, dancing, horse-riding and golf. Nordic walking was originally an off-season training method for cross-country skiers but since the 1990s has been seen as an easy-access, health-enhancing form of PA, especially for older people. In this regard, senior citizens in Finland mainly participate in 'lifestyle activities', such as walking, swimming, cross-country skiing and gym training. This is in line with adults' sports participation in general.

Settings and venues for sports participation among adults

Figure 3.1 shows that the clear majority of adult Finns participate in sport independently, either alone or in groups. Although sports-club activities have a long tradition in Finland, adults nowadays tend to prefer to exercise in unorganised or informal settings of the kinds associated with lifestyle sports and activities. Only 14% of Finnish adults participated in sports clubs in 2009–2010 and some 5% in other sports organisation settings (Finnish Sports Federation, 2010a). As the trend has been towards commercial settings and, correspondingly, away from voluntary sports clubs, the market share of the private companies has, for the first time, become bigger than that of the sports clubs (Laine, 2017).

The share of participants using other sports organisations, such as skiing associations or work-related sports clubs, was approximately 5% in 2009–2010. The share of private sport companies was 15% and the proportion accounted for in the work setting was 11% (Finnish Sports Federation, 2010a).

It is also characteristic of Finns to participate in sport outdoors by utilising different pedestrian and other outdoor routes, such as walking and cycling trails and cross-country skiing tracks. The so-called 'everyman's right' ('jokamiehenoikeus') allows the wide use of woods for outdoor activities. Only a few per cent of adults tended to use constructed facilities such as sport halls and stadia in 2013, whereas nearly 50% of all Finns used pedestrian and outdoor routes when taking part in sport and physically active recreation (European Commission, 2014). In the Eurobarometer study, 72% of Finns revealed that they participated in sport

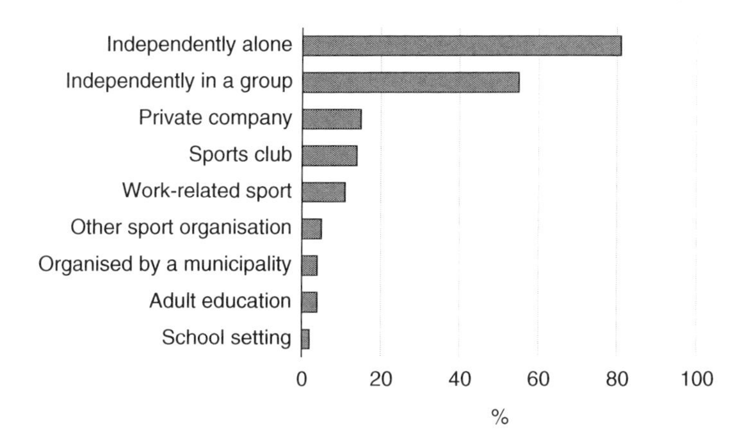

Figure 3.1 Sports participation settings of adult Finns (n = 5,588) (Finnish Sports Federation, 2010a).

in parks and outdoors. Although 'gym training' became one of the most popular forms of participation in the 2000s, Finns still exercised in fitness clubs less than, for example, Swedes (European Commission, 2014).

Sports clubs

Finnish physical and sporting culture has historically revolved around the non-profit, voluntary sports-club sector. Although Finns are relatively independent in their engagement with sport, clubs have traditionally played a central role in promoting participation. This has been especially true of sports participation among children and youth (Koski *et al.*, 2015). Gymnasts form the single largest group of adult sports-club participants. Nearly 100,000 Finns exercised within the Finnish Gymnastics Association in 2009–2010 (see Table 3.2). Most of these were girls and young women. The popularity of club-based gymnastics in Finland can be partly explained by the wide variety of different forms (e.g. apparatus, rhythmic, aesthetic group gymnastics, aerobics, family gymnastics and dance) encompassed within the category of 'gymnastics'. The second and third most popular club sports in Finland were football (soccer) and ice-hockey, respectively. These sports are also strongly organised in Finland.

Social divisions and sports participation among adults

There are at least two features of sports participation in Finland which differentiate it from many other countries, with the exception of other Nordic countries. First, Finnish women frequently participate in sport and exercise almost as much, if not more, than men. Second, although PA decreases with age in many countries, in Finland levels of PA decrease mainly during the phase of life when work

Table 3.2 The 10 most popular club sports among Finnish adults in 1994–2010 (%; participation at least once a week) (counted from Finnish Sports Federation, 2010a, and converted into percentages based on the population size at the respective time)

	1994 (n=10,972)	*1997–1998 (n=5,520)*	*2001–2002 (n=5,505)*	*2005–2006 (n=5,500)*	*2009–2010 (n=5,588)*
Gymnastics	1.9	2.4	3.2	3.0	2.7
Football (soccer)	1.4	1.1	1.5	2.0	1.9
Ice hockey	0.7	0.6	0.8	1.0	1.1
Floorball	0.6	0.9	0.9	1.3	1.0
Golf	0.5	0.7	0.7	1.0	1.0
Volleyball	1.4	1.1	0.8	0.8	0.9
Orienteering	0.9	0.6	0.7	0.8	0.6
Cross-country skiing	0.6	0.5	0.6	0.7	0.5
Horse riding	0.1	0.3	0.2	0.3	0.4
Swimming	0.2	0.3	0.2	0.3	0.3

and family are pre-eminent. Thereafter, however, when adults once again have time for themselves, their participation increases. Thus, the relationship between PA and age in Finland is more of a U-shape than a downward slope.

While differences in sports participation between different socio-demographic groups have tended to be relatively small, the situation has changed over the past two decades. Although all occupation groups have increased their sports participation, socio-economic background continues to be influential (Borodulin *et al.*, 2010). People with only primary education and lower incomes report exercising less than those with higher education and income and better positions at work. Moreover, higher socio-economic status among parents also predicts higher participation among children and youth. In addition, there is a particular correlation between certain sports and socio-demographic background variables, such as running and higher socio-economic position (Kahma, 2012; Mäkinen, 2010; OKM, 2011).

Equality has been one of the characteristics of Finnish sport and exercise. The participation differences based on education, social class, age or gender have been relatively small when compared with many other countries. The clearest differences have been found in the choices of the type of activity or sport (Zacheus, Tähtinen, Rinne, Koski & Heinonen, 2003). However, during the last few decades, economic inequality has increased and cost has increasingly appeared among the obstacles to participating when compared with even 20 years ago (Zacheus *et al.*, 2003).

There are also differences between the sexes. Men seem to identify themselves more often as competitive or fitness athletes, whereas women see themselves rather as fitness or health-enhancing participants. However, the share of competition and fitness participation has increased slightly among women, whereas with men this proportion has remained somewhat static (Finnish Sports Federation, 2010a).

Sports participation among children and young people

According to the Finnish national recommendations for the PA of children and adolescents (aged 7–18 years), everyone should be physically active for at least one to two hours per day (Tammelin & Karvinen, 2008). A recent study analysed how many young Finns were physically active in at least one hour of moderate-to-vigorous PA (MVPA) every day. Table 3.3 shows that almost one-third of the age group reached the recommended level, and boys did more often than girls. However, the share of those who met the threshold decreased sharply with age (Kokko, Mehtälä, Villberg, Ng & Hämylä, 2016).

Similar self-reported results have been found in the *Health Behaviour in School-Aged Children* study, which indicated that 23% of girls and 33% of boys aged 11–15 achieved the recommended minimum of daily PA (Tynjälä, 2016). In 2010–2015, 49% of children in primary school (40% of girls and 59% of boys) and 18% of youngsters in lower-secondary school (16% of girls and 22% of

Table 3.3 The share of Finnish children and adolescents (9–15 years) who are physically active for at least 1 hour per day (n = 7,314; %) (Kokko, Mehtälä, Villberg Ng & Hämylä, 2016: 11)

	Boys	*Girls*	*All*
9-year-olds	44	39	41
11-year-olds	46	33	39
13-year-olds	31	21	26
15-year-olds	21	13	17
All	37	28	31

boys) engaged in at least 60 minutes of MVPA each day (Tammelin, Hakonen, Kulmala & Kallio, 2015). The proportion of three-year-old children engaging in at least 60 minutes of MVPA a day was 29% (Soini, 2010).

Forms of sports participation among children and young people

Football is the most popular informal or lifestyle sport played recreationally beyond the sports-club setting among youngsters in Finland (see Table 3.4). Interestingly, the next most popular sports overall are cycling, swimming and running – all lifestyle activities typically undertaken informally, either alone or with friends and family. During the 15-year period 1995 to 2009–2010, the proportion of children and young people playing football increased from 15% to 22%

Table 3.4 The most popular sports among Finnish children and youth (3–18 years) 1995–2010 (%) (Finnish Sports Federation, 2010b)

	1995 (n=6,016)	*1997–98 (n=5,520)*	*2001–02 (n=5,531)*	*2005–06 (n=5,505)*	*2009–10 (n=5,505)*
Football (soccer)	15	18	25	23	22
Bicycling	8	17	25	20	18
Swimming	11	15	19	18	17
Running	6	8	11	13	15
Cross-country skiing	10	16	18	19	15
Floorball	9	12	16	13	15
Skating	6	9	12	12	12
Walking	7	11	12	11	12
Ice hockey	11	12	11	11	10
Athletics	6	7	7	7	6
Gymnastics	5	5	7	7	8
Dancing	4	5	7	7	8
Horse riding	4	5	5	5	6
Downhill skiing	5	5	5	5	6
Gym	2	4	3	5	6

(from 157,000 participants to 217,000). By comparison, in 1995 the number of children and young people cycling was 88,000 (8%); swimming, 112,000 (11%); and running, 58,000 (6%). In 2010, the numbers were cycling, 180,000 (18%); swimming, 166,000 (17%); and running, 149,000 (15%).

Settings and venues for sports participation among children and young people

Unorganised activities undertaken alone or among a group of friends are the most typical way of engaging in sport and exercise among young people in Finland (Figure 3.2). More than 90% of 9–15-year-olds reported participating this way at least once a week in 2016. The proportion of those who played sport independently between four to seven times per week was roughly half (51%). By comparison, four-fifths (79%) played sport independently two to three times per week and 9% did not play at all (Suomi, Mehtälä & Kokko, 2016).

When looking at the proportion of children (3–6 years) engaged in unorganised activities daily or almost daily, the results varied considerably. Sixty-three per cent of 3–6-year-olds played outdoors on weekdays (after day-care) for at least 30 minutes, and 30% played outdoors on weekends for more than two hours a day (Sääkslahti, 2016).

Sports clubs are a more common and important setting for children and youth than for adults. A recent survey revealed that more than half (53%) participated in sports-club activities at least once a week (Mononen, Blomqvist, Koski, & Kokko, 2016).

The market share of private companies has increased during recent decades. According to a recent survey, 41% of children and adolescents aged 9–15 reported participating in private-sector sport activities, such as at dance academies or riding stables. Girls (47%) participated more often than boys (34%) in these. Organised sports activities are also arranged by many other operators,

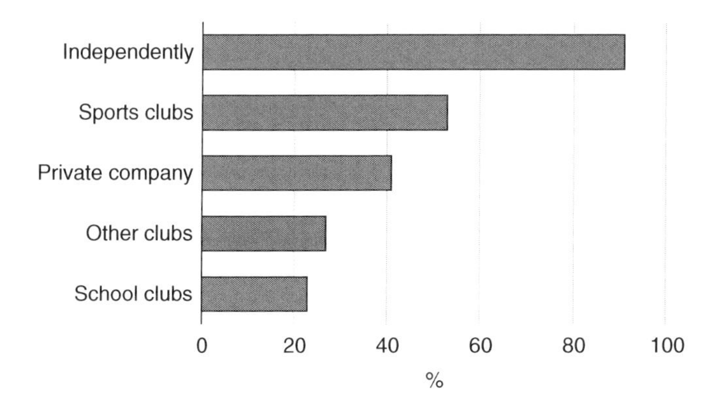

Figure 3.2 Sports participation settings of children and adolescents (9–15 years, at least once a week) (n= 5,330) (Suomi, Mehtälä, & Kokko, 2016).

such as the Finnish Scout movement, parishes and village associations, and these activities were participated in weekly by 27% of children and adolescents aged 9–15 (Suomi *et al.*, 2016). Schools also facilitate leisure-time sporting opportunities for pupils, typically during long breaks or after school. Almost one-quarter (23%) of pupils aged 9–15 participated in some organised PA during the school day at least once a week (Suomi *et al.*, 2016).

The most commonly used places to participate in sport or engage in leisure-time PA were walking and cycling routes. Seventy-one per cent of 9–15-year-old children and young people used these venues at least once a week, whereas 36% used gyms and 33% used sports fields. Interestingly, nature/outdoors (33%) was as popular as sports fields. One-quarter (25%) of 9–15-year-old boys and girls used schoolyards before or after schooldays. Girls (75%) used walking and cycling routes more often than boys (67%), as well as using nature/outdoors (girls 36%; boys 29%). However, far more boys (43%) used sports fields than girls (24%). Boys (31%) also used schoolyards more than girls (19%) (Suomi *et al.*, 2016).

Sports clubs

Almost 90% of Finnish youth participated in sports-club activities during their youth (Mononen *et al.*, 2016). However, the exact proportions participating in sports-club activities varies depending on the age of the target group and the criteria for participation. According to Mononen *et al.* (2016), 62% of 9–15-year-old children and young people participated in sports-club activities regularly or occasionally. By comparison, when age distribution is greater (7–19 years), 46% of children and young people engaged in sports-club activities at least once a week. Boys (51%) participate more often than girls (41%) (Myllyniemi & Berg, 2013). For children below school age, no accurate information is available regarding their participation in organised practice sessions at sports clubs although, according to the parents' report, 57% of children aged 3–6 take part in some kind of organised sports hobby (Sääkslahti, 2016).

In terms of trends, there has been a clear tendency during recent decades towards children beginning to participate in organised sport and exercise for the first time at an earlier age. While those born in the 1950s began (if they started at all) their sports-club participation at age 11, on average, those born in the 1970s began at around 9 years of age, and nowadays the average age is 6.6 years. Almost 60% of children participate in sports-club activities for the first time before they go to school (Koski, 2009; Mononen *et al.*, 2016). While the international trend is towards youngsters leaving the voluntary sports club scene earlier, this tendency is not so marked in Finland, at least until age 15 (Aira, Kannas, Tynjälä, Villberg & Kokko, 2013).

Participation in sports-club activities declines with age. While 49% of girls and 61% of boys aged 7–14 participated in sports-club activities every week in 2012, the corresponding percentage for youth aged 15–19 was 29% (girls) and 34% (boys) (Myllyniemi & Berg, 2013). When comparing different age groups,

Table 3.5 The main sports among children and adolescents (9–15 years) who are participating regularly in sports-club activities (%). (Mononen, Blomqvist, Koski & Kokko, 2016: 119)

	Boys	*Girls*	*All*
	n=1,582	*n=1,633*	*n=3,215*
Football	27.2	10.3	18.6
Dancing	0.5	10.3	8.7
Floorball	14.6	2.8	8.6
Riding	0.3	16.2	8.4
Ice hockey	13.5	0.9	7.1
Gymnastic	1.6	8.9	5.3
Track and field	2.2	4.7	3.5
Basketball	3	2.3	2.6
Volleyball	1.3	3.4	2.4
Swimming	2.7	2.2	2.4

the results revealed that 9- and 11-year-olds participated in sports-club activities most. The proportion of 9-year-olds who participated regularly was 68%, and was 67% for 11-year-olds. When it comes to gender, boys aged 9 (53%) participated regularly in sports-club activities more often than girls (47%). The same was true at age 11 (boys 60% and girls 52%) (Mononen *et al.*, 2016).

The most popular club-based sport among 9–15-year olds was football (Table 3.5). Twenty-seven per cent of boys and 10% of girls played football in sports clubs. Besides football, ice-hockey and floorball were also more common among boys than girls. Roughly one in seven boys played floorball (14.6%) and ice-hockey (13.6%) regularly whereas the proportion of girls was much lower (2.9%, floorball; 0.9%, ice-hockey). By comparison, girls' most popular sporting activities undertaken at sports clubs were horse-riding (16.2%), dancing (10.3%) and gymnastics (8.9%). In these sports, the proportion of boys was very low: 0.3% for horse-riding regularly in sport clubs, 0.5% dancing and 1.6% gymnastics (Mononen *et al.*, 2016).

In club-based sport, the role of team ball-games has increased markedly during the last few decades (Zacheus, 2008). Many more young people participated in the nine most-popular team ball-games, for example, than in the 21 other most-practiced sport disciplines (Koski, 2007).

Social divisions and sports participation among children and young people

Lower parental education and household income are associated with lower levels of PA in both sexes as well as in children aged 6–8 (Lampinen *et al.*, 2017) and young people aged 14 (Tammelin, Näyhä, Laitinen, Rintamäki & Järvelin, 2003).

Higher parental education and household income are also associated with sports-club participation among young people (Tammelin *et al.*, 2003).

According to Tammelin, Näyhä, Hills and Järvelin (2003), higher household incomes are associated with young people's participation in different sports. Fourteen-year-olds who took part in alpine skiing (64%), dancing (53%), horse-riding (47%) and orienteering (47%) tended to live in families with higher household incomes. By comparison, young people whose household incomes were lower were more likely to take part most often in gym (28%), walking (26%), cycling (25%) and football (25%).

Self-reported PA is also associated with parental education and household income. However, there are differences between the sexes. High parental education is associated with boys' (10–12 years) self-reported PA, but not that of girls. Half (50%) of boys whose parental education was high did sport in their leisure time seven hours or more per week compared with 24% of boys whose parental education was low. In contrast, 25% of girls (10–12 years) with high household incomes did sport in their leisure time seven or more hours per week compared with 8% whose household incomes were low. Household incomes were not associated with boys' self-reported PA (Kantomaa, Tammelin, Taanila & Näyhä, 2007).

The costs for many sports and physical activities have increased. In Finland, this trend has led to a situation where high expenses have become one of the main barriers to sports participation among young people (Hirvensalo, Jaakkola, Sääkslahti & Lintunen, 2016).

The organisation of sport in Finland

The roles and responsibilities within the Finnish sports system are defined in the Sports Act (2015). In Figure 3.3, the sports system is described in terms of state subsidies and memberships between sports organisations. The remarkable thing is the central role of the Ministry of Education and Culture (MEC), which makes almost all decisions when it comes to state sport subsidies. For example, all subsidies directed to national and regional sports organisations are determined by the MEC. Furthermore, since 2013, the Finnish state has allocated project subsidies directly to sports clubs (€3.7–4.9 million per year), even though the municipalities are mainly responsible for supporting sports clubs. Regional state agencies allocate some project subsidies to municipalities but the amounts tend to be small. The only notable exception is that the High Performance Unit (established in 2013 within the Olympic Committee) forwards subsidies to national sports organisations to develop elite and Paralympic elite sport. In 2016, the amount of forwarded subsidies was €4.9 million (NOC, 2017).

Another noteworthy feature of the Finnish sports system is the strong independency of organisations at different levels. Almost all sports clubs – around 10,000, with approximately 1.1 million members (Koski, 2013; Mäkinen *et al.*, 2015) – are

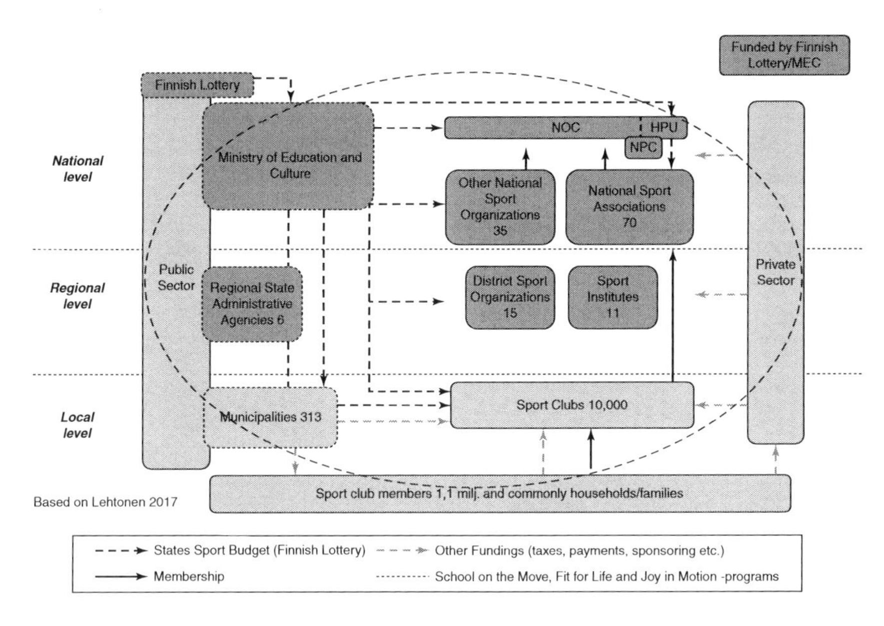

Figure 3.3 Finnish Sport System 2016 (Lehtonen, 2017: 16).

members of national sport associations such as football and ice hockey, which are, in turn, members of the National Olympic Committee (NOC). Although the Finnish model resembles the traditional sport movement model (e.g. Lindroth, 1974), where voluntary sports clubs are the backbone of sport and the central sports organisation is a negotiator and representative of the sport movement, there is no functional relationship between NOC, sports organisations and sports clubs (Heikkala, 1998; Koski & Heikkala, 1998; Lehtonen, 2015). The system-level fragmentariness gets support from the large amount of national and regional sport organisations which are funded directly by MEC but are not members of NOC. Thus, although the state has a good deal of authority due to its responsibility for funding, there are still structures that remind us of a Nordic sport movement model.

The state sports budget is almost totally (99.5%) made up of National Lottery funds. In 2015, the state sports subsidy was €189 million, including €40 million for the Helsinki Olympic Stadium renovation. Without this extra subsidy, the sports budget had been around €150 million in previous years (MEC, 2017). In 2015, one-quarter of the sport subsidies were directed to the civic sector of sport which, in practice, meant 123 national and regional sport organisations and the sports club subsidies mentioned in Figure 3.4.

The state subsidy for the municipalities was €19 million in 2015. The use of state subsidies varies because of the strong autonomy of municipalities. At the end of 2016, there were 313 municipalities in Finland (Kuntaliitto, 2017), all of which could independently decide how to use the state subsidy. Because of this,

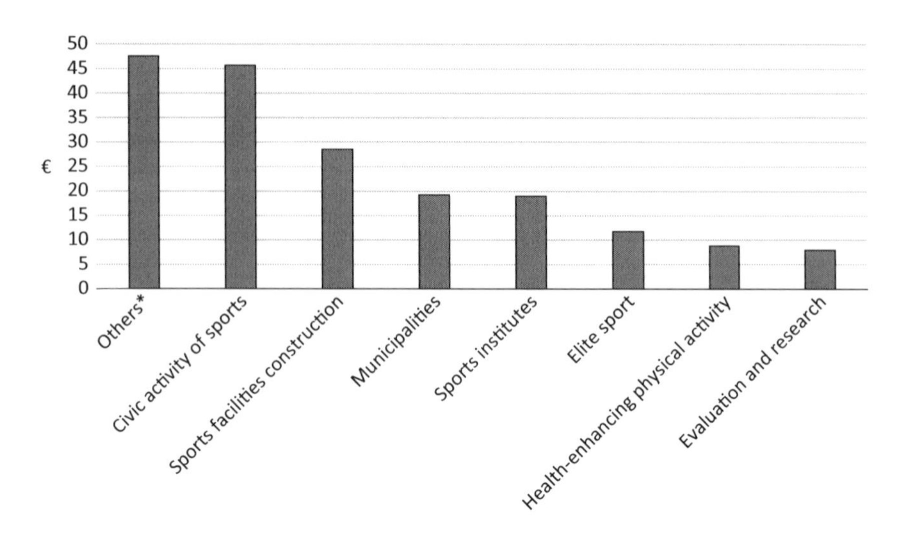

Figure 3.4 Distribution of states subsidies for sport in 2015 (€). Category "Others" includes Olympic Stadium renovation (MEC, 2017).

subsidies are not granted in every municipality, or the clubs themselves do not apply for them. According to Koski (2013), less than half of the sports clubs in the country – close to 4,700 sports clubs – received public support in the form of funding from their home municipalities. The state's subsidies for the municipalities are about 3% of the operational costs of the local sport sectors. In addition to the state subsidies, the municipalities allocate approximately €690 million tax revenue to sport and PA every year that, for example, enables the construction and maintenance of sports facilities and services that are directed at disabled people and senior citizens (MEC, 2017). In 2015, €28.5 million were directed towards sports facilities construction, €19 million to the sports institutes and nearly €12 million to elite sport. Subsidies for health-enhancing PA (€8.8 million) consist mainly of project subsidies to two national programmes (*School on the Move* and *Fit for Life*) and individual projects implemented by sports organisations. These national programmes are based on networking between the public, private and third sectors.[1]

In general, the private sector sponsored sport to the tune of €133 million in 2015 (Sponsor Insight, 2016). However, there is no detailed information about how the sponsorship was divided between, for example, sports clubs, national sports organisations or sport events at local, regional and national levels. Thus, at the system level, it is not an exaggeration to say that local level actors – municipalities and households – sustain the whole sport system. Further support takes the form of private consumption: Finnish households devoted €775 million to sport in 2012 (Hakamäki, 2014), mainly on sports equipment and participation fees.

Sports policy and politics in Finland

More than 100 years ago, when organised physical culture in Finland emerged, it was viewed as having an important societal role in the pursuit of fostering national identity, national self-consciousness, patriotism and world recognition (Koski, 2017). Thereafter, sport and PA came to be viewed as instruments for socialisation and education, particularly for the young. Subsequently, sport began to occupy a place in the programme of many non-profit associations (e.g. workers' associations, women's associations, temperance societies, voluntary fire brigades and youth associations) (see Halila & Sirmeikkö, 1960; Koski, Itkonen, Lehtonen & Vehmas, 2015). When sport began to be seen as worthwhile in its own right, the tight connections with the non-sport-specific organisations started to dissolve (Itkonen, 2000; Koski *et al.*, 2015). More recently, some areas of sport have been treated as commodities in the leisure and entertainment marketplace while, increasingly, sport and PA have been presented as playing an important role in policy towards health and well-being (Koski, 2008).

Finnish society went through rapid changes after the Second World War. Urbanisation along with economic growth and changes in the character of work, away from physically demanding jobs, increased the need for physically active leisure. At the same time that public policy began to focus on physically active leisure, the hegemony of competitive sport began to weaken (Vasara, 1992). The popular term *liikunta* covers the whole of physical culture (*liikuntakulttuuri*) and is constituted of four equal parts: 'sport for all', physical education, competitive sport and top-level sport (Koski, 1999). Adopted in public policy from the late 1960s onwards, liikunta became the basis for policy from the 1970s. In this regard, sport and PA were used as tools in building the welfare state in Finland (Kokkonen, 2015).

The Finnish social and political system is based on the operations and division of labour of three main sectors: the public sector, private business and the voluntary sector (Heikkala & Koski, 1999). Essential in the Finnish system as a whole, but in sport and leisure in particular, is the interrelationship between the public and third sectors. The recent shift away from a planned economy to a more mixed-market model has involved public administration applying the ideas of New Public Management[2] (Hämäläinen & Heiskala, 2004). For the third sector, such as sports organisations, this meant the influx of market thinking. Suddenly, voluntary sports organisations became 'service providers' with the expectation of delivering services, as manifest in the so-called 'results-based' system implemented by the government since the early 1990s. Thereafter, and until 2013, 50% of public subsidies were targeted at children's and youth sport, 25% based on results in recreational sport and health-related activities, and 25% according to results in top-level sport (Heikkala & Koski, 1999).

Finland is one of only a handful of countries that have a specific Sports Act which, while only a 'skeleton law', indicates where the emphases in Finnish sports policy should lie. The Sports Act was last renewed in 2015, with a focus on the promotion of sport and PA. Its main objectives are:

> 1) the opportunities of various demographic groups to engage in PA; 2) the wellbeing and health of the population; 3) the maintenance and improvement of the capacity for PA; 4) the growth and development of children and young people; 5) civic action in the field of PA including club activities; 6) top-level sports; 7) integrity and ethical principles in the context of PA and top-level sports; and 8) greater equality in sports and PA.
>
> (Sports Act, 2015)

In the Finnish system, the key players in delivering these objectives are the municipalities and the third sector. The role of the former revolves around the provision of sports facilities. In the 1980s, almost all sports facilities were built and owned by local authorities. Almost four decades on, 75% of the more than 30,000 sports facilities in Finland continue to be owned by the municipalities (Suomi *et al.*, 2012).

As in other Nordic countries, the role of school sport is rather small. By international comparison, the volume of Finnish school sport and physical education is not very high. The current government platform includes the aim to introduce at least one hour of PA in school days. The *Schools on the Move* programme has already reached more than 90% of municipalities and 80% of comprehensive schools (2,000 schools). The purpose of the programme is to promote PA among school-aged children.

Sámi sport in Finland

Since 1990, there has been a Sámi Sport Association in Finland (Sámi Valastallanlihttu-Finland/SVL-F), as well as in Norway and Sweden (SVL-N and SVL-S). However, unlike in Norway and Sweden, SVL-F's operations have closed down. Nowadays, SVL-F exists only on paper. This is a result of the diminishing number of Sámi sports clubs. There are no members in the SVL-F. There is only one Sámi sports club (Anára Sámisearvi) in the Inari municipality (with a membership of around 100) which also organises other activities around Sámi culture. The sports that are organised in Anára Sámisearvi consist of traditional Sámi sports (e.g. lassoing and reindeer racing) and other, more modern and international sports, such as football and floorball. Besides Anára Sámisearvi, the Finnish Sámi Youth Association (Suoma Sámi Nuorat) also organises sporting events but, in general, there is no organisation in Finland that deals exclusively with Sámi sport. Rather, it seems that Sámi people in Finland are more likely to be members of local sports clubs and integrated into these.

There are 32 sports clubs in the Sámi area of Finland – 0.3% of the total number of sports clubs in Finland. The main support to Sámi sport comes as project funding from the Sámi Parliament, which allocates subsidies from MEC to develop Sámi culture. Funding from the Sámi Parliament is mainly directed towards the organisation of sports events or taking part, for example, in the Arctic Winter Games. In 2016, the total amount of cultural allowances from MEC to the Sámi Parliament was over €170,000, from which €7,000 were directed to Anára Sámisearvi and the Finnish Sámi Youth Association for the organisation of sporting events. All-in-all, Sámi sports in Finland are poorly recognised at many levels. It seems that sport is neither part of the indigenous people's culture and cultural heritage (see, for example, Fahlen & Skille, 2016), nor organised in such a way that it could be part of the national sport system (Skille, 2012).

Explaining sports participation in Finland

In this section, we provide some explanations for why sport and physical activities are and have been so important for Finns. In addition, the current, more detailed, trends are examined. In the first instance, the historical dimension of Finnish sport needs to be explored.

In many countries, religion is an important factor in terms of culture. This is also true in Finland, where religious homogeneity has been and remains high. From the first decades of independence until the 1990s, more than 90% of citizens were members of the evangelical Lutheran church, and in 2016, the proportion was 72% (Statistics Finland, 2017). Thus, the Protestant ethic is deeply rooted in the Finnish culture and, as Seppänen (1981) states, it fits well with the values of sport. Both hard work and diligence are emphasised. In addition, for a good deal longer than many other European countries, Finland has been a traditional agricultural country where subsistence was dependent on heavy physical work in the demanding natural conditions of a sparsely populated country with thousands of lakes and forests (Kokkonen, 2015). In such conditions, it is then unsurprising that outdoor activities in nature have been such a staple of popular culture in Finland.

The social significance of sport was recognised in Finland relatively early (Koski, 2017). Once absorbed within political discourse, the concept of *liikunta* has ensured that political discussions regarding sport have retained a broad remit. At the same time, competitive and elite sport was an important aspect of building the new nation. Exceptional Olympic success during the first half of the twentieth century supported the status of sport in Finland (see Koski & Lämsä, 2015). Nationalism and national defence were important perspectives when sporting heroes were needed as role models and national soldiers. At the same time, the good physical condition of the nation was highly valued. Compulsory military service has made it possible to maintain this.

Sport and physical culture spread out relatively quickly in different parts of Finland and to all social classes (Halila, 1959; Halila & Sirmeikkö, 1960). In addition, compared with many other countries, Finnish women became involved in physical activities relatively early (Heinilä, 1989). These processes supported the development of organised sport, volunteer work for sport and the network of sports clubs which have been the backbone of Finnish physical culture ever since.

In addition to historical influences on the development of Finnish sport and PA, several other processes have affected the current situation. After the Second World War, rapid economic growth, increased levels of education and the creation of a strong welfare state have modified the Finnish way of life and physical culture. Opportunities for leisure have increased and improved and PA has been promoted effectively as a health-enhancing leisure hobby. This begins to explain why, unlike in many other countries, sports participation and PA are not decreasing in line with age in Finland.

From a political perspective, it has been important that the public resources for sport and PA come from the National Lottery. Consequently, economic fluctuations have not had a deleterious effect on the availability and allocation of economic resources for sport. The government and the municipalities, especially, have succeeded in building and maintaining versatile and high-quality sporting facilities.

Explanations regarding trends in popularity of the different sports and types of exercise in Finland can be explained partly in generational terms. Zacheus (2008) defined five PA generations in Finland. The first (born before 1950) was the generation of traditional exercise. They were active in outdoor activities. Constructed sport facilities were not available and the main sports were track-and-field athletics and cross-country skiing. The second generation, born in the 1950s, was associated with the breakthrough of keep-fit exercises. Their work was not as physically demanding as that of the former generation. Participation in keep-fit exercises, such as jogging, became typical for them. The next generation, born in the 1960s, experienced a radical change in physical culture as team ball-games, consumption-oriented activities and use of built facilities became more commonplace. This trend strengthened among those born in the 1970s, amid technological developments and the availability of more public facilities and better equipment. Everyday functional exercise declined noticeably. The last generation in Zacheus' (2008) classification was born in the 1980s and is referred to as the generation of personalised exercise. The increased variety of different forms of sport and diversification of sport in general is seen in the activities of this generation.

Conclusion

Sport and PA have long been an important part of leisure in Finland, and their societal status has been correspondingly high. The social significance of sport and PA was quickly recognised politically and has been used in the building of the nation and the welfare state. Proportionate to its population, Finland has been among the most successful countries in the world both in terms of elite sport and sports participation. One of the significant features of sports participation in Finland has been the level of women's involvement and the fact that PA rates do not decrease with age. Finns are well-informed about the health benefits of PA and, consequently, health-enhancing activities such as walking are popular.

The explanations for the high level of sport participation in Finland are cultural, political and structural. The cultural background refers to the influence of different traditions of physical culture and to the Lutheran roots of Finnish culture more generally. Political factors involve early nation building, the building of a Nordic welfare state and the concept of *liikunta* manifest in investment in public (common to all) sport facilities. Structurally, the focus upon equality has also been an important condition for sports participation.

The future for Finnish sports participation may not, however, be as promising as it has been hitherto. In international comparisons, Finnish youth are not among the highest participants in sport and PA. While the participation rates in sports-club activities are higher than ever, beyond the clubs Finnish youngsters seem to be rather passive. Participation in sports clubs begins earlier than before but drop-out also occurs earlier. The decline in PA during the early teenage years is exceptionally sharp in Finland. The battle against sedentary lifestyles has been fought through a variety of programmes carried out by non-governmental sports organisations and, in recent years, central government has become more involved. This is one of the examples of the changed relationship between the government and sports organisations. The renewal of sports organisations will be fundamental to the Finnish sport system in the future.

All-in-all, sport and exercise in Finland is currently characterised by several distinct features: first, everyday PA beyond the sport and exercise domain is decreasing; second, physical culture is becoming more and more versatile and diverse; third, sport is nowadays more often linked to consumption; and fourth, sports participation is more likely than ever before to take place in constructed facilities.

Notes

1 For that reason, they are encompassed by the large dotted-line circle in Figure 3.3.
2 New Public Management (NPM) is an approach created in 1980s to make public services apply the models of private-sector management to a greater extent (e.g. Hood 1995).

References

Aira, T., Kannas, L., Tynjälä, J., Villberg, J. and Kokko, S. (2013). Liikunta-aktiivisuuden väheneminen murrosiässä. [Decreasing PA of teenagers]. In State's Sport Council (eds.) *Miksi murrosikäinen luopuu liikunnasta?* [Why do teenagers drop-out from sport?]. (pp. 12–31). Helsinki: Valtion liikuntaneuvosto.

Blomqvist, M., Mononen, K., Konttinen, K., Koski, P. and Kokko, S. (2015). Urheilu ja seuratoimintaan osallistuminen [Sport and participation in sports club activities]. In S. Kokko & R. Hämylä (eds.) *Lasten ja nuorten liikuntakäyttäyminen Suomessa* [The physical activity behaviours of children and adolescents in Finland]. (pp. 74–82). Helsinki: Valtion liikuntaneuvosto.

Borodulin, K., Mäkinen, T. and Prättälä R. (2010). Vapaa-ajan liikuntaa ennustavat ylioppilaslakki, valkokaulus ja paksu lompakko [High education, white-collar occupation and economic wealth predict sport participation]. *Liikunta & Tiede*, 4: 4–10.

Borodulin, K., Harald, K., Jousilahti, P., Laatikainen, T., Männistö S. and Vartiainen, E. (2015). Time trends in PA from 1982 to 2012 in Finland. *Scandinavian Journal of Medicine and Science in Sports*, doi:10.1111/sms.12401.

Compass (1999). *Sport Participation in Europe. A Project Seeking the Co-ordinated Monitoring of Participation in Sports in Europe*. London: UK Sport & Walkden House.

European Commission (2010). *Special Eurobarometer 334*. Brussels: European Commission.

European Commission (2014). *Special Eurobarometer 412. Sport and physical activity*. Conducted by TNS Opinion & Social at the request of the Directorate-General for Education and Culture. Available from: http://ec.europa.eu/public_opinion/archives/ebs/ebs_412_en.pdf [Downloaded 17 April 2014].

Fahlen, J. and Skille E.A. (2016). State sport policy for indigenous sport: inclusive ambitions and exclusive coalitions. *International Journal of Sport Policy and Politics*, 9(1): 173–187.

Finnish Sports Federation (2010a). *Kansallinen liikuntatutkimus 2009–2010. Aikuisväestö*. [National Sport Survey 2009–2010. Adults]. Helsinki: Suomen Liikunta ja urheilu.

Finnish Sports Federation (2010b). *Kansallinen liikuntatutkimus 2009–2010. Lapset ja nuoret*. [National sport survey 2009–2010. Children and youth]. Helsinki: Suomen Liikunta ja urheilu.

Gratton, C., Rowe, N. and Veal, A.J. (2011). International comparisons of sport participation in European Countries: an update of the COMPASS Project. *European Journal for Sport and Society*, 8(1/2): 99–116.

Hakamäki, M. (2014). Liikuntaa kaikille? [Sport for all?]. *Liikunta ja Tiede*, *51*(2–3): 27–30.

Halila, A. (1959). *Suomen miesvoimistelu- ja urheiluseurat vuoteen 1915*. Historiallisia tutkimuksia 53. Helsinki: Suomen Historiallinen Seura.

Halila, A. and Sirmeikkö, P. (1960). *Suomen Voimistelu- ja Urheiluliitto SVUL 1900–1960*. [Finnish Gymnastics and Sport Federation SVUL 1900–1960]. Vammala, Finland: Suomen Voimistelu- ja Urheiluliitto.

Heikkala, J. (1998). *Ajolähtö turvattomiin kotipesiin. Liikunnan järjestökentän muutos 1990-luvun Suomessa* [Changes in organised sport in the 1990s Finland]. Acta Universitatis Tamperensis 641. Tampere: University of Tampere.

Heikkala, J. and Koski, P. (1999). *Reaching out for New Frontiers. The Finnish Physical Culture in the 1990s*. Jyväskylä, Finland: University of Jyväskylä.

Helldán, A. and Helakorpi, S. (2014a). *Eläkeikäisen väestön terveyskäyttäytyminen ja terveys keväällä 2013 ja niiden muutokset 1993–2013*. [Health behaviour and health among the Finnish elderly, spring 2013, with trends 1993–2013]. Helsinki: National Institute for Health and Welfare.

Helldán, A. and Helakorpi, S. (2014b). *Suomalaisen aikuisväestön terveyskäyttäytyminen ja terveys, kevät 2014*. [Health behaviour and health among the Finnish adult population, Spring 2014]. Helsinki:National Institute for Health and Welfare.

Hirvensalo, M., Jaakkola, T., Sääkslahti, A. and Lintunen, T. (2016). Koettu liikunnallinen pätevyys ja koetut esteet [Self-experienced PA competence]. In S. Kokko and A. Mehtälä (eds.) *Lasten ja nuorten liikuntakäyttäytyminen Suomessa*. [The PA behaviours of children and adolescents in Finland]. (pp. 36–40). Helsinki: States Sports Council.

Hood, C. (1995). The 'New Public Management' in the 1980s: variations on a theme. *Accounting Organizations and Society*, *20*(2/3): 93–109.

Hämäläinen, T.J. and Heiskala, R. (2004). *Sosiaaliset innovaatiot ja yhteiskunnan uudistumiskyky*. [Social innovations and society's ability for renewals]. Helsinki: Edita.

Itkonen, H. (2000). *Sport and Civil Society. Sociological Perspectives*. Joensuu, Finland: Karelian Institute: University of Joensuu.

Kahma, N. (2012). Sport and social class: the case of Finland. *International Review for the Sociology of Sport*, *47*(1): 113–130.

Kantomaa, M., Tammelin, T., Taanila, A. and Näyhä, S. (2007). Adolescents' physical activity in relation to family income and parents' level of education. *Preventive Medicine*, *44*(5): 410–415.

Kokko, S., Mehtälä, A., Villberg, J., Ng, K. and Hämylä, R. (2016). Itsearvioitu liikunta-aktiivisuus, istuminen ja ruutuaika sekä liikkumisen seurantalaitteet ja -sovellukset. [Self-reported PA, sedentary and screen time and the applications for monitoring]. In S. Kokko & A. Mehtälä (eds.) *Lasten ja nuorten liikuntakäyttäytyminen Suomessa*. (pp. 10–15). Helsinki: Valtionliikuntaneuvosto.

Kokkonen, J. (2015). *Suomalainen liikuntakulttuuri — juuret, nykyisyys ja muutossuunnat* [Finnish sports culture — roots, present time and changes]. Keuruu, Finland: Suomen Urheilumuseo.

Koski, P. (1999) Characteristics and contemporary trends of sports clubs in Finnish context. In K. Heinemann (ed.) *Sport Clubs in Various European Countries*. Series Club of Cologne, vol. 1. The club of Cologne. (pp. 293–316). Stuttgart, Germany: Hofmann Verlag.

Koski, P. (2007). Liikunnan ja urheilun seuratoiminta nuorisotyönä. [Sports clubs activities as youth work]. In T. Hoikkala and A. Sell (eds.) *Nuorisotyötä on tehtävä. Menetelmien perustat, rajat ja mahdollisuudet*. (pp. 299–319). Helsinki: Nuorisotutkimusverkosto.

Koski, P. (2008). PA Relationship (PAR). *International Review for the Sociology of Sport*, *43*(2): 151–163.

Koski, P. (2009). *Liikunta- ja urheiluseurat muutoksessa*. [Sports clubs in change]. Helsinki: SLU.

Koski, P. (2013). Liikunta- ja urheiluseuroja koskeva tietopohja ja sen kehittäminen. [Basic information of sports clubs and its development]. In Valtion liikuntaneuvosto (eds.) *Perustietoja liikunnan kansalaistoiminnasta Suomessa*. (pp. 18–37). Helsinki: Valtion liikuntaneuvosto.

Koski, P. (2017). Sociology of sport: Finland. In K. Young (ed.) *Sociology of Sport: A Global Sub-discipline in Review*. *Research in the Sociology of Sport*, 9: 133–151.

Koski, P. and Heikkala, J. (1998). *Suomalaisten urheiluorganisaatioiden muutos. Lajiliitot professionaalistumisen prosessissa*. [Finnish sport organisations in transition. Sport governing bodies in the process of professionalism]. Research in social science of sport. Researches No 63. Jyväskylä, Finland: University of Jyväskylä.

Koski, P., Itkonen, H., Lehtonen, K. and Vehmas, H. (2015). Sport clubs in Finland. In C. Breuer, R. Hoekman, S. Nagel, and H. van der Werff (eds.) *Sport Clubs in Europe*. (pp. 147–160). Heidelberg, Germany: Springer.

Koski, P. and Lämsä, J. (2015). Finland as a small sports nation: socio-historical perspectives on the development of national sport policy. *International Journal of Sport Policy and Politics*, *7*(3): 421–441.

Kuntaliitto (Association of Finnish Local and Regional Authorities) (2017). *Basic information about Finnish municipalities*. Available from: https://www.localfinland.fi/

expert-services/association-finnish-local-and-regional-authorities. Downloaded 6 April 2017.

Laine, A. (2017). The importance of the private sport sector has increased. In A. Laine and H. Vehmas (eds.) *Private Sport Sector in Europe. A Cross-National Comparative Perspective*. (pp. 107–125). Heidelberg, Germany: Springer.

Lampinen, E.K., Eloranta, A.M., Haapala, E.A., Lindi, V., Väistö, J., Lintu, N., Karjalainen, P., Kukkonen-Harjula, K., Laaksonen, D. and Lakka, T.A. (2017). Physical activity, sedentary behaviour, and socioeconomic status among Finnish girls and boys aged 6–8 years. *European Journal of Sport Science, 17*(4): 462–472.

Lehtonen, K. (2015). Suomalaisen urheiluliikkeen muutosprosessi systeemiteoreettisesti tulkittuna. [System theoretical construing to the Finnish sport movement reform]. *Administrative Studies, 34*(4): 311–325.

Lehtonen, K. (2017). *Muuttuvat rakenteet – staattiset verkostot. Liikunta- ja urheilujärjestelmä 2010-luvun Suomessa.* [Changing structures – static networks. Finnish sports system in the 2010s]. Jyväskylä: LIKES Research reports on PA and health. https://www.likes.fi/filebank/2619-Lehtonen-vaitoskirja-web.pdf

Lindroth, J. (1974). *Idrottens väg till folkrörelse. Studier i svensk idrottsrörelse till 1915.* [Athletics becomes a popular movement. Studies in the Swedish athletics movement up until 1915]. *Studia Historica Upsalensia* 60. Uppsala, Sweden: University of Uppsala.

MEC (Ministry of Education and Culture) (2017). *Liikuntatoimi tilastojen valossa 2015. Perustilastot vuodelta 2015.* [Sports statistics 2015]. Helsinki: Opetus- ja kulttuuriministeriö.

Mononen, K., Blomqvist, M., Koski, P. and Kokko, S. (2016). Urheilu ja seuraharrastaminen [Sports club activities]. In S. Kokko and A. Mehtälä (eds.) *Lasten ja nuorten liikuntakäyttäytyminen Suomessa* [The PA Behaviours of children and adolescents in Finland]. (pp. 27–35). Helsinki: Valtion liikuntaneuvosto.

Myllyniemi, S. and Berg, P. (2013) *Nuoria liikkeellä! Nuorten vapaa-aikatutkimus.* [Young people on the go! Study of young people's leisure activities]. Finnish Youth Research Society, No. 49.

Mäkinen, T. (2010). *Trends and explanations for socioeconomic differences in PA.* Lääketieteellinen tiedekunta. Diss. Helsinki: University of Helsinki.

Mäkinen, J., Aarresola, O., Frantsi, J., Laine, K., Lehtonen, K., Lämsä, J., Saari, A. and Vihinen, T. (2015) *Liikuntajärjestöjen arvioinnin kehittäminen ja lajiliittokysely.* [Evaluation of national sport organisations]. Publications of Research Institute of Olympic Sports, No 50. Helsinki: KIHU.

NOC (National Olympic Committee) (2017). *Subsidies for developing elite sport in 2016.* Available from: https://www.olympiakomitea.fi/huippu-urheilu/huippuvaiheen-ohjelma/valmennuksen-tukijarjestelma/ Downloaded 6 April 2017

OKM (2011). *Suomalaisten fyysinen aktiivisuus ja kunto 2010. Terveyttä edistävän liikunnan nykytila ja muutokset.* [PA and fitness of Finns in 2010. Current status and changes in health-enhancing PA]. Helsinki: Opetus- ja kulttuuriministeriö.

OKM (2013a). *Miksi murrosikäinen luopuu liikunnasta?* [Why do adolescents drop-out from sport?]. Valtion liikuntaneuvoston julkaisuja 2013:3, Helsinki: Opetus- ja kulttuuriministeriö.

OKM (2013b). *Liikuntatoimi tilastojen valossa. Perustilastot vuodelta 2011.* [BasicsStatistics on sport]. Opetus- ja kulttuuriministeriön julkaisuja 2013:2. Helsinki: Opetus- ja kulttuuriministeriö.

Scheerder, J., Breedveld, K. and Borgers, J. (2015) Who is doing a run with the running boom? The growth and governance of one of Europe's most popular sport activities. In J. Scheerder & K. Breedveld (eds.) *Running Across Europe: The Rise and Size of One of the Largest Sport Markets*. (pp. 1–27). London: Palgrave Macmillan.

Seppänen, P. (1981). Olympic success. A cross-national perspective. In. G.R.F. Lüschen and G.H. Sage (eds.) *Handbook of Social Sciences of Sport*. (pp. 93–116). Champaign, IL: Stipes Publishing.

Skille, E.A. (2012). Ethno-politics and state sport policy. The case of how the Sámi Sport Association–Norway challenged the Norwegian confederation of sport's monopoly for state subsidies to sport. *Scandinavian Sport Studies Forum*, *3*: 143–165.

Soini, A. (2015). *Always on the move? Measured PA of 3-year-old preschool children*. Studies in Sport, Physical Education and Health 216. Jyväskylä: University of Jyväskylä.

Sponsor Insight (2016). *Sponsoring in Finland 2015*. Available from: http://www.sponsorinsight.fi/uploads/1/1/1/0/11102604/sponsorointimarkkina_2015___sponsor_insight_finland.pdf Downloaded 6.4.2017.

Sports Act (2015). Available from: http://www.finlex.fi/fi/laki/alkup/2015/20150390 Downloaded 10 January 2017.

Statistics Finland (2011). *Ajankäyttötutkimus 2009. Muutokset 1979–2009*. [Time Use Survey 2009. Changes in 1979–2009]. Helsinki: Tilastokeskus.

Statistics Finland (2017). *Väestörakenne* [Demography]. Available from: https://www.tilastokeskus.fi/tup/suoluk/suoluk_vaesto.html. Downloaded 2 February 2018.

Suomi, K., Mehtälä, A. and Kokko, S. (2016). Liikuntapaikat ja -tilaisuudet [Sport Facilities and Events]. In S. Kokko & A. Mehtälä (eds.) *Lasten ja nuorten liikuntakäyttäytyminen Suomessa* [The PA behaviours of children and adolescents in Finland]. (pp. 23–26). Helsinki: Valtion liikuntaneuvosto.

Suomi, K., Sjöholm, K., Matilainen, P., Nuutinen, L., Myllylä, S., Glan, V., Pavelka, B., Vehkakoski, K., Vettenranta, J. and Lee, A. (2012). *Liikuntapaikkapalvelut ja väestön tasa-arvo. Seurantatutkimus liikuntapaikkapalveluiden muutoksista 1998–2009*. Helsinki: Opetus- ja kulttuuriministeriö.

Sääkslahti, A. (2016). *Taitavat tenavat results*. Unpublished information. University of Jyväskylä.

Tammelin, T. and Karvinen, J. (toim.) (2008). *Fyysisen aktiivisuuden suositus kouluikäisille 7–18-vuotiaille*. Helsinki: Opetusministeriö ja Nuori Suomi ry.

Tammelin, T., Näyhä, S., Hills, A.P. and Järvelin, M.-R. (2003) Adolescent participation in sports and adult physical activity. *American Journal of Preventive Medicine*, *24*(1): 22–28.

Tammelin, T., Näyhä, S., Laitinen, J., Rintamäki, H. and Järvelin, M.-R. (2003). Physical activity and social status in adolescence as predictors of physical inactivity in adulthood. *Preventive Medicine*, *37*(4): 375–381.

Tammelin, T., Kulmala, J., Hakonen, H. and Kallio, J. (2015). *School makes you move and sit still. Finnish Schools on the Move research results from 2010 to 2015*. LIKES: Finnish Schools on the Move programme.

Tammelin, T.H., Aira, A., Hakamäki, M., Husu, P., Kallio, J., Kokko, S., Laine, K., Lehtonen, K., Mononen, K., Palomäki, S., Ståhl, T., Sääkslahti, A., Tynjälä, J. and Kämppi, K. (2016). Results from Finland's 2016 Report card on PA for children and youth. *Journal of PA and Health*, *13*(2): 157–164.

Tynjälä, J. (2016). *Kouluikäisten lasten terveyskäyttäytyminen 2014* [Health Behaviour in school-aged children study. Results in Finland 2014]. Unpublished information. University of Jyväskylä.

Vasara, E., (1992). Toiminnan ja ohjauksen kilpajuoksu. [Race of Operation and Direction]. In T. Pyykkönen (ed.) *Suomi uskoi urheiluun: Suomen urheilun ja liikunnan historia.* Liikuntatieteellisen seuran julkaisu nro 131. (pp. 369–391). Helsinki: VAPK-kustannus.

Zacheus, T. (2008). *Luonnonmukaisesta arkiliikunnasta liikunnan eriytymiseen. Suomalaiset liikuntasukupolvet ja liikuntakulttuurin muutos.* [From natural everyday exercise to a personalized exercise experience. Finnish physical generations and the changes in physical culture]. Turku, Finland: University of Turku.

Zacheus, T., Tähtinen, J., Rinne, R., Koski, P. and Heinonen, O.J. (2003). *Kaupunkilaisten liikunta ikäpolvittain. Turkulaisten liikuntatottumukset 2000-luvun alussa.* [Physical activities of townspeople according to the age groups]. Kasvatustieteiden laitoksen julkaisut A: 201. Turku, Finland: Turun yliopisto.

Chapter 4

Sports participation in Greenland

Trygve Laub Asserhøj

Introduction

Sports participation in Greenland reflects the geography, both physical and social, of the country. The development of an arctic variation of a modern Nordic society and the recent history of Danish patronage have shaped Greenland into a land of contrasts as recognisable as that between the midnight sun of summer and month-long night of winter. The contrasts of Greenland are revealed in the isolated life of small settlements and the vibrant metropolitan life of the capital in terms of language, tradition and culture. Similarly, they are revealed in the way people in Greenland participate in sport and exercise. The contrast between the sporting activities taking place in Greenland can be great: from the kayaking family, handing traditions down through the generations, to the baseball cap-wearing youngsters, experimenting with new tricks on their BMX bikes. Perhaps the greatest contrast lies between the active and inactive elements of the population. Thus, this chapter on sports participation in Greenland provides details regarding both variations in people's participation in sport and exercise and the issue of participation versus non-participation.

Sports participation in Greenland

The survey on sports participation in Greenland (Asserhøj & Forsberg, 2015) was carried out in the spring of 2015 by the Danish Institute for Sports Studies, commissioned by the Sports Confederation of Greenland. There are no previous studies of this kind in Greenland and, therefore, it is almost impossible to make comparisons over time. The 2015 questionnaire survey was developed on the basis of extensive qualitative research and existing Danish equivalents, thereby enabling the possibility of cross-national comparisons between the two countries. The result was a comprehensive questionnaire with 37 questions for adults and a shorter version of 29 questions for children, both available in Greenlandic and Danish. The adult survey was posted to 2,419 randomly selected inhabitants in Greenland, aged 16 and above, giving them the choice to answer a printed or online questionnaire. Of the 2,419 adults invited, 863 took part in the survey – a (relatively low) response rate of 35.7%. The survey among children was carried out in public (i.e. state-funded) schools from the fourth to the tenth grade as an online questionnaire answered during school hours. Of the 23[1] schools invited, 13 took part in the survey, with a total of 378 respondents aged between 9 and 16 years.

Measurement of sports participation in Greenland involves two partially overlapping questions. An introductory question asks "Do you normally do sport/physical exercise?", to which respondents may answer 'Yes', 'Yes, but not for the time being' and 'No'. This question is used as a measure of current sports participation at the time of the survey.[2] A subsequent question asks 'Which types of sport/physical exercise have you taken part in regularly within the past year?' To this question, respondents answer either 'I have not taken part in sport/physical exercise regularly within the past year' or tick one or more boxes in a comprehensive list of specific activities. This approach is complicated somewhat by the questionnaire being made available to respondents in both Greenlandic and Danish – languages with very different origins (Eskimo and Germanic, respectively).[3]

Having said something about the measurement of sports participation in Greenland, we now turn our attention to the five main elements of the chapter. The first and second deal with sports participation among adults and children, respectively. Subsequent sections outline the organisation of sport and sports policy and politics in Greenland, followed by an explanation of current patterns and trends and a conclusion.

Sports participation among adults

As indicated above, the 2015 survey provided data on the sports participation of 863 adults (16 years of age and above). While the Greenland survey is unique and provides a new level of detail, because it is the first of its kind, it does not allow for comparisons over time; that is to say, trends. Adults' participation in sport is measured in two ways: by respectively identifying the 'normal' or current activity (at the time of the survey, spring 2015) as well as identifying those adults who have participated in sporting activities/exercise regularly within the past year (albeit not necessarily at the time of the survey). On this basis, and as indicated in Table 4.1, less than three in ten adults (29%) were normally active in 2015. A similar proportion of the adults surveyed (28%) had not participated in sport

Table 4.1 Do you normally take part in sport/exercise? (%)

	Total	*Women*	*Men*	*16–19 years*	*20–29 years*	*30–39 years*	*40–49 years*	*50–59 years*	*60 years+*
Yes	29	28	30	29	42	37	23	25	21
Yes, but not for the time being	28	28	28	37	28	27	31	24	28
No	43	44	42	35	30	36	46	51	51

or exercise, 'for the time being', while the remaining 43% had not participated at all.

There were no notable differences in 'normal' sports participation between women and men. A number of differences were evident, though, at the level of the different adult age groups. The age groups 20–29 years and 30–39 years had the highest normal/current participation in sport: 42% and 37% respectively. By comparison, 29% of 16–19-years-olds were normally/currently active, with a comparatively large proportion of 37% currently inactive. This might have to do with a number of changes taking place in the late teenage years (e.g. education, residence and career) pushing sport/exercise off youngsters' immediate agendas.

Using the alternative or, rather, supplementary measure of sports participation (based on regular activity in at least one form of sport/exercise within the previous year), a total of 67% of Greenlandic adults surveyed had been active regularly within the previous year. The remaining third (33%) had taken part in no form of sporting activity or physical exercise regularly within the previous year (Table 4.2).

The 20–29-year-old Greenlandic adults surveyed stood out as the most active group in terms of frequency of sports participation (bearing in mind that frequency data were based on active adults only – those who had participated regularly in at least one form of sport/exercise within the past year). Just under half of all active Greenlandic adults (46%) participated in sport/exercise a minimum of three times a week, while almost one-third (32%) participated in sport/exercise once or twice a week, and the remaining 22% of active adults participated in sport/exercise less frequently than that (Table 4.3).

Table 4.2 Which types of sport/physical exercise have you taken part in regularly within the past year? (%)

	Total	*Women*	*Men*	*16–19 years*	*20–29 years*	*30–39 years*	*40–49 years*	*50–59 years*	*60 years+*
One or more activities regularly within the past year	67	66	67	76	76	75	64	60	59
No activities regularly within the past year	33	34	33	24	24	25	36	40	41

Table 4.3 How often do you do sport/exercise? (% of active adults)

	Total	*Women*	*Men*	*16–19 years*	*20–29 years*	*30–39 years*	*40–49 years*	*50–59 years*	*60 years+*
More often	10	9	11	11	15	9	11	6	8
Three or four times a week	35	38	33	37	45	35	35	35	22
Once or twice a week	32	35	30	31	26	38	27	29	47
Less often	22	18	26	20	14	18	28	30	23

There were no major differences in frequency of sports participation among active men and women. When it came to differences between age groups, as mentioned earlier, the active adults aged between 20 and 29 years stood out as particularly active with six in ten (60%) having participated in sport/exercise on at least three occasions per week. In the age groups 16–19 years and 30–39 years, the equivalent share was below 50%, and that number declined with increasing age. Among active adults over the age of 60, three in ten (30%) participated in sport/exercise at least three times a week.

Time spent on sport among adults

Supplementary longitudinal data on time spent on sport/exercise among Greenlandic adults is not readily or easily accessible. However, the Greenlandic Government has, in cooperation with the Danish National Institute of Public Health, conducted surveys on public health in Greenland at varying intervals (Bjerregaard & Aidt, 2010; Bjerregaard & Dahl-Petersen, 2008; Dahl-Petersen & Bjerregaard, 2016).

In 2016, 81% of both women and men met the health authority's threshold of physical activity of at least 1 hour each day. That number was down from 85.4% in 2005 (Dahl-Petersen, 2016). When it comes to strenuous physical activity (which includes sport/exercise but also work-related activities), 58% of women and 45% of men had spent no time on such activities during the previous week, while 11% of women and 24% of men had spent at least seven hours (Dahl-Petersen, 2016).

Social divisions and sports participation among adults

Sports participation declines with age in Greenland. While approximately three-quarters of adults aged 16–39 years were active within the past year (75%–76%), just under two-thirds in the subsequent age groups (64% of 40–49-year-olds, 60% of 50–59-year-olds and 59% of those aged 60 and over) were involved. Participation in sports clubs did not differ much between age groups. However, commercially organised sport or exercise (and typically the latter) was particularly popular in the age groups 20–29 years and 30–39 years.

There were no differences in sports participation in terms of sex. Self-organised sport/exercise was equally popular among active women and men and also between the different age groups. Significantly more active men (38%) than active women (28%) were active in sports clubs. The reverse was the case for activities undertaken in commercial contexts, which more active women (25%) did than active men (18%).

Against the, admittedly narrow, definition of (normal/current) sports participation (shown in Table 4.1), a variety of socio-demographic factors appeared influential in adult Greenlanders' tendencies towards sports participation. For instance, adults who spoke only Greenlandic participated in sport less often than

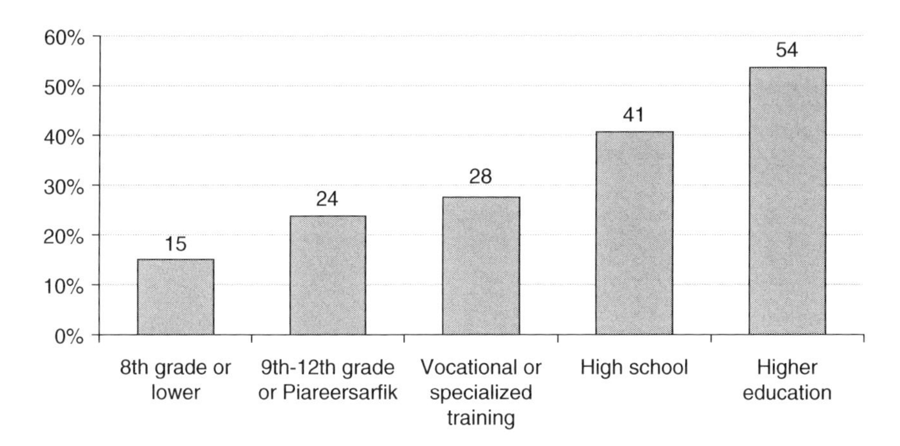

Figure 4.1 Relationship between education and sports participation among adults (%).

bilingual adults. However, when all background factors (e.g. occupation, language proficiency and residence) were taken into account simultaneously, level of education stood out as the pivotal influence in adults' sports participation in Greenland. Among those surveyed, 15% of adults with education to eighth grade or lower participated in sport. This rose to 24% among adults who completed public (state) school education or the preparatory Greenlandic education programme *Piareersarfik*.[4] Adults with vocational or specialised training had a slightly higher tendency to undertake sport/exercise (28%), while adults with high-school education (41%) or higher education (54%) had the highest rates of current sport/exercise participation. Thus, the survey reveals a significant correlation among adult Greenlanders' education and sports participation. Taking education into account eliminates the individual effects of residency and language proficiency (Figure 4.1).

Forms of sports participation among adults

In terms of specific sporting activities undertaken regularly within the previous year (see Table 4.2), 67% of adults surveyed had regularly taken part in at least one form of sport/exercise. Approximately three in ten (30%) adults had been hiking regularly within the past year, and one in five (20%) had been running/jogging. In terms of popularity, these activities were followed by football (19%), hunting (14%) and strength training (13%) (Table 4.4).

Both walking/hiking and jogging were more popular among women in Greenland than among men. The same goes for fitness exercise and gymnastics, while football and hunting were, unsurprisingly perhaps, male-dominated activities. While jogging lost a little of its popularity with growing age, hunting tended to become more popular.

Table 4.4 Which types of sport/physical exercise have you taken part in regularly within the past year? (%)

	Total	*Women*	*Men*	*16–19 years*	*20–29 years*	*30–39 years*	*40–49 years*	*50–59 years*	*60 years+*
Walking/hiking	30	36	24	35	24	26	31	35	31
Jogging	20	22	18	24	30	31	20	11	8
Football	19	12	26	29	37	24	16	9	9
Hunting	14	4	23	10	10	13	15	21	13
Strength training	13	13	14	16	25	19	10	5	6
Fitness team exercises	11	15	6	8	17	19	10	6	3
Gymnastics	7	11	4	8	12	4	3	5	12
Bike riding/mountain bike	6	7	6	8	8	6	4	10	2
Cross-country skiing	6	8	4	2	5	9	8	4	6
Futsal	5	3	7	6	13	10	4	1	0
Spinning	5	6	4	2	4	8	4	6	5
Handball	5	6	3	2	9	2	5	2	5
Swimming	5	5	5	2	8	5	3	5	3
Downhill skiing/ snowboarding	4	3	5	8	8	6	5	1	1
Dog sledding	4	3	5	4	2	5	6	5	3
Badminton	4	4	4	6	4	4	4	2	3
Dancing	3	6	1	8	5	2	4	2	1
Table tennis	3	1	5	4	4	1	3	4	3
Volleyball	2	2	2	2	6	2	2	0	1
Yoga	2	4	1	0	2	3	2	4	1
Kayaking	2	1	3	0	2	3	3	1	1
Taekwondo	1	0	2	0	1	2	1	1	1
Other martial arts	0	0	1	0	1	1	1	0	0
Skateboarding/ parkour/BMX	0	0	1	0	2	0	0	0	0
Inuit games	0	0	0	2	0	1	0	0	1
I have not taken part in sport/physical exercise regularly within the past year	33	34	33	24	24	25	36	40	41

Organisation of adults' sports participation

Active adults appear most likely to organise their sport/exercise themselves. Among all active adults surveyed, 79% did sport/exercise on their own or in informal groups with friends or family. This comes, perhaps, as no surprise, given that the most popular activities among Greenlandic adults, walking/hiking and jogging, typically take place beyond any formal organisation.

Voluntary sports clubs are the second most popular form of organisation for adult sports participation in Greenland. One-third (33%) of all active adults

Table 4.5 How is your sport/exercise organised? (% of active adults)

	Total	*Women*	*Men*	*28.12 pt*	*20–29 years*	*30–39 years*	*40–49 years*	*50–59 years*	*60 years+*
On my own	79	81	76	83	76	77	80	81	79
Voluntary sports club	33	28	38	36	44	34	38	13	33
Commercial context	22	25	18	19	33	30	17	15	9
Work-related programme	9	8	9	6	8	11	8	10	7

were or had been active in sports clubs within the past year. Furthermore, 22% were or had been active as customers in a commercial context (most often, fitness centres), while work-related programmes offering opportunities for sport/exercise had been used by 9% of active Greenlandic adults (Table 4.5).

Settings and venues for sports participation among adults

This section examines active adults' use of different settings and venues for sport/exercise in Greenland. Accessibility to venues varies substantially across the country, particularly between the cities and settlements, with the latter often tending to offer only a small community house and perhaps a gravel-covered football pitch for sporting activities besides, of course, the vast opportunities of the surrounding landscape.

Most towns of a thousand or more inhabitants will have sports halls with strong similarities – in terms of architecture and design – to their Danish counterparts, as most of the sports hall were built in the 1970s at a time of stronger Danish influence on developments in Greenland.

'Nature' is by far the most popular venue for sport or exercise participation among active adults in Greenland. Just under half (49%) of all active adults were active in natural surroundings. After nature as a setting or venue for sport/exercise comes streets and roads in the town/settlement (used by 37% of the active adults) and at home (33%). It is noteworthy that none of the top three venues were planned or constructed with sport or physical exercise in mind. Nevertheless, these are the sorts of venues that lend themselves to the kinds of so-called 'lifestyle activities' that have become increasingly popular in recent times among young and old alike in Greenland. In addition, three in ten active adults (30%) undertook sport/exercise in fitness centres, while large and small sports halls were used by 27% and 18% respectively. Large and small outdoor pitches were used by 15% and 13% of active adults, respectively, and ski-lifts or swimming halls by just under one-tenth of active adults (9% and 8% respectively) in Greenland. It should be borne in mind, however, that these types of facilities, and swimming halls in particular, are not available in all areas of Greenland. Relatively few of the active adults in Greenland used open-water

Table 4.6 Where do you do sport/exercise? (% of active adults)

	Total	*Women*	*Men*	*16–19 years*	*20–29 years*	*30–39 years*	*40–49 years*	*50–59 years*	*60 years+*
In nature	49	50	49	34	40	52	56	56	52
Streets and roads in the town/ settlement	37	44	31	31	39	44	41	34	26
At home	33	39	28	29	32	39	31	36	31
Fitness center	30	35	26	37	49	39	27	17	11
Large sports hall	27	24	30	34	45	23	25	10	25
Small sports hall	18	17	19	37	21	21	16	11	15
Large football pitch	15	8	22	23	29	15	13	7	5
Small pitch	13	8	18	20	21	14	11	10	7
Ski lifts/prepared pistes	9	8	9	3	15	10	9	3	8
Swimming hall	8	8	8	3	10	10	8	7	8
Open water	7	3	10	6	8	9	6	8	5
Outdoor facilities (skateboarding, parkour, etc.)	1	1	1	0	2	3	1	0	0

and outdoor facilities (7% and 1% respectively) for sport/exercise. On the whole, active adults' use of venues underlines the fact that adult Greenlanders' participation frequently takes place outside of established sports facilities (and, by extension, clubs) (Table 4.6).

Active women's venues for sport/exercise participation tended to be particularly disconnected from designated sports facilities, being more likely to take place on streets and roads and at home more often than was the case among active men. Active men were, in turn, more often active at sports halls and outdoor pitches, reinforcing the impression that women tend to be underrepresented in the established sports communities and associated facilities.

Differences in terms of venues for participation were also found between age groups. Older active adults used nature for sport/exercise more often, whereas the younger age groups were more often active in sports halls and fitness centres, in particular.

The next section will focus on participation in sport/exercise among youngsters in Greenland.

Sports participation among children and young people

In response to the question 'Do you normally take part in sport/physical exercise?', just over half (52%) of children in Greenland surveyed 'normally' took part in sport/exercise as a leisure-time activity in 2015 (see Table 4.7). An additional quarter (27%) of children answered that they normally took part in sport/

Table 4.7 Do you normally take part in sport/physical exercise? (%)

	Total	*Girls*	*Boys*	*9–13 years*	*14–16 years*
Yes	52	42	65	53	51
Yes, but not for the time being	27	33	19	26	28
No	21	26	16	22	20

exercise, but 'not for the time being'. The remaining 21% of children reported being non-participants.

Whereas differences between male and female adults were relatively small, differences between boys and girls in Greenland were noteworthy. While 65% of boys took part in sport/exercise, the equivalent share of girls in 2015 was 42%. There were, nevertheless, no notable differences between the age groups 9–13-year-olds and 14–16-year-olds.

The wider question regarding types of sport/exercise undertaken regularly within the past year implied that significantly larger proportions of children were active within the past year. In this context, 92% of children surveyed had regularly taken part in at least one type of sport/exercise within the past year, leaving only 8% with no regular participation in the previous 12 months (Table 4.8).

The data generated by this question indicated a less-significant participatory gap between the sexes, with 95% of boys and 90% of girls having taken part in one or more activities within the past year. The differences between age groups were also minimal.

Although generally pointing in the same direction in terms of correlations between children's sex and age and their participation in sport (i.e. boys being active more often than girls alongside no differences between age groups), the two questions on sports participation indicated markedly different levels of participation. While 52% were apparently 'normally active' (effectively meaning currently active at the time of the survey), 92% had taken part in at least one type of sport/exercise regularly within the past year.

Parental influence

Apart from the relationships between sports participation and gender and age, a number of other factors included in the survey may influence the tendency

Table 4.8 Which types of sport/physical exercise have you taken part in regularly within the past year? (%)

	Total	*Girls*	*Boys*	*9–13 years*	*14–16 years*
One or more activities regularly within the past year	92	90	95	93	92
No activities regularly within the past year	8	10	5	7	8

for children to participate in sports. These factors are living conditions (living with one or both parents, or neither),[5] language (Greenlandic-speaking, Danish-speaking or both) and parents' sports participation. Other studies show that these factors may influence children's sport participation (Pilgaard, 2012; Rask, 2017). Each of these factors prove influential on Greenlandic boys' and girls' tendency to participate in sport/exercise. Children living with both parents take part in sport/exercise more often than those living with only one parent or with neither parent. Among children whose parents do not participate in sport, 42% normally/currently participate in sport. In contrast, among children in families where one or both of the parents participate in sport (right column), 65% participate in sport while 35% do not. In addition, bilingual or Danish-speaking children participate more often than purely Greenlandic-speaking children. Finally, there is a clear relationship between parental participation in sport and that of their children, as children with one or two parents who take part in sport/physical exercise also do so themselves more often than children with parents who do not take part.

As well as being individually influential on children's sports participation in Greenland, these factors also intersect. The groups of children who do not live with both their parents, who speak only Greenlandic and who have inactive parents are, to a large extent, overlapping. Hence, data analysis of these influential factors also overlaps and reveals more or less the same thing. A combined analysis, taking into account all factors simultaneously, however, shows that the pivotal factor influencing sports participation of Greenlandic children is the sports participation of their parents (Asserhøj & Forsberg, 2015: 73) (see Figure 4.2).

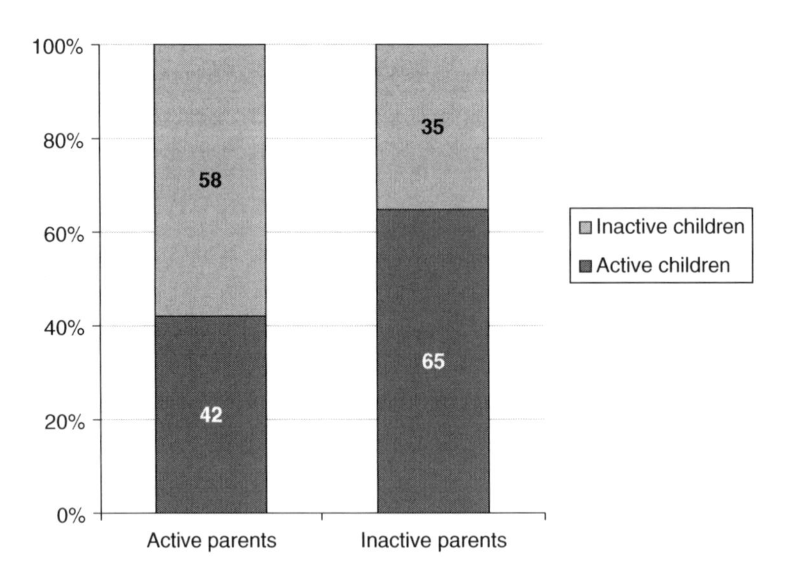

Figure 4.2 Relationship between sports participation among children and parents (%).

Forms of sports participation among children and young people

This section deals with the different forms of sport/exercise undertaken by children (9–16 years) in Greenland in the previous 12 months. The results are not necessarily, therefore, a reflection of current[6] participation in specific activities but, rather, what goes on within the course of a year. As indicated in Table 4.8, 92 % of the young Greenlanders surveyed had participated in at least one form of sport/exercise within the previous year.

Table 4.9 provides an extensive list of participation in a number of different forms of activity. By far the most popular sporting activity among the children was football. In total, almost half (49%) of all children surveyed had played football regularly within the previous year. A long way second was gymnastics, with a share of 29% of all children surveyed. Walking/hiking, with a total share of 28%, handball (25%) and *futsal* and jogging (both 24%) completed the top six most popular sports/exercise among youngsters in Greenland, according to the 2015 survey.

Table 4.9 Which types of sport/physical exercise have you taken part in regularly within the past year? (%)

	Total	*Girls*	*Boys*	*9–13 years*	*14–16 years*
Football	49	35	67	51	49
Gymnastics	29	30	28	33	24
Walking/hiking	28	34	19	32	23
Handball	25	30	18	26	24
Futsal	24	10	43	22	26
Jogging	24	22	25	22	25
Strength training	17	17	18	9	25
Badminton	15	16	15	16	15
Table tennis	12	7	18	11	13
Hunting	10	2	19	8	11
Swimming	9	7	12	9	9
Dancing	8	11	4	7	9
Fitness team exercises	7	9	5	4	12
Downhill skiing/snowboarding	7	6	9	5	9
Dog sledding	7	3	12	9	4
Cross-country skiing	6	9	4	6	7
Taekwondo	6	7	4	7	4
Volleyball	5	6	4	5	4
Skateboard/parkour/BMX	5	0	10	4	6
Inuit games	3	1	5	4	2
Kayaking	2	1	3	2	3
Martial arts	2	1	4	3	2
I have not taken part in sport/physical exercise regularly within the past year	8	10	5	7	8

The sporting activities organised within the realm of the Sports Confederation of Greenland are found both at the top and bottom of Table 4.9. Football (and *futsal*) and handball were popular activities among children, whereas volleyball, Inuit games and kayaking were somewhat less popular. Hence, the list of sports/exercises undertaken by Greenlandic children constitutes a mix of typically club-organised activities and less-/unorganised activities (so-called 'lifestyle sports'). The organisation of children's sporting activities is described in greater detail later in this chapter.

As Table 4.9 indicates, a number of activities were equally popular among both girls and boys. These included gymnastics, jogging, strength training and badminton. However, there were also significant differences. Despite being the most popular sport among both sexes, football was played by roughly twice as many boys (67%) as girls (35%). The difference was even greater when it came to *futsal*. Table tennis was also largely a boys' sport, with 18% of boys and 7% of girls playing. The same goes for a number of traditional Inuit activities with strong historical and cultural ties to the Arctic. Dog-sledding and hunting were dominated by boys, with 19% and 12%, respectively, regularly taking part in these activities. The equivalent shares among girls were only 2% and 3%. In addition, street activities such as skateboarding, parkour and BMX-biking were done by one in ten boys (10%) but by none of the girls surveyed.

Some types of sport/exercise were, nevertheless, dominated by girls. Walking/hiking was undertaken by 34% of girls compared with 19% of boys, while handball was played regularly by 30% of girls and 18% of boys. Dancing was also a largely girl-dominated activity, with 11% of girls and only 4% of boys having danced regularly within the previous 12 months.

In terms of choice of specific types of sport/exercise, differences between age groups were not as significant as those between girls and boys. Participation in gymnastics and walking/hiking dropped by about a third between the age groups 9–13 and 14–16. Participation in strength training, by contrast, involved a significantly larger proportion of the older age group (25%) than the younger (9%). Likewise, participation in fitness exercises (such as aerobics and Pilates) among children increased with age.

Finally, it is worth noting that the majority of children surveyed took part in more than one type of sport/exercise within the previous year. On average, active girls engaged in three different activities each, while the average among active boys was almost four.

Time spent on sports by children and young people

Data analysis with regard to time spent on sport and seasonality in sports participation is based only on children who have taken part in at least one form of sporting activity or exercise regularly within the previous year. This share of the youngsters surveyed (92%, as per Table 4.8) are henceforth labelled 'the active children'.

Table 4.10 How often do you do sport/exercise? (% of active children)

	Total	*Girls*	*Boys*	*9–13 years*	*14–16 years*
More often	18	12	26	14	22
Three or four times a week	25	21	32	23	28
Once or twice a week	33	39	26	35	31
Less often	24	28	16	28	19

One in three of the active children (33%) did sport/exercise once or twice a week, and almost a quarter of them (24%) were involved less frequently.[7] Furthermore, a quarter of the active children (25%) undertook sport/exercise three or four times a week, and the remainder (18%) even more often.

Active boys were typically active more often than active girls in Greenland (see Table 4.10). Among active boys, 58% were active at least three times a week. The equivalent share among active girls was 33%. The largest group (39%) of active girls were active once or twice a week, and a relatively large share of 28% were active less often. These shares were somewhat smaller among active boys, further indicating a tendency for Greenlandic boys to be active more often than girls. Although the differences between the two age groups were not as significant, they nevertheless suggest that older active children (aged 14 through 16) tend to be more active more often than younger children.

Children's time spent on sport/exercise is also covered by another Greenlandic survey – one that offers an analysis of trends over time. As part of the international HBSC cooperation, Greenlandic data on health behaviour in school-aged children are studied through surveys every four years. The latest survey is from 2014, with similar surveys conducted in 2006 and 2010 (Niclasen 2014). The Greenlandic HBSC study defines 'physically active' children as school students who spend four hours or more a week on strenuous physical activity in their spare time (Dahl-Petersen, 2014). In general terms, the Greenlandic HBSC study supports the above conclusions, confirming that boys are more often physically active than girls and older school students are physically active more often than younger school students, albeit to a less significant extent. Perhaps more interestingly, the HBSC study offers a comparison of physical activity among school children from 2006 through 2010 with the latest data from 2014. The results appear bleak. In both sexes and all age groups, the share of physically active children declined from 2006 to 2014 and, in all but two groups (girls aged 13–14 years and boys aged 15–17 years), the trend was the same from 2010 to 2014 (Dahl-Petersen, 2014) (Figure 4.3).

Organisation of children's and young people's sports participation

Many children are active in voluntary sports clubs in Greenland. Nevertheless, youngsters in Greenland also make use of commercial organisations, such as fitness centres and private dance schools. Children might also be active as part of

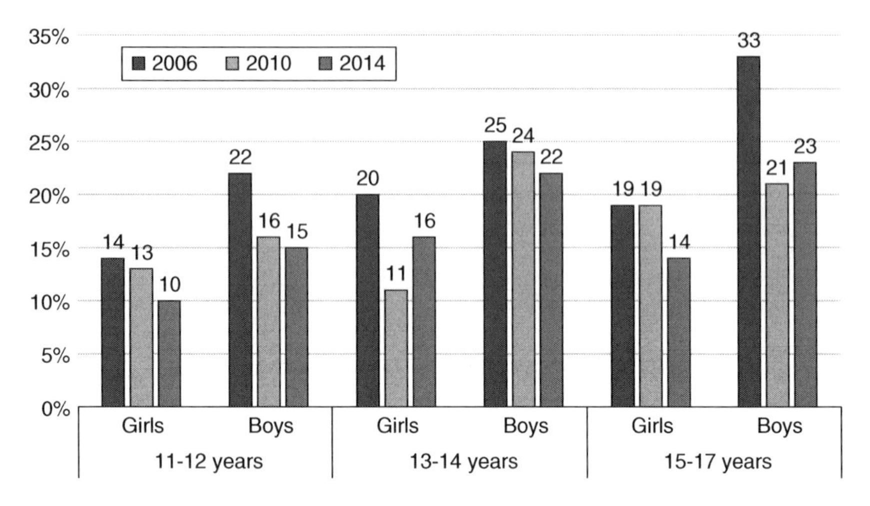

Figure 4.3 Decline in shares of physically active children from 2006 to 2014.
Source: The Greenlandic HBSC-study (Niclasen 2014).

an after-school programme or entirely on their own in informal, self-organised contexts – alone or with friends. Indeed, most of the Greenlandic children surveyed in 2015 were active on their own (54% of the active children). Being active on their own did not necessarily mean being active alone (e.g. a solo jog). Rather, it means activity in the form of an informal arrangement with friends or family (as in a family dog-sled trip or a game of football with friends).

Voluntary sports clubs were the second most widespread form of organisation of children's sport/exercise. Just under half (46%) of the active children were active in one or more voluntary sports clubs. Significantly fewer active children (19%) took part in sport/exercise in the commercial context of a private enterprise (predominantly fitness centres), and fewer still (18%) within the realm of an after-school programme.

As indicated in Table 4.11, active girls tended to be more frequently active on their own while active boys tended to be more likely to do sport/exercise in voluntary sports clubs. Doing sport/exercise in a commercial setting or as part of an after-school programme was equally popular among girls and boys. In terms of age, the active older children tended to undertake sport/exercise on their own or

Table 4.11 How is your sport/exercise organised? (% of active children)

	Total	*Girls*	*Boys*	*9–13 years*	*14–16 years*
On my own	54	61	47	45	64
Voluntary sports club	46	41	53	46	46
Commercial context	19	19	20	15	24
After-school programme	18	18	17	23	11

in a commercial context more frequently than the active younger children, who participated more often in sport through after-school programmes. Participation in voluntary sports clubs was stable at 46% of the active children, regardless of age group.

Table 4.11 indicates that there was no particular trend among teenagers to drop out of voluntary sports clubs. Nevertheless, activities organised on one's own or in commercial contexts tend to gain popularity during youth, while participation in club-organised sport remains stable, with a reach of a little less than half of the active children in Greenland.

Settings and venues for children's and young people's sports participation

Almost half of all active Greenlandic children surveyed (46%) were active in large sports halls.[8] Smaller sports halls (often on school premises) were the second most frequently used venue among active children, with 32% indicating indoor facilities as the main type of venue for sport/exercise. In all, 64% of active children made use of an indoor facility, be it a large or small sports hall, or both.[9]

Presented in order of children's usage in Table 4.12, other venues were not specifically designed for sport/exercise but were, nevertheless, used as such by a significant share of active children. These included 'at home' (used as a venue for sport/exercise by 32% of the active children surveyed), 'streets and roads in the town/settlement' (22%) and 'in nature' (20%).

Fitness centres (often adjacent to large sports halls) were used by one in five active children (20%). Slightly fewer did sport/exercise on large football 'pitches' (18%) or smaller 'pitches' (16%). These 'pitches' are predominantly gravel-covered plains, although recent years have seen the establishment of numerous artificial turf pitches, mostly small-sided, in a number of different towns in Greenland.

Table 4.12 Where do you do sport/exercise? (% of active children)

	Total	*Girls*	*Boys*	*9–13 years*	*14–16 years*
Large sports hall	46	45	49	44	49
Small sports hall	32	28	36	39	24
At home	32	42	21	25	39
Streets and roads in the town/settlement	22	18	26	16	28
In nature	20	21	19	16	24
Fitness center	20	23	17	10	30
Large football pitch	18	7	33	18	19
Small pitch	16	8	26	17	16
Swimming hall	8	7	9	7	8
Ski lifts/prepared pistes	6	5	7	2	9
Outdoor facilities (skateboarding, parkour, etc.)	5	2	9	3	7
Open water	4	1	8	3	5

Finally, relatively few of the active children surveyed (8%) were active in swimming halls, of which there are admittedly only three.[10] Ski-lifts and pistes were used by 6% of the active children, outdoor facilities for skateboarding, parkour and strength training were used by 5% and the open water was used as a venue for sport/exercise (mainly for kayaking) by 4% of the active Greenlandic children.

Table 4.12 reveals some significant differences in terms of sex and age in relation to use of venues for sport/exercise. Twice as many active girls (42%) as active boys (21%) were active at home. By contrast, active boys were significantly more likely to make use of pitches, large or small; outdoor facilities; and open water. This reflects the tendency of boys to participate more frequently in football, skateboarding and kayaking (see Table 4.9).

The use of fitness centres rose significantly between the age groups. One in ten (10%) active children aged between 9 and 13 years made use of fitness centres, whereas three in ten (30%) of 14–16-year-olds did so. The privately owned commercial fitness centres in the capital of Nuuk and the numerous centres connected to sports halls around the country tended to be popular among youngsters aged 14 and above. Consistent with young people's choice of activities, many Greenlandic children, as they grow older, prioritise flexible and individual access to their sporting venues (see Table 4.12). This might also explain the older age groups' greater use of outdoor public spaces (nature and streets/roads) as well as their own homes for sport/exercise.

Organisation of sport in Greenland

At no time prior to the turn of the twentieth century did sport/exercise take place in any form of organised setting. The Greenlandic people of the early 1900s would compete or play as part of everyday life as well as on special occasions. Actual 'sport' and regular training first occurred with the establishment of youth after-school programmes[11] and teacher training colleges during the early decades of the twentieth century (Borum, 1953).

Voluntary sports clubs

The first voluntary sports clubs were founded in the 1930s, primarily in the form of gymnastics clubs in the handful of indoor halls located at educational institutions. The organisation and activities of the early voluntary sports clubs were heavily influenced by Danish traditions and regulations as, until 1979, Greenland functioned, for administrative purposes, as a county in the country of Denmark (Heilmann, 2003). The Sports Confederation of Greenland was founded in 1953 in Sisimiut and consisted of 30 voluntary sports clubs, totalling just under 3,000 members. For the sports clubs, the primary motivation to form a confederation was to establish a closer bond in order to gain access to Danish lottery funds (Gabrielsen, 1978). A strong relationship developed between the Sport Confederations of Greenland and Denmark, most notably manifest in numerous

Danish training instructors teaching in Greenland. At the organisational level, the close communication and inspiration between Greenland and Denmark was, and remains, evident in the organisation of the confederation (with its nine separate federations) as well as in the advent of 'Elite Sport Greenland' as an overarching elite organisation based on its Danish counterpart. Today, the Sports Confederation of Greenland organises approximately 15,000 members in 135 clubs.

Public facilities and subsidies

The public subsidies for sport in Greenland are largely organised, as in Denmark, through the municipalities and they play a pivotal role in making sports facilities available for voluntary sports clubs while supporting them financially.[12] At state level, active sport policies and interventions in the everyday framework for sport are few and far between. In 2014, the public budget for sport amounted to 88.5 million DKK (Government of Greenland, 2013a; Kanukoka, 2014). Of these subsidies, by far the largest contribution (73%) came from municipalities' recurrent funding for facilities and financial support for voluntary sports clubs. The funding from Greenland's share of the lottery funds (18%) and the state-level funding via the annual Finance Act (9%) constitutes just over a quarter of the overall public funding for sport. *The Lottery Funds and Finance Act* funds are assigned to the Sport Confederation of Greenland and Elite Sport Greenland. Apart from the above recurring subsidies for sport, which vary only little from year to year, extraordinary public investments may go into establishing special facilities[13] or supporting special events[14] (Figure 4.4).

The subsidies for the Sport Confederation of Greenland and Elite Sport Greenland – two organisations working very closely together and sharing offices

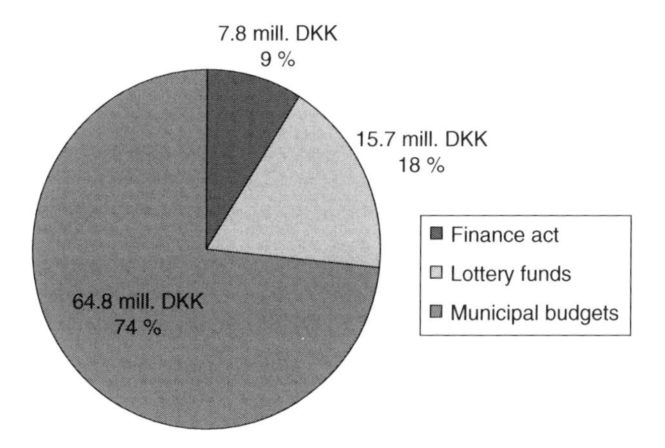

Figure 4.4 Distribution of public funding for sport in Greenland (Kanukoka 2014; Government of Greenland 2013).

in Nuuk – are provided as a fixed grant for administration, consultancy, education of staff, voluntary leaders and instructors and for travelling expenses in the different federations, such as when they hold Greenlandic championships or take part in international events. Greenland is a regular participant in the biennial Island Games and Arctic Winter Games, having hosted the latest edition in 2016 in Nuuk. Greenland can participate as an independent member state in some international federations such as handball and taekwondo, while the country is still working towards independent membership in other sports such as football and skiing and is able to organise unofficial games or compete under the Danish flag (as is the case in the Olympic Games).

Sports policy and politics in Greenland

There are no formal terms or conditions tied to the public subsidies going to sport in Greenland and, as such, the club-organised voluntary part of the sporting sector in the country stays largely out of the public agenda and state policy. In the broader scope of sport, physical activity and health, the Council for Nutrition and Exercise under the Department for Health recommends that all children and adults in Greenland be physically active for a minimum of an hour a day. This recommendation is a backdrop to the Department for Health's broadly defined policy objectives of promoting structured physical activity initiatives in children's institutions and workplace settings, urban planning and access to nature, as well as supporting organised and unorganised sport and private initiatives, including the increasingly popular campaign of 'Maaji Nuan' (be healthy in May) (Government of Greenland, 2013b). Hence, although there are no formal conditions or demands placed upon the Sports Confederation of Greenland, the organisation receives its fixed grant with the expectation that it will prioritise 'sport for all' initiatives among children and youth within all types of sport (Government of Greenland, 2013a).

Sport and physical education (PE) is part of the subject 'Local choices' in the public school system in Greenland, meaning that there is no predefined syllabus or fixed number of lessons per week or school year. The construction of the special subject 'Local choices' in Greenlandic schools is a recognition of the vast differences between the resources and possibilities in the different parts of the country and between towns and settlements in Greenland. Consequently, 'Local choices' provides a framework for doing sport/PE when, where and in what form it is most appropriate to local conditions – in terms of facilities, natural surroundings and weather. However, the framework also includes a number of other types of classes such as crafts/design, art/architecture, music and drama, leaving it open to individual schools to determine the extent to which sport/PE is part of schoolchildren's schedules, if at all. Especially in small settlements, the content of 'Local choices' classes is limited by the (very few) teachers' competencies/ interests and the possibilities available.

Economically, the four municipalities play an important role in terms of sport policy in Greenland, with the majority of public subsidies and investments in sport coming from municipal budgets. The municipal policies fall under the general regulation of the '*Landstingsforordning* nr. 10 on culture and leisure activities', which provides a framework for municipal obligations and opportunities in terms of supporting sport and leisure activities (Government of Greenland, 2002). From that basic policy, the municipalities individually shape detailed regulations. Even as the overarching legal framework of the *Landstingsforordning* offers a great deal of leeway and few limitations, all Greenlandic municipalities subsidise and support local sport quite heavily and within quite similar structures – all prioritising voluntary club-organised sport. The municipalities support sports clubs by constructing and making sports facilities (mainly sports halls) available at no or very limited charge to users, as well as providing limited grants for clubs' sports-related travelling, education and investment in equipment.

Explaining sports participation in Greenland

As longitudinal studies on sports participation in Greenland are non-existent, trends in the Greenlandic population's participation in sport are hard to describe, let alone explain. However, the broader social trends influencing sport in Greenland are discernible.

Social and economic development

Over the course of 50 years, Greenland has developed into a modern society, with the vibrant multicultural capital of Nuuk as a showcase of development and opportunity. But Greenland has also become a divided society, with small towns and settlements left out of much of the economic development and physically left behind by increased urbanisation. As fishing and hunting techniques develop and large-scale operations dominate, many places in Greenland struggle to develop new industries and maintain workplaces. And as cars and buses fill the streets of the growing towns and hunting trips, kayaking and dog-sledding make way for motorboats and snowmobiles, everyday life for the people of Greenland is becoming ever more sedentary (Dahl-Petersen, 2016). In this context, sports participation can play an important role as a potential source of both physical activity and social cohesion.

Danish influence

The Sports Confederation of Greenland, with its nine separate federations, is a testament to the development of organised sport in Greenland and, to some extent, the development of Greenlandic society more generally. Federations with indoor sports such as volleyball, table tennis, handball and badminton, in particular, would not have had the number of active members (if any) had it not been for the strong Danish influence on sport in Greenland and society as a whole during the twentieth century. Early organisational cooperation between the Greenlandic and Danish Sport Confederations introduced traditional Danish sports through the education of volunteers and the numerous indoor sports halls built after the Danish tradition (designed after the popular Danish sports, handball and badminton) in the 1970s, when Greenland was still under Danish administration.

Physical environment and cultural heritage

The Sports Confederation of Greenland is also home to sports that emanated from the geographical and cultural heritage of the Arctic. In different form and variations, football has been played in Greenland for centuries (Heilmann, 2003). The game even loans its Greenlandic name *Arsanneq* from the Northern Lights of the arctic sky, which folklore claims are gods playing ball in the sky. Today, football, and the very recent variation of *futsal*, is immensely popular among boys in particular. Participation in skiing, Inuit games and kayaking does not enjoy anything like the same participatory levels. They do, nevertheless, represent a recent rise in international ambitions and attention to Inuit history in Greenlandic society.[15] 'Inuit games' is a common denominator for a number of different physical activities and games such as 'high kick', 'head pull' and 'airplane'. Developed and formalised in Canada, Inuit games (or 'Arctic sport' as it is more often called in Greenland) have seen a rise in club and membership numbers in Greenland in the past decade. In addition, kayaking clubs, after years of the kayak being all but a museum artefact, have successfully recruited families and young people in clubs focused on preserving the art of building kayaks and offering the tough physical training required to master the vessel.

Public and commercial investment and provision

Beyond club-organised sport and publicly funded sporting facilities, a myriad of informal and unorganised activities take place, particularly among adults and females. Leisurely running, skiing and hiking alone or with family and friends are obvious examples of these types of activities. Other examples are fitness exercise or strength training in fitness centres. Being informal and unorganised, no membership data describe the participation and trends in these 'lifestyle activities', but the upturn in running and fitness events in recent years, and the increased dissemination of fitness facilities suggests a trend on the rise. Today, Nuuk is home to three privately owned commercial centres offering fitness training and 'cross-fit'. Furthermore, rooms with fitness facilities and strength-training equipment are available in a number of the indoor sports halls in the larger towns of Greenland, including some in Nuuk. These types of centres most often operate as municipal facilities to which individual members buy access on a monthly basis, doing their own exercise routines or joining the occasional classes with instructors offered in a minority of the centres. As such, some sort of public, mostly municipal, investment and attention goes into supporting the growing number of people in Greenland doing sport/exercise in flexible settings beyond club-organised sport.

The planning and funding of large facilities for sport and physical exercise is often at the forefront of public debate with underlying discussions of prioritisation between certain areas and towns and, indeed, prioritisation of economic resources in places of scarce population (and in a country with a very tight budget). Currently on the agenda in the different municipalities are a number of sport and leisure facilities with an economic magnitude requiring government funding and external funds: a national indoor football arena, indoor artificial turf pitches, swimming halls and the development of large areas for skiing and hiking. On a smaller – and economically more viable – scale, artificial turf pitches, primarily for small-sided football, have materialised in most towns of over 1,000 inhabitants over the past five years. This trend in municipal facility planning has, presumably, helped to increase participation in football, as artificial turf pitches are used intensively in both organised and unorganised settings (in the four to six snow-free months, depending on latitude).

Conclusion

The Greenlandic climate with its long, dark and harsh winters constitutes, if not extraordinary challenges to sports participation, then at least some unique conditions. These influence sports participation among Greenlandic children and adults in a number different ways, not least by creating seasonality.

A little over half of Greenlandic children and three in ten adults participated in sport/exercise at the time of the first-ever study on sports participation in Greenland, in the spring of 2015 (Asserhøj & Forsberg, 2015). However, the share of children and adults participating in sport approximately doubled when it came to regular activities within the previous year rather than current participation. This may be seen as a testament to the fact that sport in Greenland is the art of the possible. Over the course of a year, the conditions vary significantly for playing football or going hiking, the most popular activities among children and adults in Greenland, respectively.

Slightly more boys than girls participate in sport/exercise in Greenland, whereas participation is almost the same between men and women. Despite the near-gender equality in general sports participation, club-organised activities, most often football, handball, skiing and badminton, are largely male-dominated. As a consequence, boys and men are the primary users of the publicly funded sporting infrastructure in Greenland, mainly sports hall and football pitches, while girls and women more often tend to do sports on their own or in informal settings at home, in public or in fitness centres.

The development in sports participation in Greenland is hard to describe, as only one study has dealt with the issue in detail (Asserhøj & Forsberg, 2015). Public health studies, however, suggest a slow but steady trend over the last century towards a more inactive and sedentary population (Dahl-Petersen, 2014; Dahl-Petersen, 2016). With the public sector and the government a heavy investor but limited legislator in the field of sports in Greenland, it is largely left to the autonomous sports clubs to make sport and exercise initiatives to counter the trends and get more people in Greenland involved in sport and exercise.[16]

Greenland is a country in transition: from traditional culture to modern society, and from significant Danish influence to almost exclusive self-government. In the field of sport, this transition is perhaps most evident in the gradual development of the available facilities and opportunities from the quintessentially Danish sports halls for handball and badminton, dominating the sporting landscape in the 1970s, to the myriad of venues for organised as well as informal sports and exercise today in skate parks, fitness centres and artificial turf pitches and in the increased appreciation of the vast opportunities for hiking, skiing, orienteering, kayaking and so much more in the vast and wild nature of Greenland.

Notes

1 Constituting all public schools in Greenland with grades four through to ten.
2 Data collection among both adults and children took place in spring (March through May) of 2015.
3 The pivotal terms used in the questionnaires, 'sport/physical exercise', translated to *timersorneq/timigissarneq* in Greenlandic and 'sport/motion' in Danish.
4 *Piareersarfik* is a programme to educate adults to the same level as public-school pupils.
5 A number of Greenlandic children growing up in small settlements have to leave home to attend larger city schools from the fourth grade and often live with extended family or in school housing arrangements.
6 This type of specification would make little sense, as many types of sport/physical exercise are somewhat seasonal, with winter sports (skiing, dog sledding etc.) as obvious examples.
7 Among these are most of the children who, based on the introductory question, presented themselves as currently inactive but are still included in the data as they have taken part in at least one form of sporting activity/physical exercise regularly within the previous year.
8 'Large' meaning they have room for a full-sized handball pitch (20 metres × 40 metres).
9 The collective share of children using large or small sports halls is 64% and not 78% (46 + 32%) as there is a considerate overlap in children using both large and small sports halls.
10 This includes one open-air swimming facility in Sisimiut, open only in summer months. The other two are in the capital of Nuuk and Kangerlussuaq.
11 'Youth after-school programmes' is an attempted translation of the Danish 'ungdomsskoler', which offer out-of-school-time elective courses for teenagers, often arts, crafts and sports.
12 Municipal financial support directly to sports clubs most often is in the form of travel grants when clubs go to compete out of town.
13 Such as the planned FIFA-compliant indoor national football arena – yet to be financed – in Nuuk.
14 Such as the Arctic Winter Games held in Nuuk in March 2016. The Arctic Winter Games is a biennial sport and culture event for all arctic peoples, with 2,000 participants from nine arctic regions. The event was granted extraordinary funding from the finance act and the capital municipality (Sermersooq), totalling 50 million DKK in the period 2012–2016.
15 The word 'kayak' itself originates from the Greenlandic 'qajaq'.
16 The Sports Confederation of Greenland's latest strategy (2016–2019) may be seen as such an initiative (The Sports Confederation of Greenland 2015).

References

Asserhøj, T. and Forsberg, P (2015). *Idræt i Grønland [Sports in Greenland]*. Copenhagen: The Danish Institute for Sports Studies.

Bjerregaard, P. and Aidt, E.C. (eds.) (2010). Levevilkår, livsstil og helbred – Befolkningsundersøgelsen i Grønland 2005–2009 [*Living Conditions, Lifestyle and Health – The Population Study in Greenland 2005–2009*]. Copenhagen: Statens Institut for Folkesundhed – SFI.

Bjerregaard P. and Dahl-Petersen I.K. (eds.) (2008). *Befolkningsundersøgelsen i Grønland 2005–2007 – levevilkår, livsstil og helbred* [*The Population Study in Greenland 2005–2007 – Living Conditions, Lifestyle and Health*]. Copenhagen: Statens Institut for Folkesundhed – SFI.

Borum, V. (1953). Sport i Grønland [Sport in Greenland]. *Tidsskriftet Grønland*, 53(9): 337–342.

Dahl-Petersen, I.K. and Bjerregaard, P. (eds.) (2016). *Befolkningsundersøgelsen i Grønland 2014 – levevilkår, livsstil og helbred [The Population Study in Greenland 2014 – Living Conditions, Lifestyle and Health]*. Copenhagen: Statens Institut for Folkesundhed – SFI.

Dahl-Petersen, I.K. (2016). Bevægelse og stillesiddende tid [Physical exercise and sedentary time]. In I.K. Dahl-Petersen and P. Bjerregaard (eds.) *Befolkningsundersøgelsen i Grønland 2014 – levevilkår, livsstil og helbred [The Population Study in Greenland 2014 – Living Conditions, Lifestyle and Health]*. (pp. 47–50). Copenhagen: Statens Institut for Folkesundhed – SFI.

Dahl-Petersen, I.K. (2014). Motion og bevægelse i hverdagen [Exercise and physical activity in everyday life]. In B. Niclasen (ed.) *Trivsel og sundhed blandt folkeskoleelever i Grønland – resultater fra skolebørnsundersøgelsen HBSC Greenland i 2014 [Wellbeing and Health Among Public School Students in Greenland – Results From the School Children Survey HBSC Greenland in 2014]*. (pp. 79–90). Copenhagen: Statens Institut for Folkesundhed - SFI.

Gabrielsen, H. (1978). *Glimt fra GIF's historie gennem 25 år, i Idrætten i Grønland – udgivet af Grønlands Idræts-Forbund i anledning af 25 års jubilæet [Glimpses of GIF's history through 25 years – published by the Sports Confederation of Greenland on the occasion of the 25th anniversary]*. Nuuk, Greenland: Grønlands Idræts-Forbund.

Government of Greenland (2013a). *Finanslov for 2014 [Finance Act for 2014]*. Nuuk, Greenland: Grønlands Selvstyre.

Government of Greenland (2013b). *Inuuneritta II – Naalakkersuisuts strategier og målsætninger for folkesundheden 2013-2019 [Inuuneritta II – The Government of Greenland's strategies and target objectives for public health 2013–2019]*. Nuuk, Greenland: Grønlands Selvstyre.

Government of Greenland (2002). *Landstingsforordning nr. 10 af 21. maj 2002 om kultur- og fritidsvirksomhed [Landstingsforordning nr. 10 of May 21st on culture and leisure activities. Nuuk: Grønlands Selvstyre]*. Nuuk, Greenland: Grønlands Selvstyre.

Heilmann, I. (2003). Sporten fra gamle dage til nutiden [Sport from old times till present day]. In J. Lennert and N. Mølgaard (eds.) *Fællesskabets glæde [The joy of the community]*. Nuuk, Greeland: Atuagkat.

Kanukoka (2014). *De kommunale budgetter 2014 [The municipal budgets 2014]*. Maniitsoq: KANUKOKA.

Niclasen, B. (ed.) (2014). *Trivsel og sundhed blandt folkeskoleelever i Grønland - resultater fra skolebørnsundersøgelsen HBSC Greenland i 2014 [Wellbeing and Health Among Public*

School Students in Greenland – Results From the School Children Survey HBSC Greenland in 2014]. Copenhagen: Statens Institut for Folkesundhed – SFI.
Nordberg, J. (2013). *Statens stöd til idrotten [The state's support for sport]*. Växjö: Centrum för Idrottsforskning.
Pilgaard, M. (2012). *Flexible Sports Participation in Late Modern Everyday Life*. Copenhagen: The Danish Institute for Sports Studies.
Rask, S. (2017). *Teenageres idrætsdeltagelse [Teenagers' Participation in Sport]*. Copenhagen: The Danish Institute for Sports Studies.
Sports Confederation of Greenland (2015). *Strategi for 2016–2019 [Strategy for 2016–2019]*. Nuuk, Greenland: The Sports Confederation of Greenland.

Chapter 5

Sports participation in Iceland[1]

Viðar Halldórsson

Introduction

Iceland is a geographically isolated island in the middle of the Atlantic. With a population of 340,000, it is the smallest of the Nordic nations and often referred to as a 'micro-state' (Sam, 2016). Iceland's population is similar to cities such as Tampere in Finland and Malmö in Sweden.[2]

Sport has high status in Iceland. Sports play a major part in the daily lives of Icelanders (Þórlindsson *et al.*, 2015) and there is considerable interest in sporting contests among the general public. Sport is a compulsory subject in schools in the form of physical education (PE). It is practiced in local sports clubs and undertaken outdoors and, increasingly, in commercial gyms. However, sports are not only seen in terms of competition and physical fitness in Iceland. Participation in formal sports is also widely believed to provide important integration and socialisation functions for Icelandic society, especially for children and adolescents. In this regard, the formal sports clubs occupy a particularly strong position within Icelandic society, holding a virtually hegemonic position at the centre of the sporting scene.

Sport in Iceland is thriving at present. Participation rates in formal sports have never been higher. At the same time, on the international sporting scene, Iceland is experiencing the most successful period in the nation's history (Esparza, 2017; Halldorsson, 2014, 2017; Kuper & Szimansky, 2014; Young, 2017; Wieting, 2015). Nowadays, Iceland is frequently referred to as 'a sporting nation'. To Icelanders, sports are not only perceived in terms of games and contests, they are also viewed as an integral part of daily life (Halldorsson, 2017).

In the first instance, this chapter outlines levels of sports participation in Iceland, particularly in relation to participation in formal sports within sports clubs. This overview is based on data from the annual reports of the Icelandic Sport and Olympic Association and regular surveys of Icelandic children and adolescents conducted by ICSRA (Icelandic Centre for Social Research and Analysis). These data will also be used to explore social divisions in participation in formal sports in Iceland. In addition, the chapter will endeavour to establish levels of physical exercise and participation in 'lifestyle sports' among the

Icelandic population. Despite the dearth of data on these areas, survey data generated by various institutions and research companies in Iceland offer a partial insight into physical exercise and lifestyle sports.

In order to understand the relatively strong position of sports within Icelandic society – especially of the sports clubs – it is also important to frame this review in the wider social context, beyond sports *per se*. Thus, the chapter will further account for the socio-cultural and historical context of Icelandic sports and Icelandic society in general, and, in particular, highlight some of the cultural distinctiveness of Icelandic sports that sets them apart from sports in many other cultures.

Sports participation in Iceland

Sports participation in formal sport (i.e. organised, typically club-based sports) in Iceland is among the highest in the world (Halldorsson, 2017; van Tuyckom, 2016). According to official numbers from the National Olympic and Sport Association, there were 99,800 active participants in the 400 Icelandic sports clubs in 2016. This constitutes 29.5% of the population (ÍSÍ, 2017). This figure was made up of around 63,000 adults (20 years of age and above) and 36,000 children and adolescents (19 years and below). Children and adolescents are the most active participants in formal sport in the sports clubs. Research on youth sport has indicated that up to 90% of all children in Iceland take part in sports clubs at one time or another (Halldorsson, 2014). Figure 5.1 shows the percentage of young Icelanders who practice sport in sports clubs. It reveals that when children are 3–4 years old, they start practicing in club sports. There is a dramatic rise in participation through childhood, which peaks at the age of 10 for boys (where 87% of all 10-year-old boys practice sport in sports clubs) and 10–11 for girls (78% of whom practice in sports clubs). Participation rates decline slowly through adolescence.

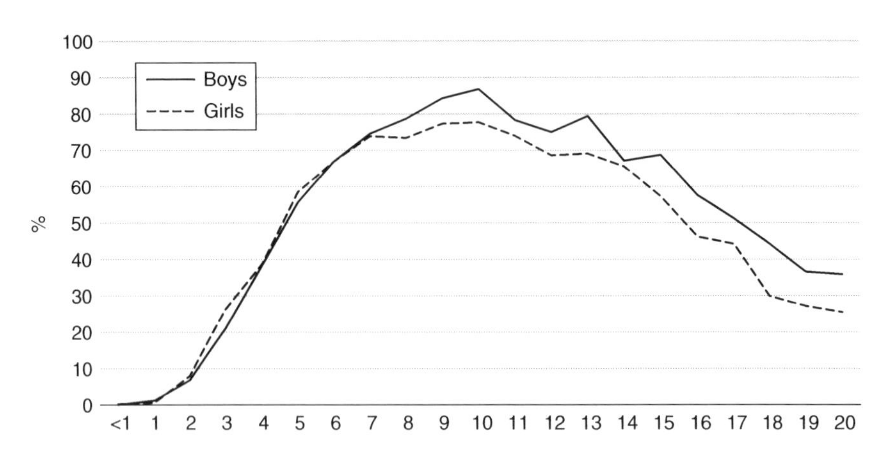

Figure 5.1 Participation of children and adolescents in sports clubs.

As in the other Nordic nations, formal sports participation has risen substantially in Iceland since the early 1990s. There has been a significant increase in the levels of active participation by all age groups within the sports clubs. Data from 1998 to 2016, from the National Sport and Olympic Association (ÍSÍ), indicate that participation rates have risen by around 70% in the age group 20–30, 100% in the age group 41–60 and almost 10 times among older adults (60 years or older) in that period[3] (see ÍSÍ, 2000, 2017). This trend towards more general and active participation in the sports clubs also holds for children and adolescents (Halldorsson, 2014). Figure 5.2 shows the trend for adolescents who practice at sports clubs on a weekly basis and those who practice more intensively.

The percentage of adolescents who practice sport once or more a week at a sports club has risen from around 40% in 1992 to 60% in 2016 (see Figure 5.1). Figure 5.1 further shows the increase in numbers of those youngsters who participate regularly, where the percentage of those who practice four times a week or more in the sports clubs has risen from around 17% in 1992 to almost 40% in 2016. The steady increase in formal sports participation among Icelandic youth is particularly noteworthy. Iceland has not witnessed the downward trend in sports-club membership experienced in many other European nations in recent years (European Commission, 2014).

When it comes to types of sport, football is the most popular formal sport in Iceland, with around 22,000 registered sports-club participants (ÍSÍ, 2015) (see Table 5.1). Golf is the second most popular sport, with around 18,000 involved, followed by gymnastics (13,000) and equestrian sports (around 11,000 participants). Prominent team sports such as handball[4] and basketball have around 8,000 and 7,000 participants, respectively. Other sports have fewer than 6,000 participants nationwide.

Table 5.1 also shows that males are more likely to participate in sport than females, and there are slightly more participants aged 16 or older than there are aged 15 or younger. In terms of age profile, golf and equestrian sports are predominantly practiced by older participants, and gymnastics by children and early

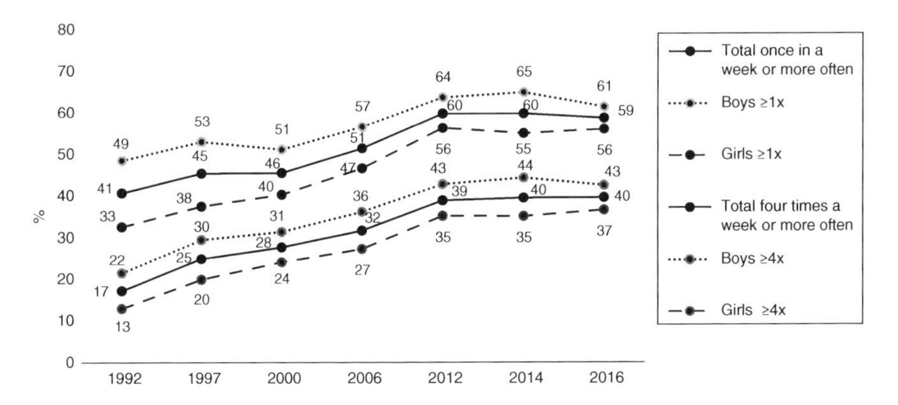

Figure 5.2 Trends in formal sports participation (ages 14–15), 1992–2016.

Table 5.1 Sports participation by sports clubs in 2013*[,1]

Sport	*Total participants*	*Male*	*Female*	*<15 years*	*>16 years*
Football	22,638	15,421	7,217	16,284	6,354
Golf	17,772	12,457	5,315	1,502	16,270
Gymnastics	13,138	4,334	8,804	12,247	891
Equestrian	10,998	5,634	5,364	2,811	8,187
Handball	8,221	5,069	3,152	5,765	2,456
Basketball	6,782	4,780	2,002	3,785	2,997
Badminton	5,521	3,166	2,355	2,574	2,947
Track and field	4,982	2,343	2,639	3,274	1,708
Shooting	4,304	4,026	278	3	4,301
Volleyball	3,149	1,068	2,081	737	2,412
Swimming	3,108	1,349	1,759	2,593	515
Dance	2,777	873	1,904	1,477	1,300
Motor sports	2,167	1,915	252	155	2,012
Tennis	1,697	971	726	405	1,292
Karate	1,493	1,078	415	1,128	365
Fencing	1,333	941	392	267	1,066
Skiing	1,295	1,071	224	142	1,153
Sailing	1,256	659	597	922	334
Weight lifting	1,252	899	353	29	1,223
Judo	1,016	900	166	571	495
Other	18,7333	11,570	7,113	7,242	11,441
Total	**133,632**	**80,524**	**53,108**	**63,913**	**69,719**

* Since some practitioners take part in more than one sport, the numbers in Table 5.1 do not represent actual number of individuals who practice sports in sports clubs, rather the combined number of sports they practice.

1 Official data from the Icelandic National Olympic and Sport Association (see Halldorsson, 2017).

youth. The introduction of team gymnastics has especially widened the appeal of the sport in recent years for Icelandic youngsters, who now have the opportunity to train through their adult years.

There is a general emphasis in Iceland on multi-sport participation until late adolescence (see Figure 5.3). The clubs provide opportunities to train in a variety of sports. Children can begin to play some specific sports, like football and gymnastics, from an early age, but some clubs also provide opportunities to register for general sports in the formative years of sports participation. Figure 5.3 shows that children in Icelandic sports clubs start to play more than one sport from the age of 6. The peak of multi-sport participation is age 11 for boys (who by then are practicing 1.9 sports on average) and age 10 for girls (1.7 sports on average). When young participants reach the age of 15, this figure is 1.5 sports for boys and 1.4 for girls. These numbers have been steady for years (see ÍSÍ, 2009, 2013).

Drop-out from formal sports is regarded as a problem in youth sports (Halldorsson, 2014), where there is a steady decline in participation rates from the

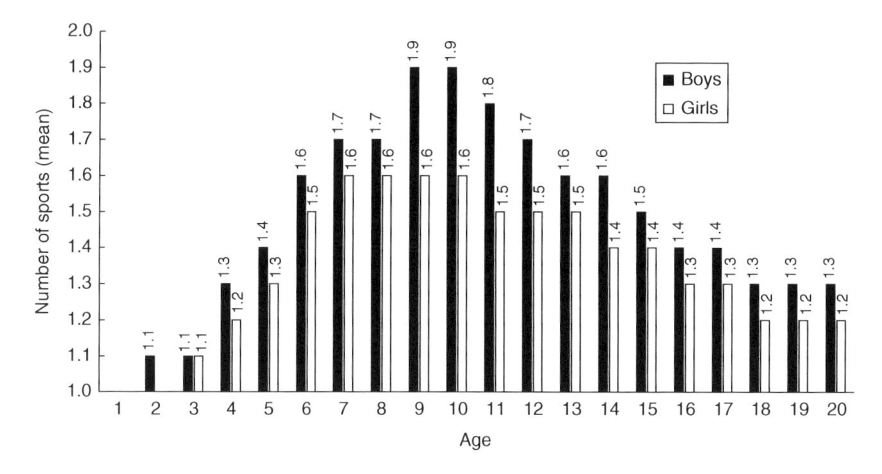

Figure 5.3 Number of sports that children and adolescents play within sports clubs.

age of 12 onwards. Sports participation rates are highest among 11–12-year-olds where over 80% practice formal sport (see Figure 5.4). Nevertheless, over 50% of 15-year-olds still participate via sports clubs, as do one-third of 18–20-year-olds.

The main underlying reason for adolescents dropping out of formal sport is that sports cease being fun. Around 85% of those who dropped out of formal sports claimed that they had lost interest in training, 55% that they no longer had time for training, 45% because their friends quit, 42% because it was too expensive, 38% because of lack of transport to/from training, 33% because they

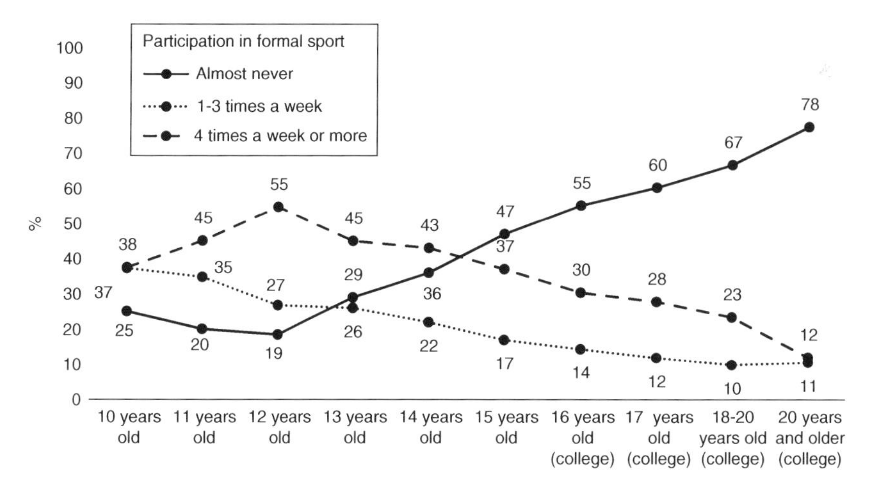

Figure 5.4 Age trends in formal sports participation (ages 10–20).

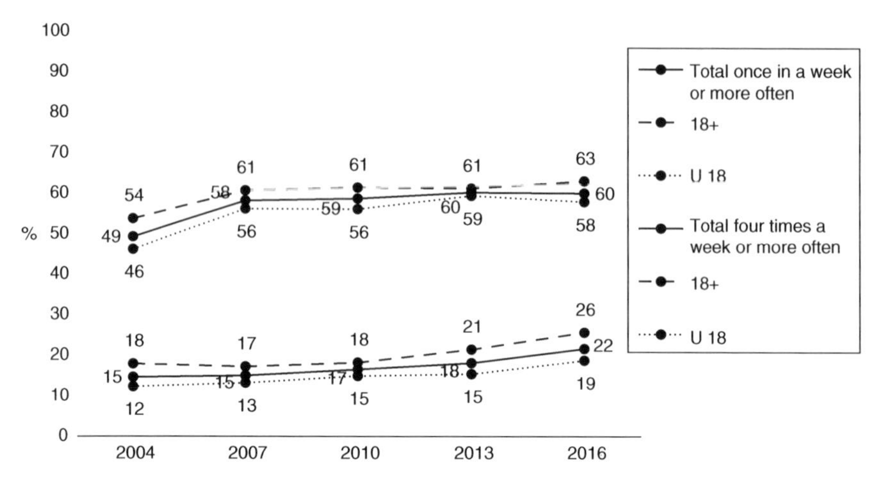

Figure 5.5 Trends in informal sports participation (ages 16–20), 2004–2016.

had to focus on school, 30% because there was too much competition and 28% because training was too demanding (Menntamálaráðuneytið, 2012).

However, although participation rates in formal sport decline with age, this trend appears to be compensated by increased levels of informal participation in physical exercise and fitness outside of traditional sports clubs (see Figure 5.5). Thus, although young people drop out of formal sport as they grow older, many appear likely to remain active in more informal settings beyond sports clubs, in what is often termed 'lifestyle sports or activities' (see the Introduction to this collection). Figure 5.5 shows that around 20% of young adults (18-year-olds) take part in sport or exercise four times a week or more, beyond formal sports clubs, and this proportion has increased around 7% in the last 12 years. This is in part due to the increasing opportunities in recent years to partake in various activities in physical fitness and exercise such as 'working out' in fitness gyms and/or running or cycling outdoors.

Figure 5.6 further reveals that around 90% of adolescents in Iceland report engaging in strenuous physical exercise on a weekly basis. This proportion appears constant over time. Around 58% of boys claim to do strenuous exercise four times a week or more while half of adolescent girls say they do so. Figure 5.5 shows that there has been an increase in the level of strenuous physical exercise by girls in recent years.

Figure 5.7 analyses the general participation of 14–15-year-old adolescents in specific sporting activities or physical exercise on a weekly basis, within or outside of sports clubs. The most popular activities among the adolescents are physical fitness, which 56% partake in on a weekly basis, and ball sports, which half of the adolescent population plays every week. The adolescents are, however, more likely to play ball sports regularly, where almost one-third play ball sports four

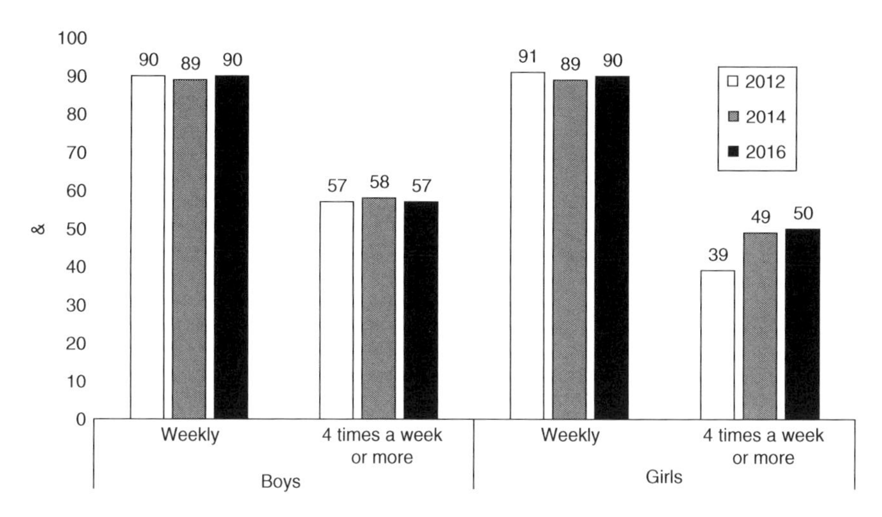

Figure 5.6 Proportion of 14–15-year-old adolescents who do physical exercise to the point that they strain physically or sweat: trend from 2012–2016.

times a week or more while around 12% participate in physical fitness to the same extent. Around 17% take part in gymnastics, around 16% in winter sports, 14% in outdoor activities, 12% in dancing, 11% in racquet sport and 8% in martial arts. Girls are more likely than boys to take part in dancing and gymnastics while boys are more likely to take part in ball sports and martial arts than girls.

From the age of 6–19, all children in Iceland take part in compulsory school sports. Sports lessons are usually three times per week in elementary school

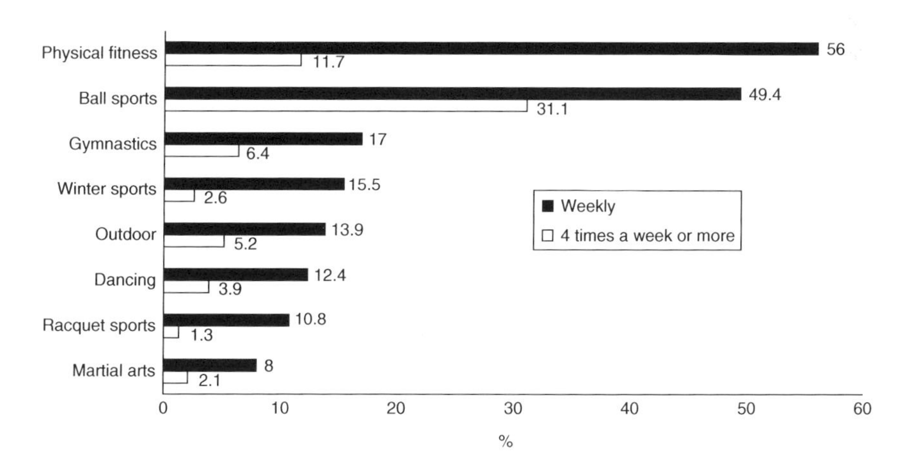

Figure 5.7 General sports participation of 14–15-year-old adolescents, according to sport.

(age 6–15), with two school hours (2 × 40 minutes) for PE lessons and one school hour (1 × 40 min) for swimming, and once a week in high school (age 16–19).

Unfortunately, not much data exist on the sports participation of adults and the general public in the growing 'lifestyle sports' arena, beyond the sports clubs, in Iceland.[5] Nonetheless, surveys have indicated an increase in the general participation in sport and regular physical exercise in recent decades, although there is an indication that this growth has recently come to a halt (Embætti Landlæknis, 2017). According to a survey from 1999, around 55% of the general population did regular physical exercise once a week or more (PriceWaterhouse Coopers, 1999). Another survey from 2008 showed that over 70% of people in the age group 16–67 years undertook regular physical exercise (once a week or more) (ÍBR, 2008). Numbers from 2016 further show that around 20% of adults walked or biked to work or school at least three times per week (Embætti Landæknis, 2017).

There is a further indication of increased physical exercise among senior citizens in recent years. A survey from 2007 showed that around 60% of seniors undertook physical exercise once a week or more (Capacent Gallup, 2007). A more recent study estimated that over 75% of senior citizens undertook sport or physical exercise once a week or more (Guðmundsson & Sturludóttir, 2017). Thus, the participation numbers in sport and physical exercise seem to have been growing since the turn of the century.

Social divisions in participation in formal sport

One of the reasons for the increased participation of Icelandic youth in sports clubs in recent years is that participation in formal sports has been associated with the positive development of its participants through sport (see Halldorsson, 2014; Þórlindsson, Karlsson & Sigfúsdóttir, 1994; Þórlindsson *et al.*, 2000). Sports are seen to be important for individual well-being and, more generally, for public health. This is especially the case for formal sports in sports clubs, but not necessarily the case for informal sports outside of sports clubs – where informal sport participation can even be counterproductive (see Halldorsson, Thorlindsson & Sigfusdottir, 2014; Thorlindsson & Halldorsson, 2012). However not all social groups are participating to the same degree in the sports clubs (see Green & Smith, 2016). There seem to be some important social divisions in participation among some groups.

First, sport in Iceland has traditionally been the preserve of males rather than females. For most of the twentieth century, sports in the sports clubs were organised by men, coached by men and played by men – like in most Western nations (see Coakley & Pike, 2014; Wright, 2017). Today, men are still more likely to play, coach and organise sports than women in Iceland. However, women's participation in formal sports has steadily increased since the 1980s (Eiðsdóttir et al., 2008; Halldorsson, 2014). Accordingly, females have been increasingly prominent in the elite sport scene in Iceland in recent years and the women's national teams in football, handball and team gymnastics, as well as individual female athletes in swimming and track and field, have become household names in Iceland (see Halldorsson, 2017). Figure 5.2 shows that the participation of adolescent girls is sports clubs has almost doubled since 1992 and tripled among girls who take sport seriously, that is, those who practice four times a week or more. The increase in participation is not as robust for boys as it is for girls. Thus, the gap in participation between boys and girls has been slowly diminishing.

In addition, there has been a substantial increase in female coaches, and women have begun to occupy key executive positions in the main sports organisations in Iceland, such as the Icelandic Sport and Olympic Association, The Youth Association of Iceland and the Football Federation of Iceland. This trend towards increased female leadership at the highest levels of Icelandic sports organisations – as well as in coaching – is helping to change the traditional male culture of sport, empowering women to make their mark on the Icelandic sports scene.

Second, Iceland is considered a largely homogeneous nation in terms of class and ethnicity, and class divisions have not been as great as in some other countries (see Halldorsson, 2017; Scheerder & Vandermeerschen, 2017). This has been noted in Icelandic sports. The local community sports clubs are intended for everyone, and through the years there have not been any significant class differences noted in youth sport participation in sports clubs (Þórlindsson, Karlsson & Sigfúsdóttir, 1994; Þórlindsson *et al.*, 2000). This, however, could be changing. A recent study on Icelandic youth sports has indicated a positive relationship between sports participation in sports clubs and parents' education and/or socio-economic status. In other words, children and adolescents who have more educated parents and higher socio-economic status are more likely to partake in formal sport than those with less educated parents and lower socio-economic status. The relationship has, nevertheless, been shown to be weak and not statistically significant. The study also demonstrated that there was no class difference between those who practice sports in sports clubs and those who practice sports outside formal sports clubs (see Halldorsson, 2014).

Third, other areas of the social divisions of formal youth sports participation in Iceland are largely under-analysed. However, there are recent indications that children and youth from immigrant families – growing steadily in Iceland – are less likely to partake in formal sport than those of Icelandic origins and, similarly, gay and lesbian youngsters are less likely to take part compared with their heterosexual peers (Guðmundsdóttir *et al.*, 2016). Finally, studies show that children with an intellectual disability are less likely to practice sports in sports clubs, as well as to be physically active, than their peers (Einarsson *et al.*, 2016). The same probably applies to those with physical disability (Goodwin, 2017), according to the main sources in the field, although no research exists in Iceland to confirm such a hypothesis.

The policy and organisation of sports in Iceland

The history of sports in Iceland can be traced back to the early settlers. In the famous Icelandic sagas, there were frequent mentions of Viking games, which were built on physical strength, such as wrestling, and games with weapons as well as ball games (Jónsson, 1983; Wieting, 2015). The Viking heritage is still, today, linked to Icelandic sports, both within Icelandic society as well as in the international discourse – where successful Icelandic athletes are often described as Vikings, both in traditional sporting contests (see Halldorsson, 2017) as well as in strongmen and fitness competitions (see Wieting, 2015). Thus, Icelanders have developed a national identity closely tied to physical activity, strength and sports (Wieting, 2015). This shows in the interest of Icelanders in their national sporting teams which, when playing in major tournaments, can be watched on television by over 80% of the population (Halldorsson, 2017).

Sports in Iceland were informal pastimes until the turn of the twentieth century when they took on the characteristics of modern sports as we know them today. In the early twentieth century, the Icelandic sports clubs and associations were mostly built around the national sentiments associated with Iceland's fight for independence from Denmark (Halldorsson, 2017). Iceland gained its independence in 1918 and became a republic in 1944. Modern sport in Iceland can be traced to the turn of the twentieth century when the first sports clubs were established – particularly under Danish influence. In 1906, shortly after the formation of the first sports clubs, the Icelandic Youth Association was established (in part to fight for Iceland's independence from Denmark) and the National Olympic and Sport Association in 1912.[6]

The Icelandic sports clubs were rooted in the volunteer movements, as in other Nordic nations, in the early twentieth century and were intended to foster democracy and civic society (Andersen & Ronglan, 2012; Halldorsson, 2017; Peterson, 2008; Seippel, 2008). Sports were further taken up in school curricula and slowly progressed to become an important part of the daily lives of Icelanders in the latter part of the twentieth century. While UMFÍ has a more general role in promoting healthy lifestyles and social issues for Icelandic society, ÍSÍ serves as an umbrella organisation for the specific sports federations and sports clubs. All sports clubs are members of ÍSÍ and many clubs are also members of UMFÍ, but ÍSÍ has a near-monopoly on competitive sports in Iceland.

For most of the twentieth century, Icelanders were heavily influenced by their Nordic neighbours with regard to which sports to play and how to organise and administer sports. In this respect, Icelandic sports remain largely built around 'the Nordic sports model' – the foundation of sports in the Nordic nations (see Bairner, 2010). The Icelandic sports organisations work in close collaboration with their Nordic colleagues and follow their conduct in most sports-related matters. Sports for the Icelanders are, however, still seen as important for their independence and identity on the world stage (Halldorsson, 2017).

Funding for sports

Formal sports in Iceland are built around the local sports clubs: grass-roots clubs that serve the local community, especially children and adolescents. The clubs work at the community level and are open to everybody. The clubs are mainly funded by the municipalities – which provide sports facilities and employ some staff for administrative work – as well as the state – which supports the sports governing bodies and the sports federations. The overall proportion of funding is, however, almost exclusively provided by the municipalities, which provide 40 times more funding for formal sports than does the state through the Ministry of Education (see Þórlindsson *et al.* 2015). The sports associations further receive lottery funds which are distributed to the sports federations through ÍSÍ and to various projects through UMFÍ.

The municipalities are mainly responsible for providing sports facilities to the local community sports clubs. Building facilities for sport as well as providing basic equipment and maintenance[7] constitutes the municipalities' largest expense. Accordingly, since the local sports clubs are subject to public funding, they correspondingly serve the local community by working to promote positive development through sport – as indicated above. The typical local sports complex of an Icelandic sports club consists of an indoor multi-sports hall (which serves many sports as well as PE courses for the local schools) and an outdoor football pitch or pitches. Historically, those pitches have developed from gravel (commonplace until the late 1980s), to grass, to AstroTurf fields in the 2000s. Most sports clubs have more than one football pitch. Most sports complexes, especially in the countryside, also possess swimming pools (mostly outdoor), which also serve the general population. Icelandic sports club complexes often also function as community centres, hosting all kinds of local activities such as concerts, community gatherings and festivals. In this manner, the local sports complexes often serve as the hub and 'heart' of local communities in Iceland.

Since the turn of the century, there has been an upsurge in the building of special facilities for specialised sports, in contrast with multi-sport halls. The Icelandic Football Association (KSÍ), in particular, has invested in football facilities by supporting sports clubs in changing to AstroTurf surfaces, building indoor football halls in the clubs and introducing mini-football pitches all around the country. In total, there are now 179 full-size football pitches in Iceland (natural grass or AstroTurf, outdoor or indoor), which equates to approximately 1,800 inhabitants for each full-size football pitch and one for every 128 registered players. Due to the increasing interest in gymnastics – especially team gymnastics – there has also been a growth in the incorporation of special gymnastics halls within local sports complexes. In 2018, there were eight large gymnastics halls in Iceland, with four more under construction.

Besides formal sports clubs there have, in recent years, been increased opportunities to undertake physical exercise in various kinds of fitness centres in Iceland. Privately owned commercial sport and fitness facilities, aimed at the general public, have appeared in all towns and most neighbourhoods in Iceland. Some of these fitness centres are attached to the traditional sports complexes while others are situated elsewhere, even in industrial districts and shopping malls.

Finally, despite the weather in Iceland, which is typified by long, cold and dark winters and very short and bright summers, the natural resources in Iceland facilitate recreational outdoor activity to some extent. Running, cycling, climbing and hiking have, for instance, become more popular in recent years and there has been an upsurge in the building of walking and cycling paths in urban areas.

Coaches

Sports clubs employ some full-time staff as well as coaches for all participants. For the most part, the coaches work part-time alongside other employment beyond the sports clubs. Iceland contrasts with some other Nordic nations in this respect. While most nations tend to depend more on the volunteering work of parents to coach the younger age groups, the sports clubs in Iceland provide paid and specialised coaches for all participants, from the beginning of participation at around the age of three to four. The Icelandic sports federations also place great emphasis on coach education in formal sports. To varying degrees, depending on the sport, most club coaches have coaching qualifications. This is most notable in football. As a result of an initiative of the Icelandic Football Federation in the early 2000s, Iceland now has far more coaches with UEFA coaching certificates, per capita, than its neighbouring countries (there is one qualified UEFA coach for every 500 Icelanders, compared with approximately one for every 15,000 elsewhere in Europe). Of all the head coaches in Icelandic football, over two-thirds hold the UEFA B license or more and around 30% have the UEFA A license or more (KSÍ, 2018). Though such high numbers of educated coaches are not to be found in all sports in Iceland, all sports underscore the importance of providing qualified and paid coaches for all their participants from the beginning of formal sports participation.

Volunteers

Funding aside, Icelandic sports clubs rely heavily on the work of volunteers (Gísladóttir, 2006). Around 10% of Icelanders are said to work as volunteers in Icelandic sports clubs (Hrafnsdóttir, Jónsdóttir & Kristmundsson, 2014). Among other things, the volunteers – most often parents of participants and other enthusiasts – sit on boards and committees, raise funds and assist in the organisation of games and tournaments. It is also customary for employed staff in Icelandic sports to put in more working hours per working week than the average worker, particularly on evenings and weekends. In effect, therefore, the employed staff members also work as part-time volunteers in the Icelandic sports movement!

Furthermore, parents and other volunteers were also a driving force in the building of sports facilities in the twentieth century. This is still the case in small towns around the country, where the sports clubs are run by enthusiastic visionaries and where it takes the collective effort of the town's inhabitants to build sports facilities and run the day-to-day operations of the sports clubs. Thus, it can be argued that without the work of the volunteers, the sports clubs system in Iceland (and, for that matter, in most other countries) would not exist as it does today (Downward, Dawson, & Dejonghe 2009; Gísladóttir, 2006).

Explaining sports participation in Iceland

The upsurge of sport in Iceland can be linked to the international trend which Crum (1991) has termed 'the sportization of society'. The high rates of participation in sport among Icelanders also rests on various socio-cultural, structural and historical factors which have increased the general status of sport in Icelandic society. The formal sports clubs play an exceptionally important role in this context, where participation in the clubs is high and the clubs have gained hegemonic status in Icelandic sports. Almost all youngsters take part in sport through the club system in the first instance and early sports participation is a good indicator of sports participation later in life (Vanreusel & Scheerder, 2016). For one thing, the sports clubs provide the younger generations with opportunities to take part in formal activities after school, in safe environments, from early on. The clubs are, in this sense, a part of the structural fabric of Icelandic society. There is general consensus in Iceland around the idea that sport and sports clubs provide suitable opportunities to foster positive development among young people (Halldórsson, 2014; Þórlindsson, Karlsson & Sigfúsdóttir, 1994; Þórlindsson *et al.*, 1998; Þórlindsson *et al.*, 2000; Thorlindsson, Vilhjalmsson & Valgeirsson, 1990; Vilhjalmsson & Thorlindsson, 1998).

This ideology of positive development through sport has encouraged parents to send their children to sport after school as well as for authorities to invest in building the infrastructure for sports in the local communities. Furthermore, the municipalities try to support the parents and sports clubs by helping local families to send their children to practice sport in the sports clubs by, for example, subsidising participation fees (and even paying for those children who cannot afford to practice sports) and providing buses to enable younger children to travel to sports clubs straight after school. Belief that sport builds character is a further reason why Iceland offers paid and educated coaches for all in Icelandic youth sport.

The community-based sports clubs serve the local neighbourhoods in this respect and function as social centres for big and small communities all around Iceland. Despite the emphasis on paid and educated coaches and the public funding of sports clubs, the clubs can be defined as amateur and open to everyone in return for a modest participation fee to pay the coaches' salaries. Furthermore, there is no exclusion from the clubs on the grounds of skill level. Anyone can participate in the sports clubs, despite a lack of skill in the sport, at least until the age of 20. In this sense, the sports system in Iceland is a 'sport-for-all' system.

In addition, there are no professional sports clubs in Iceland predisposed towards selecting those youngsters with the highest prospects for a career in sports while rejecting others, like there are in most Western countries (Andersen & Ronglan, 2012; Halldorsson, 2017). The youngsters play in their local sports clubs and they do not change sports clubs even though there is no contract system in Icelandic youth sports. They stay in their local club where it is easy to go to practice and where they can play with friends. There are, therefore, no incentives for youngsters to change clubs to play for another team, at least not until the age of 18. The youngsters only change teams if their parents move to another town or neighbourhood.

Nor does Iceland have a 'sports science support' infrastructure which prevails in the professional world of sport (see Andersen & Ronglan, 2012; Beamish & Ritchie, 2006; Halldorsson, 2017). Icelandic sports clubs are formal in the sense that they provide formal coaches and sometimes follow a formal curriculum. They are, however, informal in the sense that the conduct in the sports clubs resembles playground games. Sport in sports clubs is based on friendships and functions as play within formal settings – research demonstrates that even at the elite level, Icelandic athletes largely approach sport as play rather than work (see Halldorsson, 2017; Halldorsson, Helgason & Thorlindsson, 2012; Halldorsson, Thorlindsson & Katovich, 2014, 2017). Surveys on Icelandic youth have reinforced this impression and demonstrated that up to 90% of adolescent participants in the sports clubs are happy with their club and their coach, and view sports training as fun (Guðmundsdóttir *et al.*, 2016).

There is, nevertheless, an interesting dichotomy within Icelandic youth sports. On the one hand, the sports clubs are underpinned by a 'sport-for-all' ideology (as noted above). On the other hand, however, they maintain a focus on developing players for elite competition: what Peterson (2008) has described as an affiliation between 'democratic fostering' and 'competitive fostering'. Thus, despite the democratic nature of the youth sport system, participants are, in most cases, partly divided into ability-based groups according to skills from early on – depending on the sport – which is not always the case in the other Nordic nations. The intent of such competition in practice and games is to motivate the participants to do their best and to provide everyone with opportunities to compete among their peers. Friends within different ability groups tend, however, to train together for the most part and to do social activities together within the sport. They also tend to have similar training schedules so that they can play together after sports practice. Accordingly, research shows that youth sports coaches emphasise healthy living and fair play, while at the same time underscoring competition and winning (Rannsóknir & Greining, 2014).

It is also customary to award individual and team prizes for good achievement in youth sport – such as for winning tournaments, top goal scorer and best player. This acknowledgement of skill and achievement through competition is somewhat contrary to youth sport in some Nordic nations, such as Norway, where the emphasis is more on communal values than keeping score and celebrating individual achievements (see Gregory, 2018). In this regard, some scholars have argued that individualism is stronger in Iceland than in some of the other Nordic nations, which could explain why Iceland places more emphasis on individual achievement in sport than some of the other Nordic nations (Mixa & Vaidman, 2015).

Thus, this simultaneous emphasis on positive development through sport and sports achievement represents a duality which is a fundamental characteristic of Icelandic youth sports. This duality can also be described in terms of a relationship between amateur and professional sports, where amateurism emphasises play and friendships and professionalism emphasises competition and winning (see Halldorsson, 2017; Telseth & Halldorsson, 2017). Hence, the sports clubs in Iceland are open to everybody and therefore reach both those participants who just want to have fun and play with their friends (highlighting the positive development and amateurism of sport) as well as those who aspire to an elite career in sport (highlighting competition and professionalism in sport).

Thus, the general sports participation of Icelanders rests on the strengths and the pervasiveness of the formal sports club system. The sports clubs are attractive to children and adolescents because they provide opportunities for everybody to play sport in a formal and safe environment with their friends on a regular basis. The sports clubs are also attractive to parents who see the clubs as an extension of school, in taking care of their children after school while simultaneously building character and preparing them for life in general. The clubs also interest the general public in relation to sporting performance and sporting achievement, which is especially the case when Icelandic athletes and teams do well on the international stage, as in recent years (see Halldorsson, 2017).

Almost all sports participation in Iceland starts in the local community sports clubs and from there spreads to other settings and other forms, at various stages in people's lives. Playing sport in the sports clubs thus becomes the norm for children in Iceland, which further draws their peers to participate as well – even when they do not have a particular interest in sport *per se* – and, thus, generates a general consensus around the significance of sport in Icelandic society and provides sports with legitimacy and currency.

Participation in sport establishes social networks and connections between participants (Christakis & Fowler, 2009; Granovetter, 1985) as well as linking parents, grandparents and other enthusiasts. In this sense, it generates a form of social capital (Bourdieu, 2006 Putnam, 2000) for Icelandic society. The smallness of Icelandic society further provides closeness and familiarity between the general public and the national sporting heroes (see Halldorsson, 2017). Sporting heroes serve as role models, which positively affects participation in traditional sports such as football, handball and athletics as well as in commercial physical activities. The power of successful athletes is even stronger in such a small society like Iceland than in bigger countries, as only one prominent athlete can be highly influential for a whole generation of youngsters to take up his or her sport, and also because the role models are closer to the Icelanders than to people in larger societies (people in Iceland are usually within 'one degree' of separation from other Icelanders).

Thus, the main strength of the Icelandic sports scene lies in the formal sports-club system, which supports high levels of participation in formal sports and also works as a gateway to other forms of sports participation, such as lifestyle sports. The strength of the formal sports-club system is reflected in the fact that the clubs have been able to withhold and even strengthen their position, despite the emergence and increasing popularity of various lifestyle sports in recent years. Thus, lifestyle sports have supplemented rather than displaced the traditional sports and formal sports-club scene.

Conclusion

The globalisation of sports, alongside increased professionalisation and standardisation, can threaten the cultural distinctiveness of local, country-wide sports (Andersen & Ronglan, 2012; Beamish & Ritchie, 2006). While grounded in the Nordic sports model (Andersen & Ronglan, 2012; Bairner, 2010; Peterson, 2008), Icelandic sports have inevitably been influenced by the wider global sports world. Notwithstanding cultural and structural similarities with the Nordic nations with regard to sport, there are nuances and peculiarities which characterise sports in Iceland as quite apart from how sports are organised and played among their Nordic neighbours or elsewhere – as becomes evident in relation to other chapters in this book (see also Andersen & Ronglan, 2012). Sports are cultural productions, played for different reasons, in different contexts, in different cultures (Thorlindsson & Halldorsson, 2018). Those special characteristics contrast sport in Iceland with sport in many other countries – e.g. that Iceland does not host professional sports, that all sports clubs provide qualified coaches for all participants and that the sports clubs simultaneously emphasise positive development through sport as well as competition and achievement from early on. These characteristics of Icelandic sports – which deviate somewhat from sports in the other Nordic nations – are, in part, due to the smallness of Icelandic society and Iceland's geographical isolation, which has enabled Icelanders to develop their own language and culture apart from their Nordic neighbours (Halldorsson, 2017; Karlsson, 1995).[8]

It can be argued that the current structure and organisation of sports in Iceland has been effective. Sports participation in Iceland is at an all-time high (Esparza, 2017; Halldorsson, 2014; 2017; Kuper & Szimansky, 2014; Wieting, 2015; Young, 2017). Sport has a strong position in Icelandic society and participation is at its peak among all groups. In addition, Icelandic athletes and teams do well in international competition and the interest in sport is huge. The sports clubs, which first and foremost emphasise youth sports, have gained a hegemonic position in the Icelandic sports scene. The sports clubs serve the local communities as well as developing elite athletes. The sports clubs are built on a solid infrastructure, especially at the youth level, with support from the municipalities and the recognition of the general population. Nevertheless, the Icelandic elite sports system is financially and structurally weak (see Halldorsson, 2017). The sports clubs have further been able to resist the emergence of the growing lifestyle sports (see Borgers, Seghers & Scheerder, 2017) – which take place outside of the traditional sports clubs – and withhold and even strengthen their position in Icelandic society in recent years.

However, despite the present and positive status of Icelandic sports, Iceland – owing to its small and dispersed population – is faced with major challenges in terms of the organisation of sport, both at the amateur recreational level and at the elite competitive level (see Benedict, 1967; Halldorsson, 2017). Micro-states like Iceland are, in this context, vulnerable to global sporting influences (Sam, 2016). While Icelandic sports are presently flourishing, they stand at a crossroads. They have been characterised by a 'sport-for-all' amateur sports model that emphasises positive development, friendship and play, but are developing towards a more professional model of sports that emphasises formal training, competition, specialisation and work – which some have referred to as 'the professionalization of play' (see Ford & Williams, 2017; Gregory, 2017). These trends are becoming more evident in Icelandic sports. The recent success of Iceland's national sporting teams (see Halldorsson, 2017) has suddenly made Iceland a player on the global stage of international elite sports. This success has drawn Iceland further into the global and professional sporting world, and the country stands at risk of experiencing fundamental changes in its sports system in the coming years. The progression from amateurism to professionalism provides significant challenges, wherein Icelandic sports could lose their 'innocence' (Telseth & Halldorsson, 2017) in favour of more global, professional and commercially organised sports. Thus, sport in Iceland appears in a state of flux, capable of developing in a variety of directions.

Notes

1 I would like to thank ICSRA (The Icelandic Centre for Social Research and Analysis) for granting me access to its large database on Icelandic youth. I would also like to thank Jón Finnbogason, Margrét Lilja Guðmundsdóttir and Viðar Sigurjónsson for providing important information (and comments) for this chapter.
2 Interestingly, the population of Iceland is lower than the number of Norwegians who are registered members of the Norwegian Football Federation (see Norges Idrettsforbund, 2013, p. 65).
3 The increase in participation numbers may be overstated since registration procedures have improved considerably within the National Sport and Olympic Association since the 1990s.
4 Handball has historically been Iceland's most prominent and successful sport on the international stage. The men's handball team has been at the forefront of Icelandic sport for most of the country's sporting history. Iceland has been referred to as a 'handball nation', and the national team players have regularly been referred to as 'strákarnir okkar' (our boys) in the general discourse (see Thorlindsson and Halldorsson, 2018).
5 The numbers in this section could include those who take part in formal sport in sports clubs.
6 First as the Icelandic Sport Association, which emerged with the Icelandic Olympic Association in 1997.

7 The sports clubs, national sport federations, the state and private investors also take part in raising and maintaining the sports facilities, to different extent in different cases.
8 Furthermore, Iceland is not a member of the European Union.

References

Andersen, S.S. and Ronglan, L.T. (2012). *Nordic Elite Sport: Same Ambitions, Different Tracks*. Oslo: Universititetsforlaget.

Bairner, A. (2010). What is Scandinavian about Scandinavian Sport? *Sport in Society*, *13*(4): 734–743.

Beamish, R. and Ritchie, I. (2006). *Fastest, Highest, Strongest: A Critique of High-Performance Sport*. London: Routledge.

Benedict, B. (ed.) (1967). *Problems of Smaller Territories*. London: The Athlone Press.

Borgers, J., Seghers, J. and Scheerder, J. (2017). Dropping out from clubs, dropping in to sport light? In K. Green and A. Smith (eds.) *Routledge Handbook of Youth Sport*. (pp. 158–174). London: Routledge.

Bourdieu, P. (2006). The forms of capital. In H. Lauder, P. Brown, J.-A. Dillabough and A.H. Halsey (eds.) *Education, Globalization and Social Change*. (pp. 105–118). Oxford: Oxford University Press.

Capacent Gallup (2007). Hagir og viðhorf eldri borgara: Viðhorfsrannsókn [The Behavior and Attitudes of Senior Citizens: Results from a Survey]. Retrieved from: https://www.velferdarraduneyti.is/utgefid-efni/utgafa/nr/4729.

Christakis, N.A. and Fowler, J.H. (2009). *Connected: The Surprising Power of Our Social Networks and How They Shape Our Lives*. New York: Little Brown & Company.

Coakley, J. and Pike, E. (2014). *Sport in Society: Issues and Controversies*. Boston: McGraw-Hill.

Crum, B.J. (1991). *Over Versporting vand de Samenleving: Reflecties over de bewegingsculturele ontwikkelingen met het og op sportbeleid* [Sportification of Society. Reflections for policy]. Rijswijk, The Netherlands: WVC.

Dawnward, P., Dawson, A. and Dejonghe, T. (2009). *Sport Economics: Theory, Evidence and Policy*. London: Elsevier.

Eiðsdóttir, S.T., Kristjánsson, Á.L., Sigfúsdóttir, I.D. and Allegrante, J.P. (2008). Trends in physical activity and participation in sport clubs among Icelandic adolescents. *European Journal of Public Health*, *18*(3): 289–293.

Einarsson, I.Ó., Ólafsson, Á., Hinriksdóttir, G., Jóhannsson, E., Daly, D. and Arngrímsson, S.Á. (2016). Differences in physical activity among youth with and without intellectual disability. *Medicine & Science in Sports & Exercise*, *56*: 60–70.

Embætti Landlæknis [Directorate of Health] (2017). *Talnabrunnur* (Statistics), 11(5). Retrieved from: https://www.landlaeknir.is/servlet/file/store93/item32432/Talnabrunnur_Mai_2017.pdf.

Esparza, P. (2017). El secreto de Islandia para que sus jóvenes dejaran de beber alcohol y de fumar [Iceland´s secret for young people to stop drinking alcohol and smoking]. *BBC.com*. Retrieved from: http://www.bbc.com/mundo/noticias-internacional-38932226?ocid=socialflow_facebook.

European Commission (2014). *Special Eurobarometer 412. Sport and Physical Activity*. Brussels: Directorate-General for Education and Culture.

Ford, P.R. and Williams, A.M. (2017). Sport activity in childhood: Early specialization and diversification. In J. Baker, S. Cobley, J. Schorer & N. Wattie (eds.). *Routledge Handbook of Talent Identification and Development in Sport*. (pp. 117–132). London: Routledge.

Gísladóttir, T.L. (2006). *Hagræmt gildi íþrótta í íslensku nútímasamfélagi* [The Economic Value of Sport in Icelandic Society]. Unpublished M.A. dissertation from Bifröst University, Iceland.

Goodwin, D. (2017). Youth sport and dis/ability. In K. Green and A. Smith (eds.) *Routledge Handbook of Youth Sport*. (pp. 308–320). London: Routledge.

Granovetter, M. (1985) Economic action and social structure: the problem of embeddedness. *American Journal of Sociology*, *91*(3): 481–510.

Green, K. and Smith, A. (eds.) (2017). *Routledge Handbook of Youth Sport*. London: Routledge.

Gregory, S. (2017). How kids' sports became a $15 billion industry. *Time.com*. Retrieved 21 March from: http://time.com/magazine/us/4913681/september-4th-2017-vol-190-no-9-u-s/

Gregory, S. (2018) Norway crushed the competition at the Winter Olympics. Here is the tiny country's secret. *Time.com*. Retrieved 21 March from: http://time.com/5168048/norway-olympics-medals-winter-games-skiiing/

Guðmundsdóttir, M.L., Sigfússon, J., Pálsdóttir, H., Tölgyes, E.M., Kristjánsson, A.L. and Sigfúsdóttir, I.D. (2016). *Ánægja í íþróttum 2016* [Satisfaction in youth sport 2016]. Unpublished report for The National Olympic and Sport Association of Iceland.

Guðmundsson, H. and Sturludóttir, G.J. (2017). *Greining á högum og líðan aldraðra á Íslandi 2016* [The lives of the elderly in Iceland in 2016]. Reykjavík: Félagsvísindastofnun Háskóla Íslands.

Halldorsson, V. (2014). Íþróttaþátttaka íslenskra ungmenna: Þróun og helstu áhrifaþættir [Sport participation among Icelandic youth: Development trends and analysis of social factors affecting sport participation]. *Netla – Veftímarit um uppeldi og menntun*, 20 December. http://netla.hi.is/greinar/2014/ryn/007.pdf

Halldorsson, V. (2017). *Sport in Iceland: How Small Nations Achieve International Success*. London: Routledge.

Halldorsson, V., Helgason, A. and Thorlindsson, T. (2012) Attitudes, commitment and motivation amongst Icelandic elite athletes. *International Journal of Sport Psychology*, *43*(3): 241–254.

Halldorsson, V., Thorlindsson, T. and Katovich M.A. (2014). The role of informal sport: the local context and the development of elite athletes. *Studies in Symbolic Interaction*, *42*(1): 133–160.

Halldorsson, V., Thorlindsson, T. and Katovich M.A. (2017). Teamwork in sport: a sociological analysis. *Sport in Society*, *19*(9): 1281–1296.

Halldorsson, V., Thorlindsson, T. and Sigfusdottir, I.D. (2014). Adolescents' sport participation and alcohol use: the importance of sport organization and the wider social context. *International Review for the Sociology of Sport*, 46(3–4): 311–330.

Hrafnsdóttir, S., Jónsdóttir, G.A. and Kristmundsson, Ó.H. (2014). Þátttaka í sjálfboðaliðastarfi á Íslandi [Volunteer work in Iceland]. *Stjórnmál og Stjórnsýsla*, *10*(2): 427–444.

ÍBR [Reykjavik Sports Union] (2008) *Könnun á íþróttaiðkun Reykvíkinga* [Survey of sport participation in Reykjavik]. Reykjavík: ParX Viðskiptaráðgjöf.

ÍSÍ [The National Olympic and Sport Association of Iceland] (2000) *Ársskýrsla ÍSÍ 2000* [Annual report 2000] Reykjavík: ÍSÍ.

ÍSÍ [The National Olympic and Sport Association of Iceland] (2009). Tölfræði 2009 [Statistics 2009]. Retrieved from http://isi.is/library/Skrar/Efnisveita/Tolfraedi/Tölfræði %20ÍSÍ%202009.pdf?=

ÍSÍ [The National Olympic and Sport Association of Iceland] (2013). Tölfræði 2013 [Statistics 2013]. Retrieved from: http://isi.is/library/Skrar/Efnisveita/Tolfraedi/tolfraedi_ISI_2013.pdf?=

ÍSÍ [The National Olympic and Sport Association of Iceland] (2015). *Kostnaður Vegna Afreksíþróttastarfs á Íslandi* [The economic costs of elite sports programmes in Iceland] Reykjavík: ÍSÍ.

ÍSÍ [The National Olympic and Sport Association of Iceland] (2017). *Ársskýrsla ÍSÍ 2017* [Annual report 2017]. Reykjavík: ÍSÍ.

Jónsson, I. (1983). *Ágrip af sögu íþrótta: Ísland* [Synopsis of the history of sports in Iceland] Reykjavík: Menntamálaráðuneytið.

Karlsson, G. (1995). The emergence of nationalism in Iceland. In S. Tägil (ed.) *Ethnicity and Nation Building in the Nordic World*. (pp. 33–62). Carbondale, IL: Southern Illinois University Press.

KSÍ [The Football Federation of Iceland] (2018). *Why has Icelandic football been so successful recently?* Press information from KSÍ. Winter 2018.

Kuper, S. and Szimansky, S. (2014). *Soccernomics: Why Spain, Germany and Brazil Win, and Why the USA, Japan, Australia – and Even Iraq – Are Destined to Become the Kings of the World's Most Popular Sport*. London: HarperSport.

Menntamálaráðuneytið (2012). *Ungt fólk 2012: Menntun, menning, íþróttir, tómstundir, hagir og líðan nemenda í 8., 9. og 10. bekk grunnskóla* [Youth in Iceland 2012: Education, culture, sports, leisure and wellbeing of 8th–10th grade of elementary school students]. Reykjavík: Menntamálaráðuneytið.

Mixa, M. W. and Vaidman, V. (2015). Individualistic vikings: culture, economics and Iceland. *Icelandic Review of Politics and Administration*, *11*(2): 355–374.

Norges Idrettsforbund (2013). *Årsrapport 2013* [Annual report 2013]. Retrieved from: www.idrettsforbundet.no/globalassets/idrett/idrettsforbundet/om-nif/arsrapporter/aarsrapport2013.pdf.

Peterson, T. (2008). The professionalization of sport in the Scandinavian countries, *Idrottsforum.org*. Retrieved from: http://www.idrottsforum.org/articles/peterson/peterson 080220.pdf.

PriceWaterhouseCoopers (1999). *Fréttabréf* (Newsletter). Reykjavík: Iceland.

Putnam, R. D. (2000). *Bowling Alone: The Collapse and Revival of American Community*. New York: Simon & Schuster.

Rannsóknir and Greining (2014). *Ánægja í íþróttum: Niðurstöður rannsókna meðal framhaldskólanema* [Enjoyment in sport: Results from a survey of high-school students]. Reykjavík: Rannsóknir&greining.

Sam, M. (2016). Youth sport policy in small nations. In K. Green and A. Smith (eds.) *Routledge Handbook of Youth Sport*. (pp. 535–542). London: Routledge.

Seippel, Ø. (2008). Public policies, social capital and voluntary sport. In M. Nicholson and R. Hoye (eds.) *Sport and Social Capital*. (pp. 233–256). Oxford: Elsevier.

Scheerder, J. and Vandermeerschen, H. (2017). Playing an unequal game? Youth sport and social class. In K. Green and A. Smith (eds.) *Routledge Handbook of Youth Sport*. (pp. 265–275). London: Routledge.

Telseth, F. and Halldorsson, V. (2017). The success culture of Nordic football: the cases of the national men's teams of Norway in the 1990s and Iceland in the 2010s. *Sport in Society*, DOI:10.1080/17430437.2017.1390928.

Thorlindsson, T. and Halldorsson, V. (2012). Sport and the use of anabolic androgenic steroids among Icelandic high school students: a critical test of three perspectives.

Substance Abuse, Treatment, Prevention and Policy, 5: 32. Retrieved from: https://substanceabusepolicy.biomedcentral.com/articles/10.1186/1747-597X-5-32

Thorlindsson, T. and Halldorsson, V. (2018). The cultural production of a successful sport tradition: a case study of Icelandic handball. *Studies in Symbolic Interaction*, *50*(1): (in press).

Thorlindsson, T., Vilhjalmsson, R. and Valgeirsson, G. (1990). Sport participation and perceived health status: a study of adolescents. *Social Science & Medicine*, *31*(5): 551–556.

Vanreusel, B. and Scheerder, J. (2016). Tracking and youth sport. In K. Green and A. Smith (eds.) *Routledge Handbook of Youth Sport*. (pp. 148–157). London: Routledge.

Van Tuyckom, C. (2016). A comparison between European member states. In K. Green and A. Smith (eds.) *Routledge Handbook of Youth Sport*. (pp. 61–71). London: Routledge.

Vilhjalmsson, R. and Thorlindsson, T. (1998). Factors related to physical activity: a study of adolescents. *Social Science & Medicine*, *47*(5): 665–675.

Young, E. (2017). Iceland knows how to stop teen abuse but the rest of the world isn't listening. *Independent.co.uk*. Retrieved from: http://www.independent.co.uk/life-style/health-and-families/iceland-knows-how-to-stop-teen-substance-abuse-but-the-rest-of-the-world-isn-t-listening-a7526316.html.

Wieting, S. (2015). *The Sociology of Hypocrisy: An Analysis of Sport and Religion*. London: Routledge.

Wright, J. (2017). Sexuality, gender and youth sport. In K. Green and A. Smith (eds.) *Routledge Handbook of Youth Sport*. (pp. 276–286). London: Routledge.

Þórlindsson, Þ., Halldórsson, V., Hallgrímsson, H., Lárusson, D. and Geirs, D.P. (2015). *Íþróttir á Íslandi: Umfang og hagræn áhrif* [The scope and impact of sports in Iceland]. Reykjavík: Félagsvísindastofnun Háskóla Íslands.

Þórlindsson, Þ., Karlsson, Þ. and Sigfúsdóttir, I.D. (1994). *Um gildi íþrótta fyrir íslensk ungmenni* [The value of sport for Icelandic adolescents]. Reykjavík: RUM.

Þórlindsson, Þ., Sigfúsdóttir, I.D., Bernburg, J.G. and Halldórsson, V. (1998). *Vímuefnaneysla ungs fólks: Umhverfi og aðstæður* [Substance Use Among Icelandic Youth]. Reykjavík: RUM.

Þórlindsson, Þ., Sigfúsdóttir, I.D., Halldórsson, V. and Ólafsson, K. (2000). *Félagsstarf og Frístundir Íslenskra Ungmenna* [The Leisure Activites of Youth in Iceland]. Reykjavík: Æskan.

Chapter 6

Sports participation in Norway

Ørnulf Seippel and Eivind Åsrum Skille

Introduction

There have now been many years of continuous growth in participation in sport and exercise in Norway, a trend which continues with traditional as well as new participatory patterns. Patterns of participation in sport and exercise reflect the fact that Norway, like other Western countries, experienced strong economic growth during the post-Second World War period and this, combined with changing gender roles, delayed entrance into the adult world, increased multi-culturalism and leisure time, and health policies has resulted in an overall increase in participation. Increased differentiation has accompanied growth, both in society at large and in sports and exercise more specifically. There are now more activities available as well as more arenas for participation, more explicit sports policies and a more complex system of funding for sports.

Having said that, two caveats are worthy of note: first, multi-culturalism is a well-established phenomenon in Norway. The indigenous Sámi population, for example, has always been part of the northern parts of Norway. Second, while new and global trends have influenced the Norwegian sport and exercise picture, participation in traditional activities – with their roots in Norwegian culture and nature – remains strong. This mix of stability and change in sports participation in Norway has challenged the organisation of and policies towards sport and exercise, especially during recent decades.

In this chapter, we describe and explain the development of Norwegian sport and exercise, and discuss some of the challenges stemming from it. We will first present the larger picture of participation, including a separate section on social divisions in participation in sport and exercise. Having described the situation and the development of sport and exercise, we will outline the organisation of sports in Norway and state policies towards sports and exercise, and try to identify key devevelopments within these policies. After describing sports participation and the organisation of sport in Norway, we discuss how the development of participation in and policy for sport and exercise is part of, and influenced by, global societal and policy trends. In conclusion, we identify some challenges confronting the field of sport and exercise in Norway.

Sports participation in Norway

In this section, we first describe the historical background for participation in sport and exercise in Norway. Thereafter, we focus upon developments over the past 30 years, both because these are relevant but also because we have data that make it possible to address the pivotal developments in this period. In the first instance, we look at the general levels of participation: *how often* people participate in sport and exercise. Thereafter, we look at *how* people are exercising: which activities are dominant, which are on the rise and which are in decline. We then explore *where* people are exercising: which arenas they use – club, fitness centres or on their own.

The historical dimension to sports participation in Norway

Norway has a long tradition of sport and exercise. At least since the time of the Vikings, some 1,000 years ago, men (mostly) have competed in running, skiing, rowing, swimming, man-to-man battles with and without tools (e.g. swords and shields) and even poetry (similar to the performances commonplace at the ancient Olympics). The omnipresence of nature (coasts, fjords, rivers, mountains, fields and forests) in a sparsely populated country necessitated a closeness to nature, not least in terms of the use of natural resources for survival (gathering, hunting, fishery, forestry, agriculture). Subsequently, the processes of industrialisation and urbanisation and the corresponding development of leisure time coincided with more romantic and idealised perceptions of the relationship between Norwegians and nature, manifest in use of the term *friluftsliv* (outdoor living) to describe recreational activity in nature.

About the same time, modern sport – a child of modernisation – was imported to Norway from England. The first national umbrella sports organisation was established in 1861, in the period where the modernisation of Norway really took off. Subsequently, local exercise traditions (e.g. skiing and shooting) were supplemented with more modern forms of organised and competitive physical activities – usually referred to as English sports (especially football) – and, alongside the influence of German and Swedish gymnastics traditions, these have dominated the Norwegian sport and exercise scene ever since.

In the second half of the twentieth century, participation rates increased – markedly since the mid-1960s – with the explosion in organised and competitive sport (the so-called 'sports revolution'). The revolution was effective mainly because sport opened up to, and even encouraged, new participant groups, especially youngsters and women. Subsequently, the 1970s and 1980s witnessed waves of recreational activities, including lifestyle sports such as jogging, swimming and cycling. The growth of more individual and instrumental exercise during this latter period was associated with a development in the fitness sector. In sum, the current situation stems from a mixture of historical and more contemporary influences and developments.

The data used in this study are from three sources: Norsk Monitor, a biennial study, representative of the Norwegian population over 15 years of age (Breivik, 2013; Hellevik, 2015); NOVA's[1] analyses of young people (Seippel, Strandbu & Sletten, 2011); and Statistics Norway's studies of children's participation in sport (Vaage, 2015).

Rates of participation

Nowadays, while sports clubs remain important in participatory terms, involvement in exercise and fitness activities is increasingly widespread. Figure 6.1 reveals that while in 1985 only 15% of the adult population reported never being physically active,[2] 30 years later, in 2015, this proportion had decreased to 9%. The clearest and most consistent decline took place among those who were physically active less often than weekly: from 28% in 1985 to 14% in 2015. At the other end of the participatory spectrum, the proportion reporting exercising three times each week or more grew steadily from 23% to 41% between 1985 and 2015. Those exercising once or twice a week remained relatively stable, at around one-third (between 34% and 39%) of the population.

Data from Statistics Norway on exercise among children aged 6–15 (Figure 6.2) provides a similar picture. From 2004 to 2013, the proportion on a very low exercise level was low and stable. Those exercising once or twice a week were in decline, whereas the proportion exercising three times a week or more was rising (from 30% in 2004 to 38% in 2013). It should be noted that the

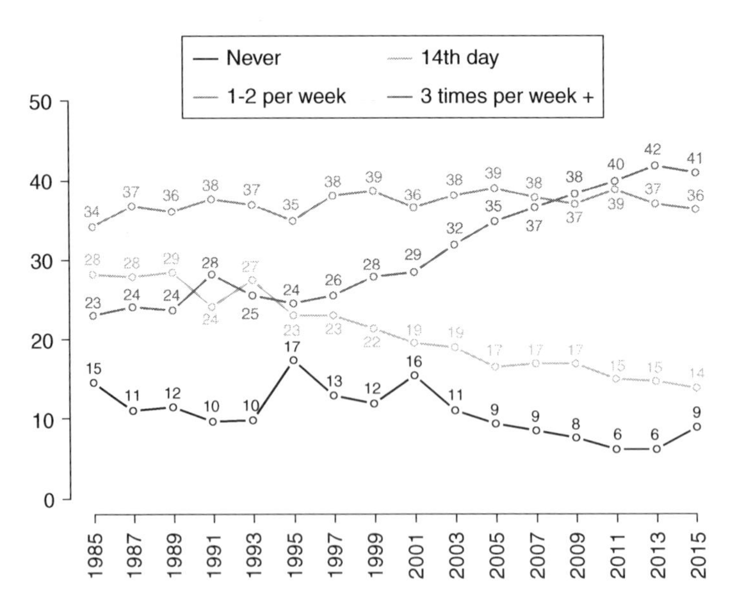

Figure 6.1 How often do you take part in physical activity? (age 15–96).
Data: Norsk Monitor, 2015.

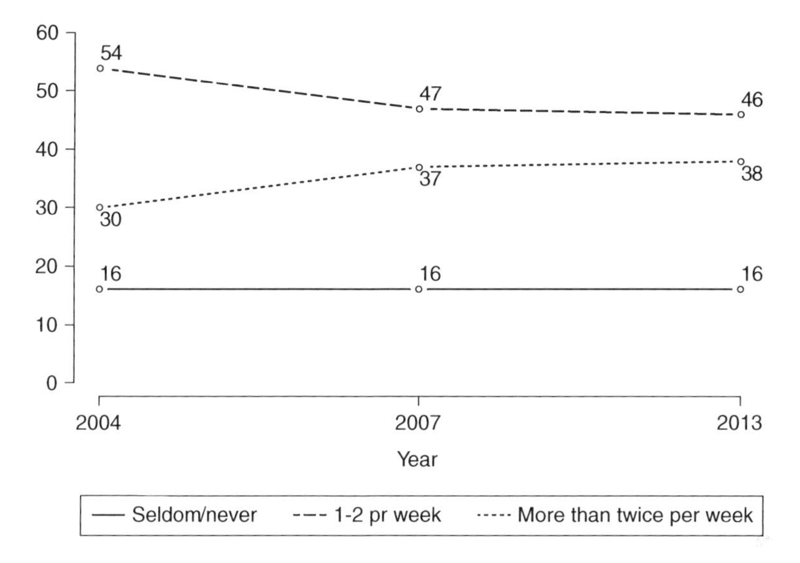

Figure 6.2 Percentages who have been physical active during leisure time the previous 12 months (age 6–15).

Data: SSB, 2015.

participation level differs across social strata (sex, age, education) – outlined in more detail below.

Even though there has been an overall increase in participation since the mid-1990s, the trends differ between various exercise arenas. There are three trends worth paying particular attention to. First, the most traditional sports arena – the sports clubs – is struggling to retain adult members, witnessing a decline of roughly one-quarter between 1985 (16%) and 2015 (12%) (Figure 6.3a). As part of the sports-clubs sector, company sports ('bedriftsidretten') participation has also seen a significant decline in recent years (Figure 6.3b). By contrast, 'lifestyle sports' have experienced substantial growth in recent decades. The fitness sector, for example, has experienced significantly increased recruitment over the past three decades or more: tripling from 10% in 1985 to close to 30% in 2015 (Figure 6.3c). Thus, exercising alone (Figure 6.3d) or with friends and/or family has increased markedly (Figure 6.3e).

Regarding children and the sporting arenas in which they are active, NIF's data[3] on participation in organised sports provides an insight into one especially important trend in recent decades: the enormous growth in children's participation in organised sports (Figure 6.4a and 6.4b). NIF changed the way they categorised age from simply distinguishing between those above and below 16 to the more fine-grained version we report here. This in itself is an indication of a shift in emphasis towards the younger age segments.

Comparing different age segments, we see very clearly that growth over the past 15 years has occurred among the two youngest age segments and the oldest.

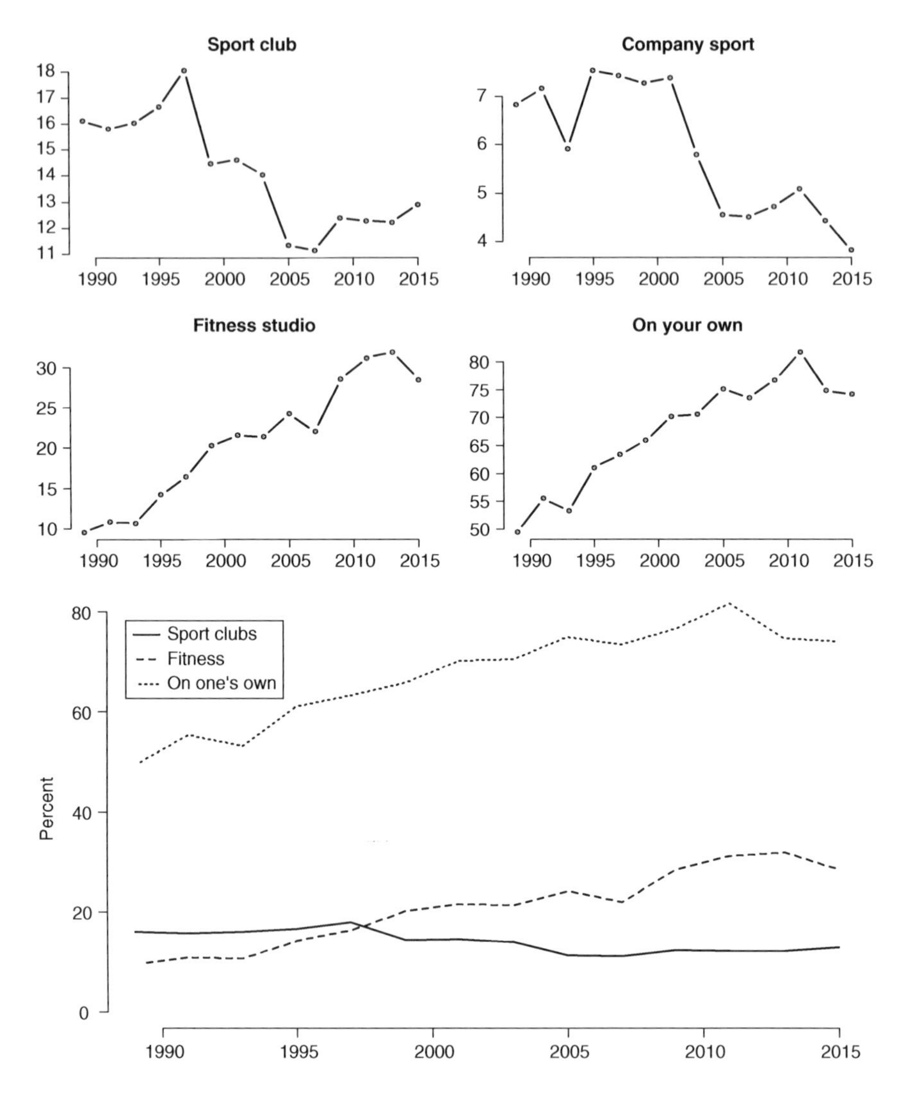

Figure 6.3a–e Percentage of adult population (age 15–96) in specific arenas for exercise (a: sports club, b: company sport, c: fitness centre, d: on one's own and e: a comparison of the three most common).

Data: Norsk Monitor, 2015.

It is also interesting to note that the sex differences are smaller for the younger cohorts, with girls most active in the youngest age group.

From NOVA data we can follow youth from lower secondary school to higher secondary school (high school). More precisely, the data are collected in school year 8 (13–14-year-olds) and school year 12 (17–18-year-olds) (see Figure 6.5).

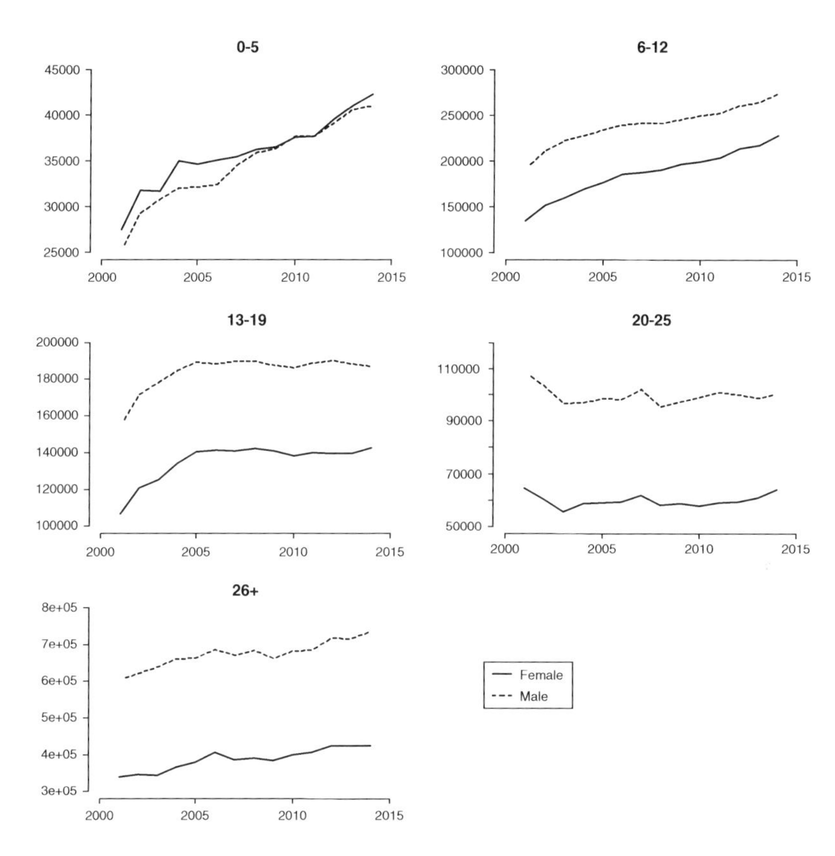

Figure 6.4a–e Memberships in Norwegian sport clubs for different age segments, 2000–2014 (a: age 0–5, b: age 6–12, c: age 13–19, d: age 20–25, e: age 26 and over).

NIF, 2016.

Among young Norwegians, exercising on one's own is widespread, whereas participation in sports clubs and fitness centres is most commonplace among the youngest and oldest, respectively (see Figures 6.5a–c). Figure 6.5b shows how the exercise habits among Norwegian youth have developed and, while participation via sports clubs has remained stable, health and fitness-related exercise increased substantially during the period. Figure 6.5c reveals that the frequency of participation was also relatively stable, with two exceptions. First, a smaller proportion of youth took part never or seldom (once a week) in 2010 compared with 1992. Second, there was a considerably larger group exercising five times per week (or more often) in 2010 than in 1992.

Forms of participation

The overall impression is that conventional sports – such as football, swimming and golf – are on the wane whereas jogging, cross-country skiing, climbing and

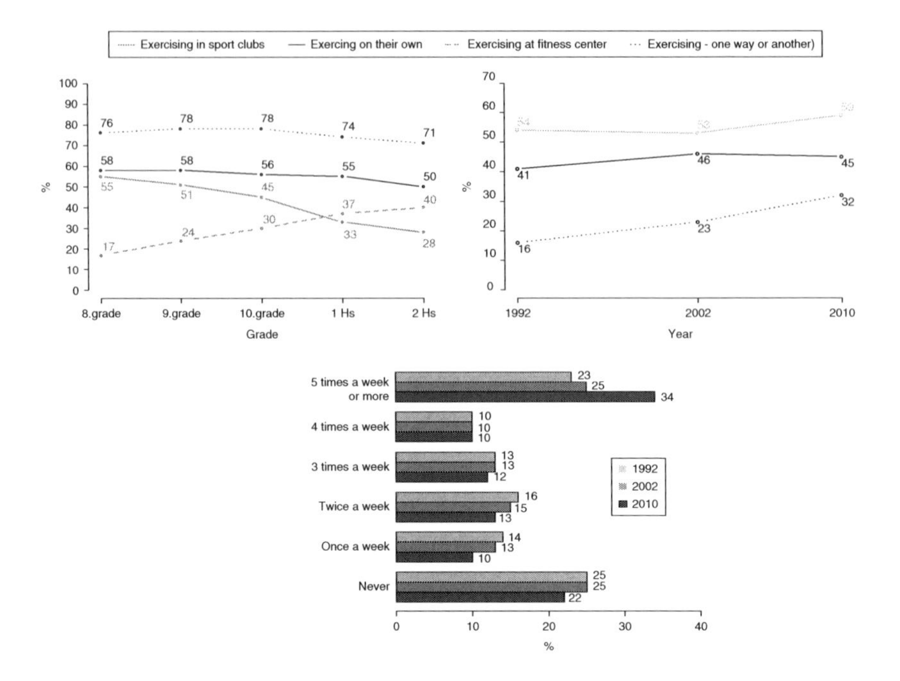

Figure 6.5a–c (a, upper left) Percentage of youngsters in different school years exercising in different arenas; (b, upper right) percentage of youngsters (school years 8 and 12) participating in specific activities in the previous week in 1992, 2002 and 2010; and (c, bottom) how often youngsters exercise *at all* in 1992, 2002 and 2010.

Data: NOVA, 2011.

hiking (in the less organised, lifestyle versions of these activities) are growing. This general pattern is, however, complicated. First, for all three sports included in this study, only golf is almost exclusively linked to organisational forms. Both football and swimming also take place in less organised and more recreational as well as organised settings.

For all lifestyle sports – that is, those activities that are characteristically less organised and more informal and recreational – the main trend is, overall, upward. However, jogging, hiking and cross-country skiing appear to have peaked in the late 1990s. By comparison, participation in climbing and cross-country skiing seems to be increasing.

In light of these wider trends, there is an overall increase in participation in sport and exercise, and while organised sport may be struggling among the adult population (see, for example, football in Figure 6.6), the less-organised activities continue to grow (such as cross-country skiing and climbing in Figure 6.6). This also resonates with the popular arenas for participation. For children, the pattern is much more stable (Figure 6.7).

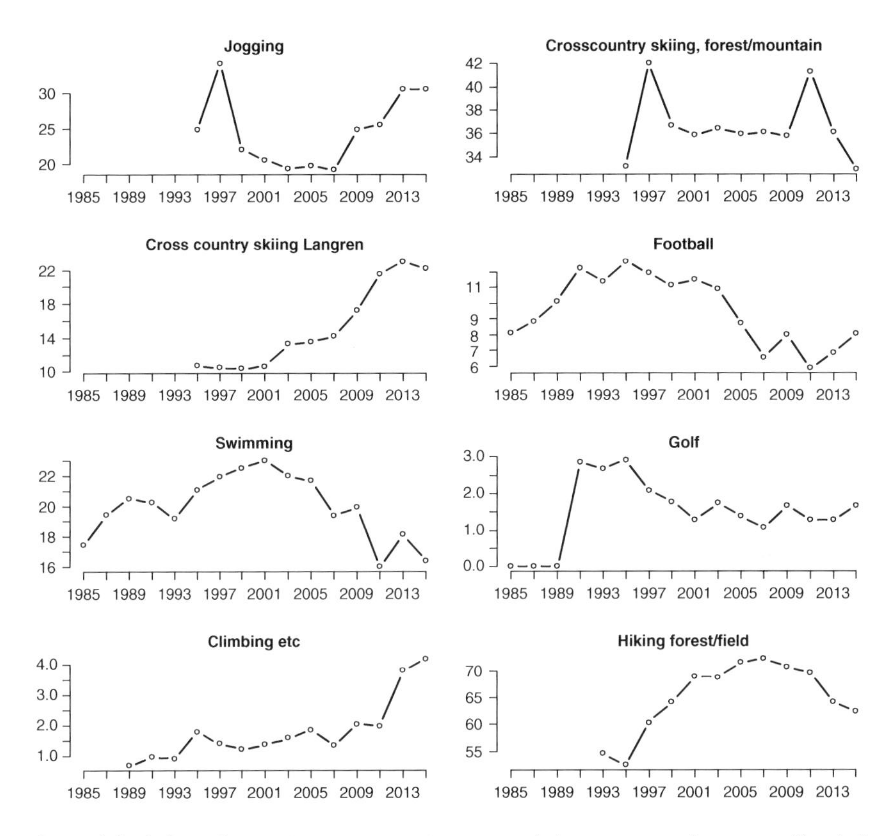

Figure 6.6a–h Specific activities representing some of the most popular sports (football, swimming and golf) and self-organised activities (age 15–96).

Data: Norsk Monitor, 2015.

Moreover, the overall trends also reflect a generally high – and recently increasing – participation in *friluftsliv* (Vaage, 2015), also among younger people. In general, more take longer tramping trips and ski trips in the woods and mountains than did some decades ago.

Facilities

As most of the state subsidies for sport in Norway go to financing the building of new facilities or the maintenance/renovation of older facilities (see below), it is important to appreciate the population's use of sports facilities. A presentation of the most-used facilities – in rank order – is presented in Figure 6.8.

The types of facilities used clearly reflect the prevalence of various types of activities. The two most used – tramping tracks and fields (in the wilderness) – are for hiking/walking/tracking and outdoor life. The third most popular facility

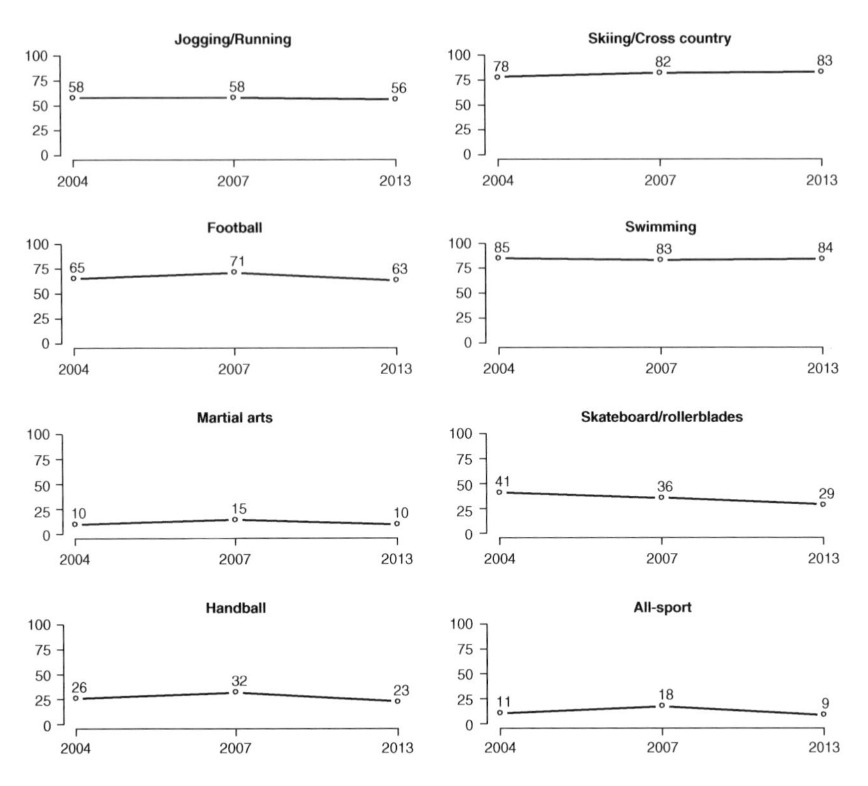

Figure 6.7a–h Specific activities representing some of the most popular sports and self-organised activities (children age 6–15).

SSB, 2015.

(training centres) relates primarily to fitness and weights activities and the rapidly developing health and fitness sector. These are followed by still more facilities for lifestyle activities: parks and floodlit cross-country ski tracks. Other facilities tend to cater to more conventional sports: sports halls, gymnastic halls, swimming pools and football pitches.

Unsurprisingly, perhaps, the trends in the use of facilities are broadly correlated with the trends in activity. While facilities suitable for more informal and recreational exercise and fitness activities have been used increasingly, the picture for competitive sports facilities is more mixed. The use of outdoor fields, parks and walking/hiking paths (Figures 6.9a–c) has increased relatively steadily since the turn of the millennium. So has the use of fitness centres (Figure 6.9d). All four types of arenas for organised and competitive sports (Figures 6.9e–h), however, experienced upwards and downwards trends in the same period. The overall trend for use of two of the four (golf courses and swimming pools) was downwards, while the use of sports halls and football pitches trended upwards.

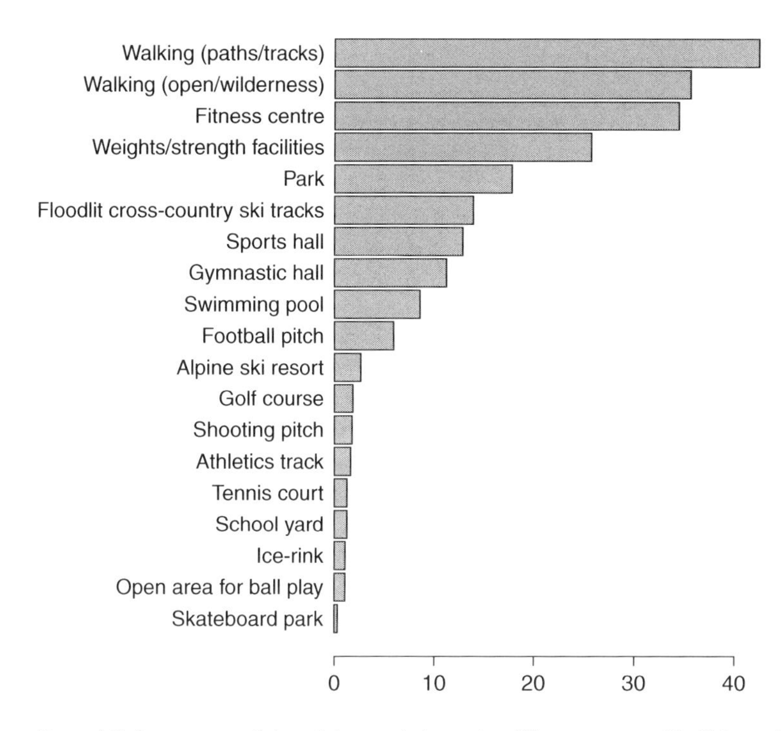

Figure 6.8 Percentage of the adult population using different types of facilities twice a week or more (age 15–96).

Data: Norsk Monitor, 2015.

Social divisions and sports participation in Norway

Besides questions of intensity and type, we are also interested in looking at social inequalities in sport and exercise: which social inequalities do we find and how do these inequalities change over time? If sports are seen as 'social goods' – whether for health, social factors, fun or more political and/organisational learning – the question of how this 'good' is distributed is of course important. Traditionally, sports have been marked by various forms of social inequalities, and we will look more closely at how these differences play out along three dimensions: sex, age and class. In addition, we comment on divisions based on ethnicity and ability/disability. The first figure (Figure 6.10a) shows that the percentage of Norwegian men and women exercising have increased from about 60% in the mid-1980s to between 70% and 80% today. This increase is clearer for women than for men.

Sex and sports participation

Even though sport has traditionally been male-dominated, recent data indicate that sex differences have become less significant and that, in some instances, women have higher levels of participation than men (Figure 6.10c).

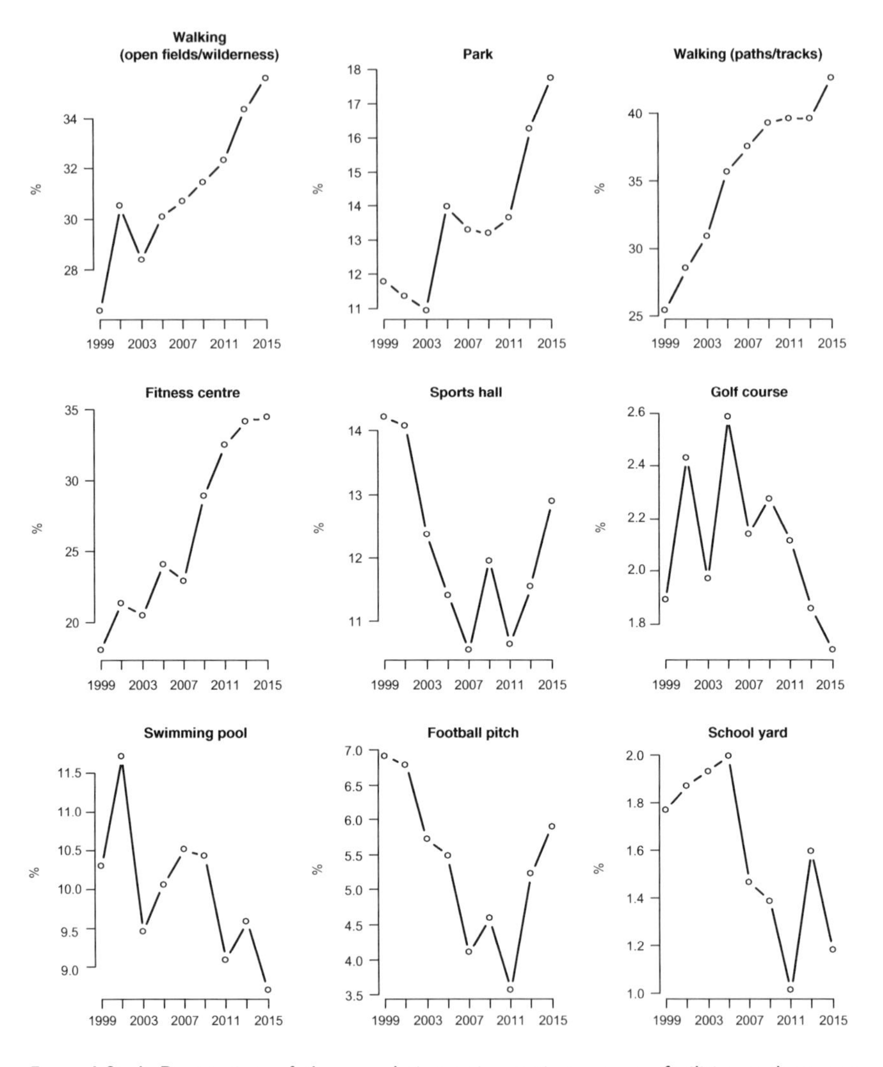

Figure 6.9a–h Proportion of the population using various sports facilities at least two times a week over time (age 15–96).

Norsk Monitor, 2015.

As Figure 6.10a indicates, from 1985 onwards men became less dominant in participatory terms in sport and exercise. While sex differences were small and shifting up to 1993, from 1995 onwards women became more involved in sport and exercise at every point in time. The difference in 2015 was around 5% in favour of women.

Looking at the use of the three different sporting and exercise venues, we find two arenas with clearly sex-divided activities. Sports clubs remain predominantly

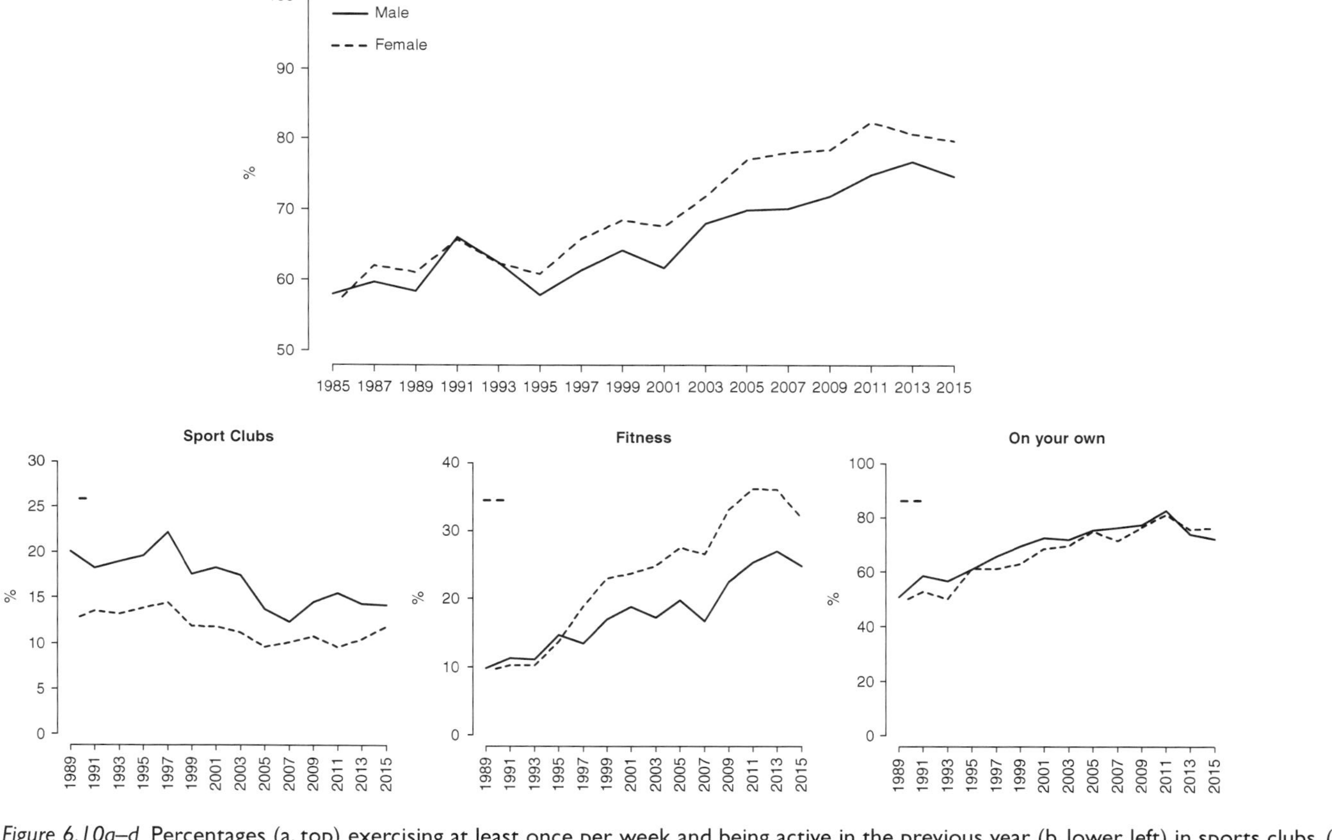

Figure 6.10a–d Percentages (a, top) exercising at least once per week and being active in the previous year (b, lower left) in sports clubs, (c, lower middle) at fitness centres and (d, lower right) while exercising on one's own, and sex (age 15–96).

Norsk Monitor, 2015.

male arenas (Figure 6.10b). Whereas about 15% of men participate via sports clubs, around 10% of women do the same. Participation in health and fitness activities has a somewhat different pattern (Figure 6.10c). In 1985, men and women participated at about the same rate: 7%–8%. Thereafter, there was an increase in participation for both men and women, yet the increase in women's participation was higher than for men such that, with the exception of the last few years, women were better represented in the health and fitness arena. The last arena, exercising on one's own, is less gendered (Figure 6.10d). For most of the period, men were marginally more active than women, but the main trend was a steady increase for females.

All-in-all, the data for the three participatory arenas explain the general pattern of Figure 6.10a, insofar as, in the male-dominated arenas, the gap has been closing between the sexes, whereas in the female-dominated arena the gap has – until recently – increased.

Regarding various levels of exercise among young people (aged 6–15), the sex pattern is relatively clear. The lower level of exercise (defined as exercising twice a month or less) shows similar patterns – and trends from 2004–2013 – across the sexes. There are marked differences when it comes to medium-level (defined as exercising one to two times a week) and high-level (defined as exercising 3 times a week or more) exercise, in two respects. First, it is more common for female than for male youth to exercise at a medium level, and more common for male than female youth to exercise at a high level. Second, these relative relationships seem stable, although there are clear changes in the number of youth within each level of activity category: there is a general drop in the number of youth exercising 'some' from 2004 to 2013 (Figure 6.11b), and a general increase in the number of youth exercising 'much' (Figure 6.11c).

Age and sports participation

In general terms – whether taking part once a week or more – there are small age differences (Figure 6.12). In terms of divisions between the sexes, participation

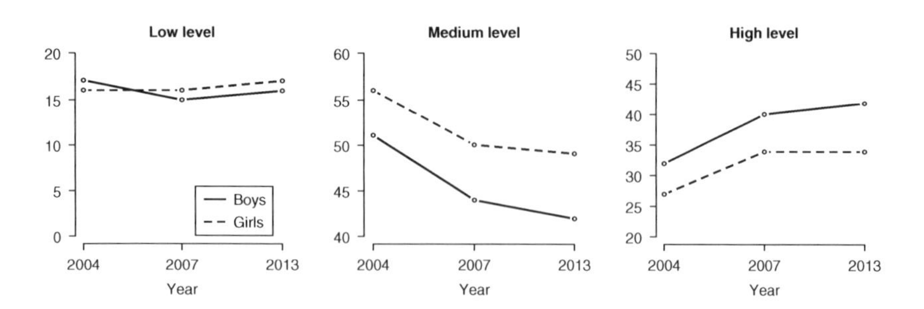

Figure 6.11a–c Percentages exercising at various levels by sex (age 6–15). (a, left) Low level: never, less than once a month, 1–2 times per month; (b, middle) medium level: 1–2 times per week; (c, right) high level: 3–4 times per week or more.

Data: SSB, 2015.

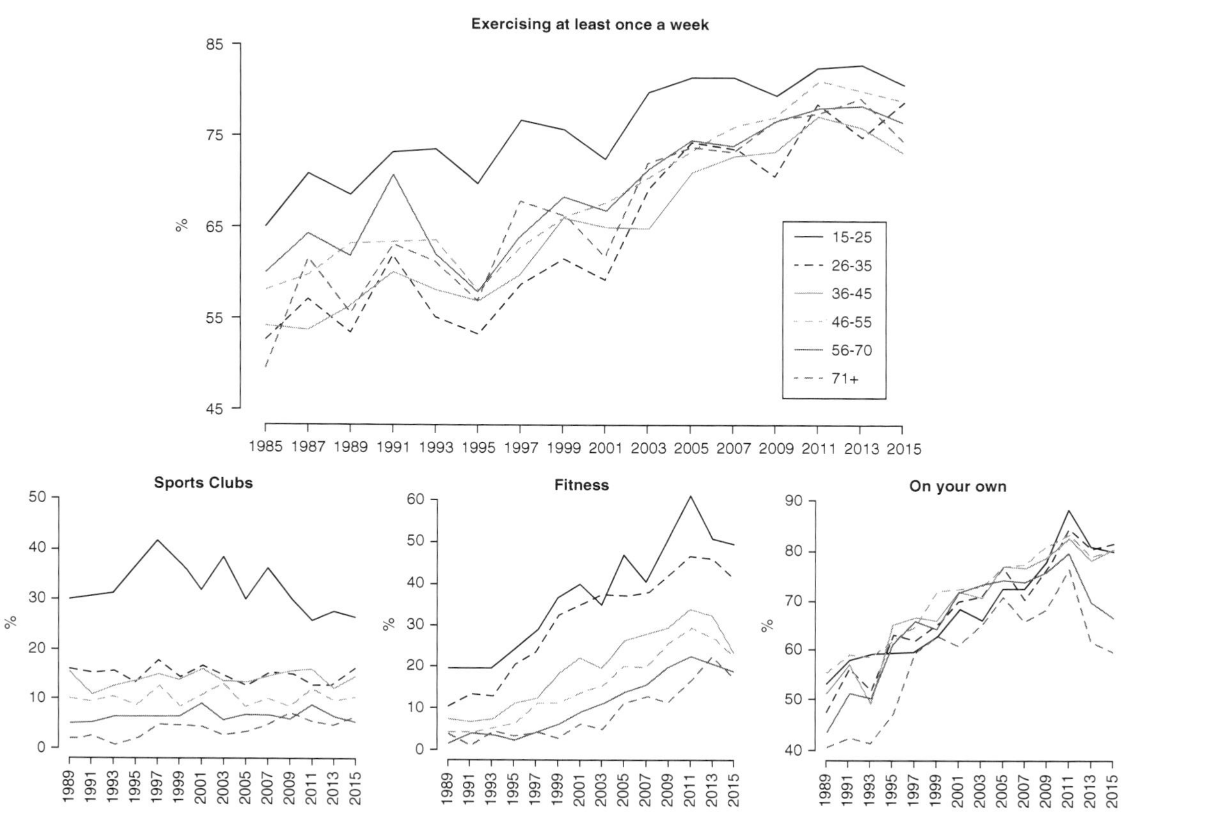

Figure 6.12a–d Percentages (a) exercising at least once per week and being active in the previous year (b) in sports clubs, (c) at fitness centres and (d) while exercising on one's own, and age (15–96).

Norsk Monitor, 2015.

at sports clubs and fitness centres is differentiated by age, whereas there are small age differences in relation to exercising on one's own. Unsurprisingly, perhaps, sports clubs remain predominantly an arena for young people. Older Norwegians are less likely to take part in organised sport and, as a result, to be active members of sports clubs. Much the same pattern is to be found in health and fitness activities. The small age differences in overall participation are largely attributable to the popularity of non-organised, or lifestyle, activities plus the fact that there is a clear overlap between exercise at different arenas.

Class/education and sports participation

In Norway, education is the best available operationalisation of, or proxy for, social inequalities related to class. It represents the social inequality dimension with a relatively consistent pattern. The exception is sport clubs, where it is difficult to see the clear imprint of education (Figure 6.13b). For general participation and for fitness and non-organised activities, the picture is uniform (Figure 6.13d): those with higher education participate to a greater extent than those with lower education. The differences are largest and, up to a point, increasing for health and fitness activities, whereas the differences in non-organised activity have the same patterns, albeit decreasing with time.

Among youth, sex differences are significantly smaller than some years ago and have in many respects disappeared to all intents and purposes among some age groups at particular frequencies of participation. In health and fitness activities and exercising on one's own, females are better represented than males, and this is also the case for the youngest cohort (0–5 years) of members of sporting organisations. For age and youth sports, the big challenge is the problem of drop-out. A very large proportion of youngsters begin as members of a sports organisation (e.g. sports clubs), but drop out thereafter.

With the caveat that it is risky to compare different measures of social class used at different times, Strandbu, Gulløy, Andersen, Seippel and Dalen (2017) suggest that social class had a strong influence on sports participation in the early post-war era, was less present during the 1970s and 1980s but seems to have resurfaced more recently. Bakken (2017) shows that there are very clear social differences – social gradient rather than social class[4] – in participation in organised sport in Norway. Where participation in youth sport has become more serious and committed, there has been an increasing demand for parents' involvement, especially in relation to economic subsidies. This is due both to developments within modern societies as well as to various aspects of sports – commercialisation, professionalisation and commodification, which drive the cost for participation. This creates a gradient where the possibility to partake in sport increases with the socio-economic status of the family. Figure 6.14 also shows that there is biased participation in some children's sports – e.g. cross-country skiing, alpine skiing, skateboarding – when it comes to parental income.

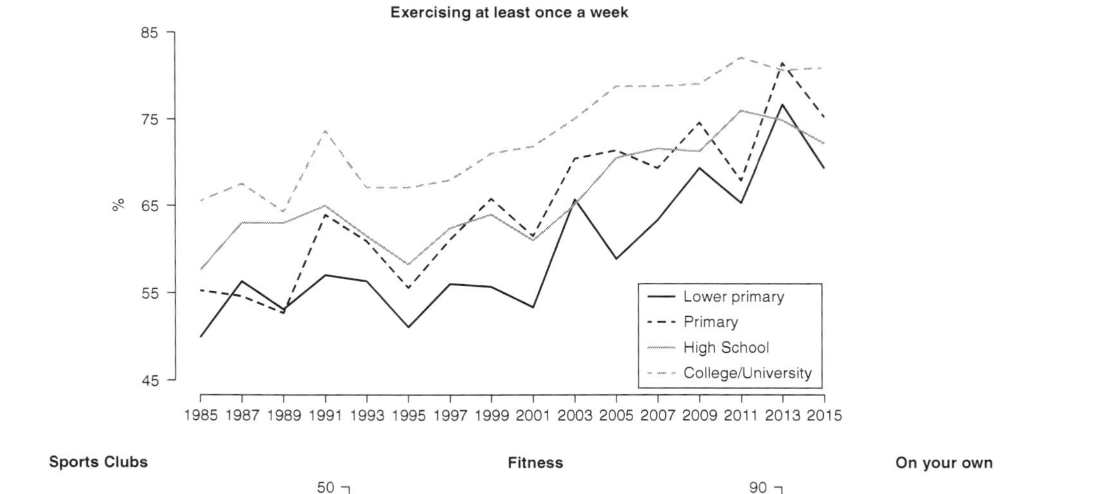

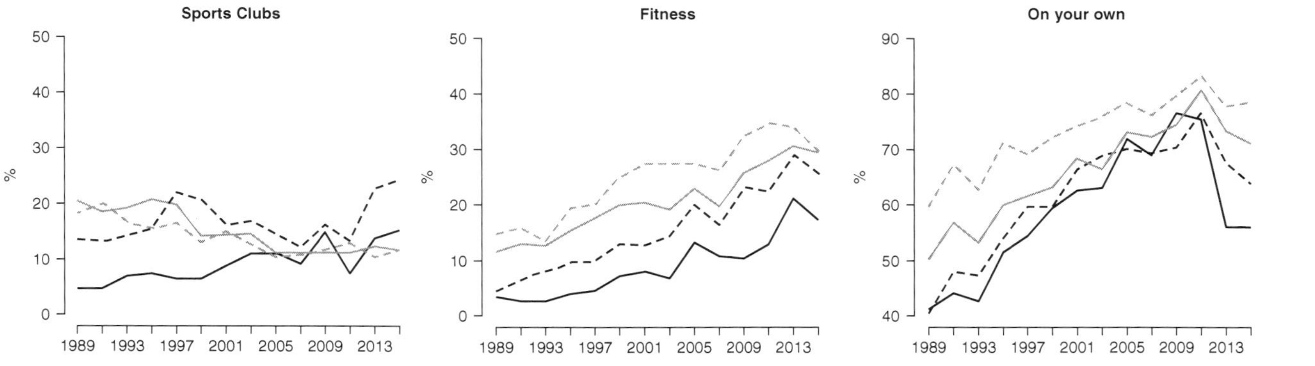

Figure 6.13a–d Percentages (a) exercising at least once per week and being active in the previous year (b) in sports clubs, (c) at fitness centres and (d) while exercising on one's own, and education (age 15–96).

Norsk Monitor, 2015.

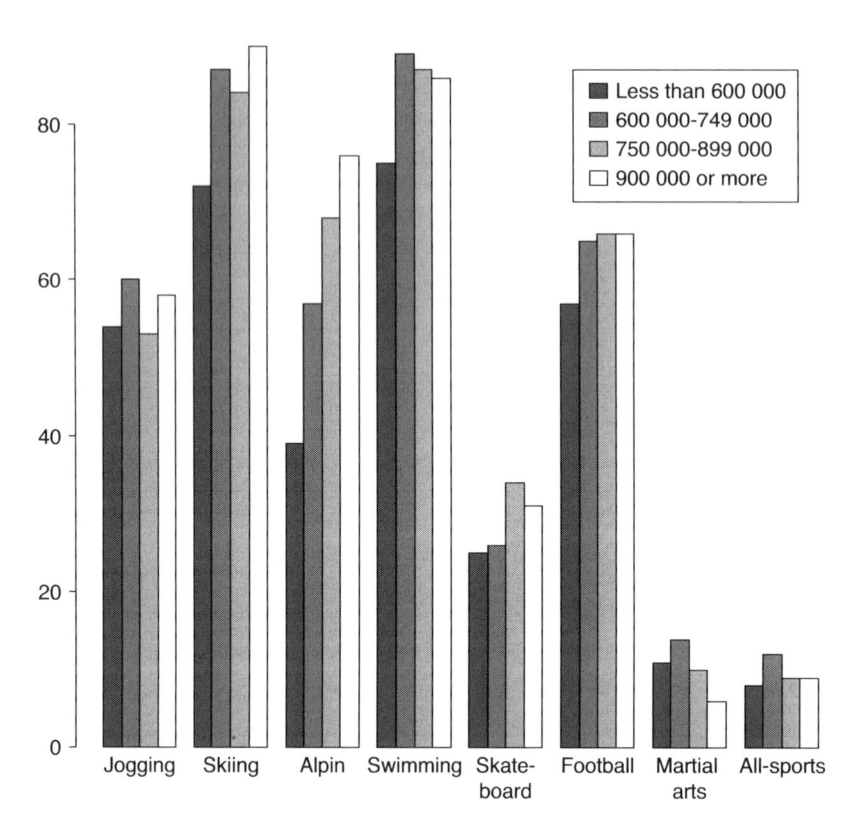

Figure 6.14 Percentages taking part in various physical activities in the previous 12 months, age 6–15, and parental income (reported in NOK; 9 NOK ≈ 1 €).

Data: SSB, 2015.

Ethnicity and sports participation

The question of ethnicity and youth sport in Norway has two elements to it. First, research shows that youth with immigrant backgrounds participate less than ethnic Norwegian youth. More precisely, boys with immigrant backgrounds participate on relatively similar levels to ethnic Norwegian boys, and participation rates among adolescent girls with immigrant backgrounds are lower than participation rates among adolescent boys with immigrant backgrounds and lower than participation rates among ethnic Norwegian girls (Strandbu, Bakken, & Sletten, 2017). These patterns relate to exercise in general but are clearest when it comes to participation in sports clubs (Seippel *et al.*, 2011). The challenge related to the inclusion and integration of immigrant girls into sport is sufficiently politically potent for there to be a specified state-initiated project (NOU, 2014).

Second, Rafoss and Hines (2016) compared participation among Sámi and Norwegian adolescents in Finnmark, the northernmost county of Norway and the county with the highest density of Sámi in the population.[5] They found that Sámi and Norwegian boys have similar participation patterns in sport and exercise. For females, Sámi girls participate less than boys (and Norwegian girls) and show similar patterns to immigrant girls. One distinct pattern is that Sámi youth partake more in traditional outdoor activities than Norwegian youth. A distinct sub-pattern of the latter is that traditional gender roles seem to be at play: boys hunt and fish – in rivers in the summertime and on the frozen ice on lakes during wintertime – while girls 'gather' – specifically, they pick berries.

Disability and sports participation

The last aspect of social division in need of mention is sport for the disabled, not least because it functions as a transition to the subsequent sections on sports organisation and sports policy. While the share of participants does not differ between the able-bodied and disabled in voluntary organisations in general, there is a slightly smaller number of disabled than able-bodied participants in sport (Eimhjellen, 2011). This remains a challenge for the sports organisations (Eimhjellen, 2011), although there are several examples of policy – or at least symbolic – efforts to do so. Of highly symbolic value, the Norwegian sports organisations staged the Paralympics as a direct continuation of the Winter Olympic Games at Lillehammer in 1994. Moreover, the closure of the Norwegian disabled sports federation in 2007 was followed by the integration of disabled sports into the ordinary sports federations. For example, wheelchair table tennis is now organised within the table tennis association, and the same is true for sledge hockey in the ice hockey association. In this regard, the Paralympic Committee has been merged with the Olympic Committees and Confederation of Sports since 2008 to form the Norwegian Olympic and Paralympic Committees and Confederation of Sports.

The organisation of sport in Norway

Using the above observations as a point of departure, it becomes clear that people have a range of possibilities for organising their participation in sport and exercise: sport clubs, health and fitness centres, or on their own and/or in informal groups (cf. Figure 6.3). Of course, the same individual can partake in several organisational contexts and even in several organisations (for example, in more than one sports club). To understand this phenomenon, we present the two umbrella sports organisations in Norway (Figures 6.15 and 6.16), and sum up by visualising the three organisational forms (Figure 6.17).

Conventionally, sports participation has been taken to imply membership of a sports club. When an individual is a member of a sports club, it implies that s/he is also a member of a broader system of sports organisations, which usually implies being a member of the Norwegian sports organisation (the NIF system, Figure 6.15). This remains the norm among Norwegians. However, another possibility is to be a member of the Sámi sports organisation or, third, a combination of the two.

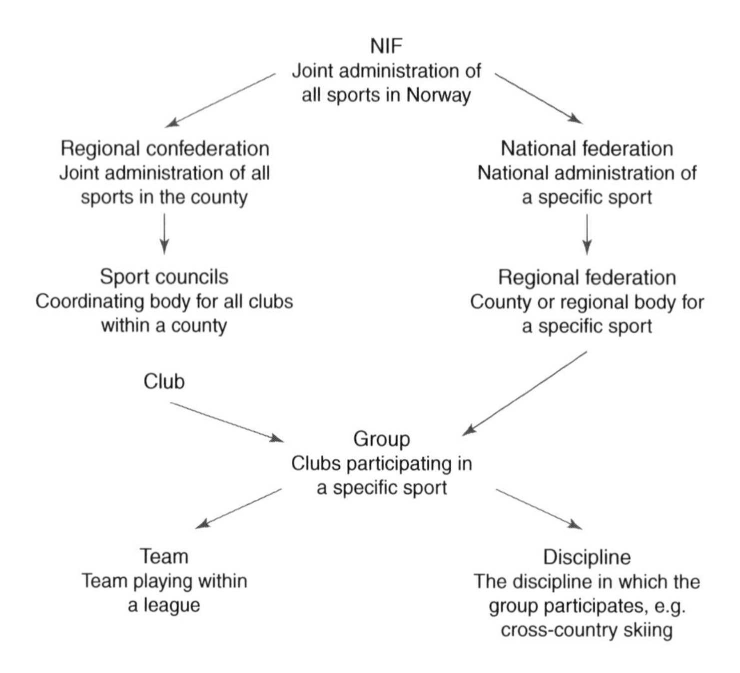

Figure 6.15 NIF system (https://www.idrettsforbundet.no/english/ (15 January 2018)).

A sports club can organise one sport or several sports. A so-called 'specialised' sports club organises only one sport: e.g. a football club or a cross-country skiing club. Multi-sport clubs are dived into specialised groups (e.g. a football group and a ski group). While there were approximately 50% of each type of sports club at the turn of the millennium, four out of five newly established sports clubs at the time were specialised, single sports clubs (Skirstad, 2002). In any respect, every sports club is a member of one (if a specialised sports club) or more (if a multi-sport

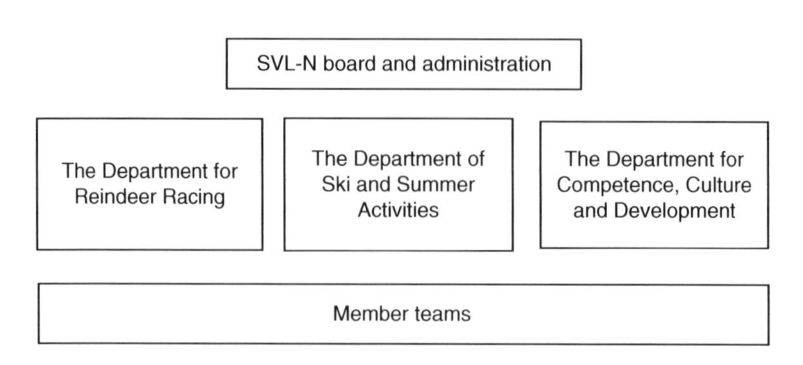

Figure 6.16 SVL-N system (Based on http://svl.no/web/index.php?bajitsladja=1&bajitvsladja=4&giella1=nor (22 February 2017)).

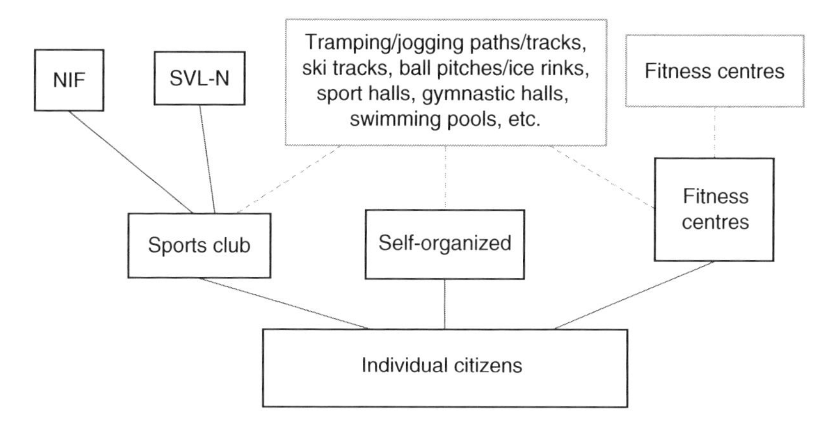

Figure 6.17 The relationship between individuals and organisations (full lines) and facilities (dotted lines).

club) national federations. All federations are members of NIF (see Figure 6.15). Thus, being a member of a sports club in Norway implies being a member of a national federation[6] and, thereby, in the Norwegian Confederation and Olympic and Paralympic Committee of Sport (NIF).[7] As one person can be a member of several sports clubs or take part in different groups in a multi-sport club, one single individual can be a member of several national federations. Inevitably, therefore, when NIF seeks to establish its membership by aggregating reports from all the national federations, the number of memberships surpasses the number of unique individuals who are members of NIF. The total number of memberships in NIF is approximately 2 million (NIF, 2017). However, it should be noted that the number of memberships includes individual members with more than one membership. An estimate of the unique individual members in Norwegian sport is 1.5 million.

There are 11,500 sports clubs federated to 'the NIF system'. The NIF system comprises the organisations that connect the sports club to NIF as the umbrella organisation via two distinctive and interrelated lines of affiliation. The two lines are a legacy from a merger of two former organisations into NIF in 1946. Following the so-called NIF or membership line (Figure 6.15, left side), there are local sports councils in each municipality with three or more sports clubs (n = 360), and there are district sports organisations at the county level (n = 19). Representation in local sports councils and district sports organisations is based on democratic structures and procedures from sports clubs. The purpose of local sports councils and district sports organisations is to coordinate sporting interests towards the public sector authorities on the same level. Variations regarding economy and employees result in variations in how sports councils function around the country. District sports organisations are extensions of the NIF central administration, and all have paid staff.

Following the so-called specialised federation or activity line (Figure 6.15, right side), specific sports clubs or groups of multi-sport clubs are members of a national federation via the national federation's district unit. The district units schedule the regional competitions (e.g. leagues and series); allocate referees and delegates; and educate referees, coaches and the like. The national federations govern their sport(s) in Norway, administrate laws and sports rules and are the links to international federations. They schedule national competitions and are responsible for elite sport, including national teams. All sports federations organise both mass and elite sport. On top of the NIF system (see Figure 6.15) is the NIF board and the NIF administration. That includes the elite sports department (Olympiatoppen), providing sports-science support for the federations' sporting elite and, specifically, for Olympic preparations. Taken together, the NIF system provides for almost all sport in Norway, both mass and elite.

Another possibility (rather than affiliation to NIF) is that the sports club is a member of the Sámi sports association – Norway (Sámiid Valáštallanlihttu-Norga, SVL-N; see Figure 6.16). Three ideal types of clubs can be members of SVL-N (Skille, 2013): (i) sports clubs that are exclusively Sámi (only one), (ii) sports clubs that are also members of NIF and (iii) Sámi associations that include sport in their repertoire. In other words, a sports club can be a member of both NIF and SVL-N. Out of the 30 clubs that are members of SVL-N, 16 are also members of NIF. This means that most of the 4,400 members of SVL-N are also members of NIF. The Sámi associations that are members of SVL-N are exclusively so because of reindeer racing.[8]

The SVL-N is organised into three departments: The Department for Reindeer Racing, The Department of Ski and Summer Activities, and The Department for Competence, Culture and Development. The first two are directly related to the provision of sport and sporting competitions, while the latter is dedicated to cultural issues, a handbook and guidelines.[9] In addition to the two sports organisations NIF and SVL-N, there are two main ways into exercise contexts for an individual[10]: health and fitness centres or self-organised activities (see Figure 6.17).

Sports policy and politics in Norway

Sports policy in Norway is structurally associated with the organisation of sport presented above (the NIF system). The sports organisations with a 'political purpose', sports councils, district sports organisations and NIF, are tuned-in to work with and lobby local, regional and national authorities, respectively. The state's sports policy has changed slightly in recent decades. Regarding policies, physical activity has partly replaced sport and other organisations in receipt of state funding.

The history of sports policy in Norway is a history of the relationship between the state and the Norwegian Sports Confederation. Since 1863, two years after the establishment of the first national organisation for sport in Norway, the state subsidised the Confederation – initially for military purposes but, subsequently, for various societal reasons, such as health and upbringing (Goksøyr, 1992). Paralleling the NIF merger in 1946, the Norwegian state's office for sporting affairs and the state gambling agency (Norsk Tipping A/S) were established. Since then, there has been an organisation to administrate sports policy and a reliable and predictable income for sport. Hence, it was possible for the state to make policies and to influence their implementation. Ever since, the state's sports policy has focused on two main strands. The first has been the building of facilities. As the norm, in order to be supportable, the application for state subsidies has to prove that the planned facility follows the rules and regulations of specific sports – for example, regarding the size and the surface of a football or handball pitch. Nonetheless, self-organised activities also receive support. About 60% of state subsidies for sport go on facilities. The second main strand of sports policy is to support the voluntary sports organisations. That is, first and foremost, NIF and its member organisations. The point is that there is no such thing as public-sector sporting activity organisations (such as there is with public – state – schools, with teachers employed by pubic authorities; or as there is in the public health service, with publicly employed doctors and nurses). The state (and other levels of public authorities) is fundamentally dependent on the voluntary sports organisations for sports policy to be implemented.

Since the 1970s, the Department of Sport Policy (DSP) has been located in the Ministry of Cultural Affairs.[11] Sport was included in white papers in the 1970s and the 1980s on culture in general, with separate sections on sport (Skille, 2010). Since 1991, there have been three white papers exclusively on sport. The white papers treat the reasons for state subsidies to sport along two main lines. On the one hand, and consistent with the idea of sport as culture, there are intrinsic values justifying state subsidies to sport: sport is said to be valuable in itself. On the other hand, state subsidies are justified in terms of the societal or instrumental values sport is believed to promote.

Two instrumental values have stood at the forefront of Norwegian sports policy in recent decades. First, following increased levels of sedentary lifestyles and their consequences, health is the most widely used justification given for state subsidies. Second, following immigration, and the associated challenges of multiculturalism, social integration is another societal issue in which sport is claimed to be a potential partner. Given sport's potential multiple purposes, other governmental ministries can be relevant to sports policy in Norway. Other reasons for state subsidies are that sport generates employment. In addition, participation in sporting organisations is said to generate social and cultural capital in a democratic society. Elite sports achievement, on the other hand, is claimed to generate national pride and contribute to nation-building and national unity.

While there has been a high degree of stability in state sports policy since the Second World War, there have been three distinct changes in sports policy more recently which appear to be mutually reinforcing. First, there is more focus on physical activity and exercise nowadays, rather than sport as merely an organised and competitive phenomenon. Second, health is now emphasised as the most important element of the instrumental values that justify state sports policy. Third, there are now more openings for other organisations (than NIF) to receive economic state support. Throughout all white papers that included sport, the state's sports policy vision was 'Sport for All' (Skille, 2010: 24). This changed with the second exclusively sport-related white paper, where 'sport and exercise for all' (St. Meld. nr. 14, 1999–2000) was defined as the current state sports-policy vision. One interpretation is that high rates of participation had become politically more important than high numbers of international medals. A related interpretation is that it has been more important, politically, to be physically active than to participate in organised sport. This impression is supported by formulations in the same white paper indicating that other organisations (than NIF) can receive subsidies (St. Meld. nr. 14, 1999–2000). A recent state-appointed council evaluating the situation and advising the minister on future sports policy emphasised opportunities for supporting self-organised activities (KUD, 2016).

Explaining sports participation in Norway

There are many reasons for the general development in levels of participation in sport and exercise in the Norwegian population. We have touched upon some of them already, but they comprise both general trends alongside those more germane to particular activities. A simple explanation is trends such as a richer population with post-material values, more leisure and equal gender roles and age roles regarding opportunities for children, youth, adults and older people. When patterns and trends in sports participation in Norway are considered alongside developments in state policy towards sport, the latter's adjustment of policy in favour of self-organised activities becomes comprehensible.

Two overall conclusions can be drawn regarding sports participation in Norway: first, high levels of participation in sport and exercise and, second, a shift in the dominant context for participation, from conventional (organised and competitive) sport and sports clubs to commercial and self-organised activities. The former – generally high levels of participation – fits with the traditional picture of Norway as a social democratic welfare state – including the notion of providing fair chances for *all* individuals. According to Esping-Andersen (1990), Norway is a social democratic welfare state, recognised by an egalitarian society comprising a strong state and a strong *and* large civil sector with a high degree of participation in civic organisations. In other words, the large proportion of the Norwegian population participating in sport can be seen to be rooted in the egalitarian ideology of Norway as a social democratic welfare state. At the same time, the stable and high participation rates in relatively cheap, readily accessible and self-organised activities, such as skiing and hiking in forests and mountains, confirms the high influence of traditions related to exercise in Norway.

Norwegian sport is a voluntary phenomenon. Three different and complementary elements of volunteerism support this argument. First, as stated above, sport is a large and significant part of the civil sector. Sports organisations are non-profit and non-governmental organisations and thus, by definition, voluntary. The Norwegian Confederation of Sport (NIF) is a voluntary organisation at arm's length from the state. Second, participation in the organisation is based on individual and voluntary membership. Third, the work of (elected) leaders, coaches and others at all levels of the organisation is voluntary. It should be noted, however, that there is an increasing number of sports clubs with paid coaches and/or paid administrative staff.

The characteristics of sport as the main part of the voluntary sector are also evident at the club level, wherein the role of sports clubs in local communities cannot be overestimated. It is one of the few social institutions everyone has a relationship to, one way or another – whether one likes sport or not. The other main institution which influences sports participation significantly (and involvement in sports clubs, in particular) is school. All local communities comprise one or more sports club and one or more schools. As the majority of the participants in organised sport are of school age, young people's activity is the centre of gravity for communities. Moreover, the community sports club is an arena for interaction between parents, through voluntary work. This interaction would never have taken place without the sports club's need for a free/voluntary workforce. The way voluntary sport functions is so rooted in community practices and general conventions that when a new sporting organisation such as SVL-N is established, it inevitably adapts to the existing and dominant NIF to a large degree. While Sámi sport is a voluntary phenomenon very similar to NIF, it is perhaps not surprising that the four organisational values are shared between NIF and SVL-N (volunteerism, democracy, loyalty, equality). In that respect, the new organisation represents both distinction and conformity.

Changes in participatory patterns reflect the ways in which sport is inevitably intertwined with general societal processes, and neo-liberalism, in particular. In Norway, that means moving from social liberalism (with state regulation and civic-sector provision) – providing all individuals with opportunities for participation – to a focus on the individual as a consumer. We apply neo-liberalism (commonly understood as politics oriented towards market economics) to explain how individuals choose different sports and physical activities. That is, in modern Norway. This is manifest in how individuals have high economic power and freedom, combined with a high degree of accessibility to new products and services. Another feature of neo-liberalism is that the state wants more control over (and, as a consequence, more measures of) whether money is spent appropriately. This is often referred to as 'New Public Management'. The report into future sports policy (KUD, 2016: 60) proposes more holistic responsibility for the government regarding the population's physical activity. What form this will take, in practice, remains to be seen. However, it is plausible to claim that the above-mentioned trends are associated with pervasive processes in the Western world: namely, trends that are often in sociology referred to as globalisation and individualisation.

Globalisation – here operationalised as how relevant elements from outside Norway influence Norwegian sport and exercise patterns, policies or organisation – can be identified in several ways. First, fitness centres, imported from America in the 1980s, took off as a cultural element of some significance in 1990s (Steen-Johnsen, 2004). Having said that, the fitness sector in Norway is an interesting case of how new elements are combined with old – national cultural elements (in processes of 'glocalisation'). Second, there are new sports influencing participation patterns. While skiing is a traditional Norwegian sport and leisure activity, the import and adaption of snowboarding as a lifestyle sport has impacted participatory patterns. Moreover, the youth-oriented culture of emancipation has challenged the established culture of Norwegian sports organisation.

Conclusion

The pattern of participation in sport and exercise in the Norwegian population is one of both continuity and change, and similarities and differences. All-in-all, the past three decades reveal trends of increased complexity. Nevertheless, levels of participation, combined with neo-liberal trends more generally, make further strengthening of the 'sectors' of self-organised and fitness-centre-based exercise a relatively safe prognosis to propose. Another anticipated development is that complexity will continue to increase regarding participation trends as well as policy and organisation. An interesting element to follow up on in future research is the degree to which the state will be more involved in steering the main receiver of state sports subsidies, NIF. Consequently, it would be interesting to explore, first, whether the state will welcome new organisations in order to achieve policy aims and, second, if completely new ideas can develop and receive subsidies outside the very idea of sports organisation.

Despite Sámi sport's small size regarding both number of members and state subsidies, the development of the relationship between the state and the Sámi sport organisation is also of future research interest. That is because that relationship includes, and symbolises, elements of larger policy issues with a potential global overtone. To be more precise, there are elements related to international organisations and policies of ethnic issues including, for example, policies towards human rights.

While the trends described above can be interpreted as a call for an adjusted organisation of subsidies to sport and exercise, there are few signs of change. Despite developments in sporting and exercise trends, the main context of sports participation remains the same. Organised sport will probably stay relatively stable, in two respects. First, the organisation of the NIF system has stayed the same for seven decades. There are no signs of re-organisation. Second, the convention related to sport at the community level appears stable (Skille and Stenling, 2017). For most people, the local sports club is where children spend their leisure time. Moreover, the sports clubs reproduce a competitive sporting tradition, feasible for most children but resulting in drop-out among many adolescents.

Nevertheless, there are recent signs of more – or, at least, a changed – involvement in sport, on the state's side. There are two illustrations of this development. First is the re-organisation of the DSP into a merged department of civil society and sport. It is too early to say whether this re-organisation mirrors actual policy change, but we offer two bureaucratically oriented interpretations: sport is de-valued in the bureaucratic hierarchy, by losing the exclusive department name and, with that, a person primarily interested in and working for sport in the minister's leadership group. Second, a Minister of Culture has never before been involved in NIF's issues to the same extent as in 2016 (Broch and Skille, in progress). These two elements together create a paradox, where the minister makes sport 'more political' and, at the same time, devalues sport in the bureaucratic hierarchy. Time and further research will reveal whether any of these elements result in changes in the field of sport and the participation in exercise.

All-in-all, the Norwegian population is relatively active, across age groups, sexes and classes. Nevertheless, there are still underrepresented groups – especially immigrant girls and, increasingly, youth (and adults?) living in poverty – that are of concern for policy-makers and are hard to reach via the traditional sporting organisations. In that respect, the differentiation of forms and arenas for participation is probably a good thing, as long as sport and exercise for all is the vision.

Notes

1 NOVA = Norwegian Social Research.
2 A study into physical activity from a physiological perspective, focusing on energy expenditures, shows that there is a tendency for people to report higher levels of physical activity than they actually do. While over half of the population claimed to follow the levels of physical activity recommended by the Norwegian health authorities, studies with objective measures revealed that only 32% actually did (and females significantly more than males) (Helsedirektoratet, 2015).
3 NIF's register data are the sport clubs' membership reports to the national federations, which add up to an accumulated number of memberships of the umbrella organisation, NIF.
4 Bakken (2017) refers to social differences as being on a spectrum (gradient), rather than being categorical (such as class).
5 To be specific, there are no direct measures for Sámi ethnicity, the operationalisation of Sámi and Norwegian based on language primarily used at home (Rafoss and Hines 2016).
6 A national federation is a specified organisation governing one specific sport, such as the Norwegian Football Association or the Norwegian Ski Association. However, there are variations regarding the formulation 'one specific sport' as, for example, the ski association governs seven different disciplines: cross-country skiing, ski jumping, Nordic combined, alpine skiing, Telemark, freestyle and free skiing.
7 We use the Norwegian abbreviation NIF as it relates to the confederation function of the organisation, while the English abbreviation NOC relates primarily to its Olympic function.
8 Being active in the sport of reindeer racing implies access to reindeer. Owning a reindeer is legally limited to Sámi and family specific heritage (https://lovdata.no/dokument/NL/lov/2007-06-15-40).

9 SVL is under re-organisation, and may take on a different organisational appearance beyond January 2019.
10 A number of other organisations promoting physical activity, specifically organisations for *friluftsliv* mentioned in the report on future sports policy (KUD, 2016: 29–31).
11 The cultural aspect of state policy has had different affiliations with other aspects. The point here is that sport has always followed culture. The Minister of Culture is the minister of sport.

References

Bakken, A. (2017). Sosiale forskjeller i ungdomsidretten – fattigdomsproblem eller sosial gradient? In: *Oppvekstrapporten 2017. Økte forskjeller – gjør det noe?* (pp. 148–167). Oslo: Barne-ungdoms- og familiedirektoratet. (Available from https://www.bufdir.no/bibliotek/Dokumentside/?docId=BUF00003918, 22 April 2017).

Broch, T.B. and Skille, E.Å. (in progress). Norwegian sport's scapegoat – a media analysis of the minister's and the state's sport policy and the voluntary sport organization's openness.

Breivik, G. (2013). Jakten på det gode liv. Fysisk aktivitet i den norske befolkning 1985-2011. Oslo: Universitetsforlaget.

Christensen, O. (2001). *Sidelengs ungdomskultur*. Oslo: University of Oslo.

Eimhjellen, I. (2011). *Inkludering av funksjonshemmea i frivillige organisasjoner*. Oslo: Institutt for Samfunnsforskning.

Esping-Andersen, G. (1990). *Three Worlds of Welfare Capitalism*. Cambridge: Polity Press.

Goksøyr, M. (1992). *Staten og idretten*. Oslo: Kulturdepartementet.

Hellevik, O. (2015). Hva Betyr Respondentbortfallet i intevjuundersøkelser. *Tidsskrift for samfunnsforskning* 56(2): 211–231.

Helsedirektoratet (2015). *Fysisk aktivitet og sedat tid blant voksne og eldre i Norge. Nasjonal kartlegging 2014–2015*. Oslo: Helsedirektoratet.

KUD (2016). *Statlig idrettspolitikk inn i en ny tid*. Report from a government-appointed council. Oslo: Kulturdepartementet.

Meld. St. 26 (2011–2012). *Den norske idrettsmodellen*. Oslo: Kulturdepartementet.

NIF (2017). *Årsrapport 2016*. Oslo: Norges Idrettsforbund og Olympiske og Paralympiske Komité.

NOU (2014). *Kom igjen, jenter! Jenter med minoritetsbakgrunn og deltakelse i organisert idrett*. Oslo: Kulturdepartementet. (Available from https://www.idrettsforbundet.no/globalassets/idrett/idrettsforbundet/inkludering-i-idrettslag/rapport_minoritetsutvalg_kom-igjen-jenter-01april2014.pdf, 22 April 2017).

Rafoss, K. and Hines, K. (2016). Ung i Finnmark – en studie av bruk av fritidsarenaer og deltakelse i fritidsaktiviteter blant Sámisk og norsk ungdom. In H. C. Pedersen and E. Å. Skille (eds.). *Utafor sporet?* (pp. 169–196). Vallset: Oplandske Bokforlag.

Seippel, Ø.N., Strandby, Å. and Sletten, M.A. (2011). *Ungdom og trening. Endring over tidog sosiale skillelinjer*. Oslo: NOVA.

Skille, E.Å. (2010). *Idrettslaget – trivselsarena eller helseprodusent?* Vallset: Oplandske Bokforlag.

Skille, E.Å. (2013). Lassoing and reindeer racing versus 'universal' sports: Various routes to Sámi ethnic identity through sports. In C. Hallinan and B. Judd (eds.) *Native Games: Indigenous Peoples and Sports in the Post-Colonial World*. (pp. 21–41). Melbourne: Emerald.

Skille, E.Å. and Stenling, C. (2017). Inside-out and outside-in: applying the concept of conventions in the analysis of policy implementation through sport clubs. *International Review for the Sociology of Sport*. (Available from https://doi.org/10.1177/1012690216685584, 22 April 2017).

Skirstad, B. (2002). Norske idrettslag. Oversikt og utfordringer. In Ø.N. Seippel (ed.) *Idrettens bevegelser. Sosiologiske studier av idrett i et moderne samfunn*. Oslo: Novus.

Steen-Johnsen, K. (2004). *Individualized Communities*. Oslo: Norwegian School of Sport Sciences.

St. Meld. Nr. 41 (1991–1992). *Idretten. Folkebevegelse og folkeforlystelse*. Oslo: Kulturdepartementet.

St. Meld. Nr. 14 (1999–2000). *Idrettslivet i endring*. Oslo: Kulturdepartementet.

Strandbu, Å., Bakken, A. and Sletten, M.A. (2017). Exploring the minority–majority gap in sport participation: different patterns for boys and girls? *Sport in Society*. DOI:10.1080/17430437.2017.1389056.

Strandbu, Å., Gulløy, E., Andersen, P.L., Seippel, Ø.N. and Dalen, H.B. (2017). Ungdom, idrett og klasse: fortid, samtid og framtid. *Norsk sosiologisk tidsskrift*, *1*(2), 132–151.

Vaage, O.F. (2015). *Fritidsaktiviteter 1997–2014*. Report 25/2015. Oslo: Statistics Norway.

Chapter 7

Sports participation in Sweden

Josef Fahlén and Magnus Ferry

Introduction

In this chapter, we aim to provide an understanding of sports participation in Sweden by placing it in a socio-political context. As we will argue throughout, understanding the self-image of Swedish society – in terms of belonging to the Scandinavian and Nordic community and being ideologically grounded in the notion of 'the people's home' (Schön, 2012) – is key to untangling complex phenomena such as sport and physical activity participation patterns in Sweden. As Fahlén (2016) has argued, the hallmarks of the modern welfare state have been instrumental not only in the economic growth, social security and general development of Sweden but also in the outstanding achievements in sport, one aspect of which is a physically active and sporting population. Many others (e.g. Bergsgard & Norberg, 2010; Lindroth, 1988; Lindroth & Norberg, 2002; Norberg, 2002; Sjöblom, 2006) have similarly argued that high participation rates and international recognition would not have been possible without the general political developments that included voluntary and membership-based club sport in the social engineering of the modern Swedish welfare state. These, in turn, gave sport a leading role in the fostering and promotion of health and democracy and were aided by substantial financial support (Fahlén & Stenling, 2016).

In this chapter, we will show how this support, together with civic engagement and enthusiasm, has been turned into participation in sport and exercise in Sweden. While focussing primarily on who does what and how, how much and where, we will also sketch the context surrounding these activities in terms of organisation, politics, culture and commerce, before concluding with an outline of current issues in, and prognoses for, future sports participation in Sweden.

Sports participation in Sweden

In this section, we will focus on participation in sport in its broadest sense.[1] The section contains the most recent available data, at the time of writing, as well as trends over time regarding the different types of activities, participants and settings. Since 1975, Statistics Sweden (SCB) has charted and analysed the development of Swedish citizens' lives through the *Survey of Living Conditions* (ULF/SILC). The survey is performed every other year and has had a specific focus on leisure-time activities on several occasions (1976, 1983, 1991, 1999, 2006 and 2015), as well as children's leisure-time activities twice (2005 and 2009). Most data from these surveys are accessible via SCB's open databases (www.scb.se).

The survey is based on interviews with a random sample of 7,000–13,000 individuals, aged 16 and older (up to age 74 until 1980, 84 until 2001 and no upper age limit thereafter). Although the areas covered by the survey have remained largely the same over the years, some questions have been omitted or altered, limiting the possibilities for comparison. Despite this, the available data enable rough comparisons over time: that is, trends. The results from these surveys are divided by age, gender, ethnicity and education level, which provides the structure for this section. Data on living conditions for people with disabilities were part of the first surveys. However, these data are no longer collected and will, therefore, not be presented here. In addition to SCB's surveys, the Swedish Sports Confederation (RF) and the Swedish Research Council for Sport Science (CIF) have published reports on sporting habits and physical activity levels among the Swedish population. Taken together, these studies provide the basis for this section.

Sports participation among adults

During the past four decades, participation in sport and physical activity in Sweden has increased gradually among those aged 16 years and over. Most notably, the proportion of individuals who participate at least two times a week has increased to over 60% of the total population aged 16–84 years, and over 70% in the age group 16–24 years during 2013 (Figure 7.1). Results from the SCB survey in 2015 indicate that 74% of all women and 70% of all men practiced sport or

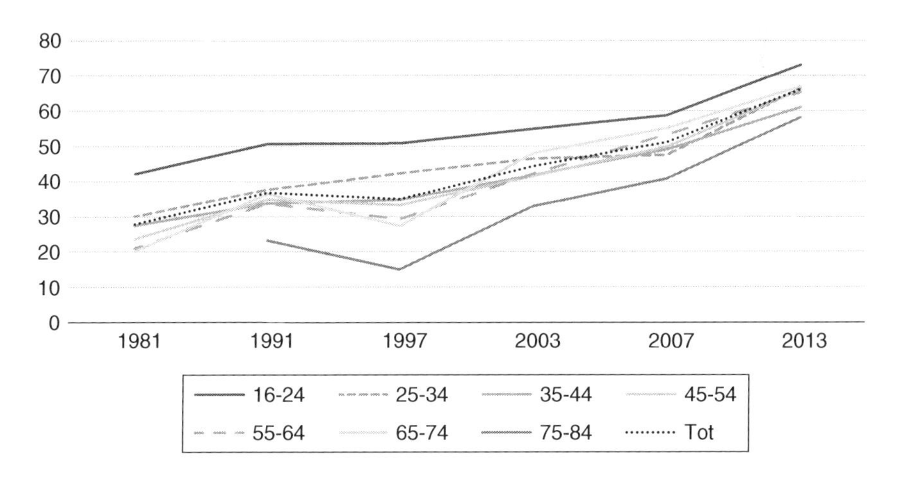

Figure 7.1 Proportion of the population in different age groups exercising at least two times each week (SCB, n.d.).

exercised 'often' (20 times per annum or more), outdoors or indoors. A large part of this increase resulted from increased participation in outdoor activities and exercise, where the greatest increase has been among the older age groups.

Closer inspection of developments between 2009 and 2015 reveals only minor changes in relation to participation in sport and exercise. In 2015, over 40% of all men and nearly 50% of all women exercised at least three times a week and fewer than 20% of all men and women hardly ever exercised (Figure 7.2).

By contrast, using the measure 'at least 30 minutes of exercise each day' – the World Health Organisation (WHO) recommendation – rather than participation *per se*, reveals decreasing levels of exercise between 2009 and 2015. The highest levels of exercise in 2015 existed among the 16–29-year-olds and the lowest among those aged 45–64 (Figure 7.3).

Dividing sport and exercise habits by outdoor–indoor indicates that the proportion of the population participating often (i.e. 20 times per annum or more) in an outdoor activity during the previous year was over 50% in 2015 and almost 70% among those aged 16–24 years. The proportion of individuals participating often in indoor activities also increased during the same time period, albeit slightly less than outdoor activities: 60% of 16–24-year-olds and 25% of those aged 65–74.

Breaking these data down by sex, no major differences existed between the proportion of men and women who exercised at least twice a week between 1981 and 2013 (Figures 7.4 and 7.5). However, the proportions increased significantly during this period (28% in 1981, 66% in 2013). The trend over time has been for a larger proportion of women than men to exercise on a regular basis. CIF's 2016 report also noted such differences – the proportion of men (63%) and women (69%) who exercised at least two times a week had increased.

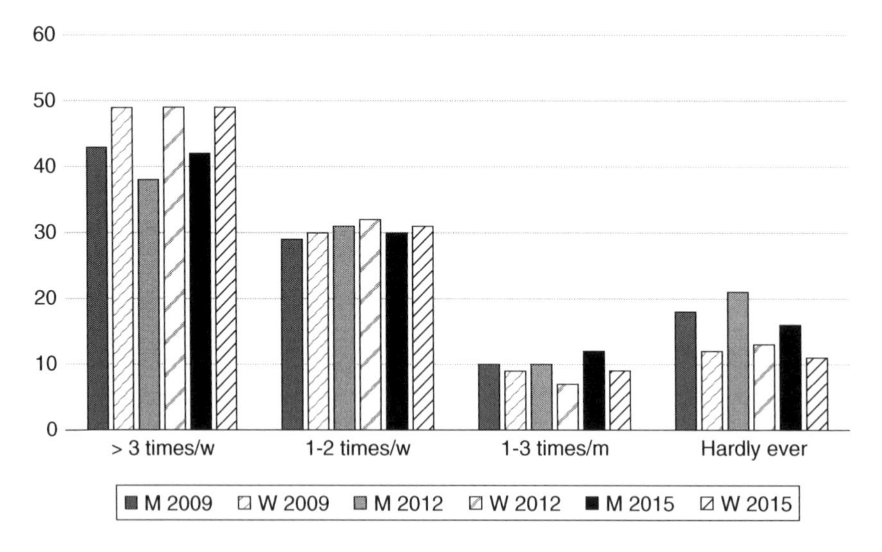

Figure 7.2 Participation in sport and physical exercise, proportion of the population (CIF, 2010; 2013; 2016).

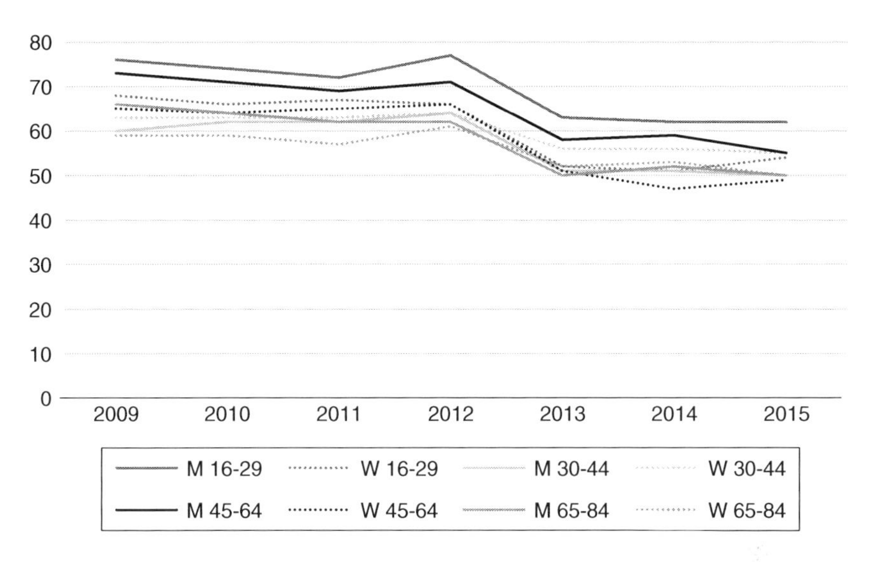

Figure 7.3 At least 30 minutes of physical exercise each day, proportion of the population (CIF, 2010; 2011; 2012; 2013; 2014; 2015; 2016).

In terms of ethnicity, a greater proportion of those with a Swedish background participated in sport or exercise (both indoors and outdoors) than those with foreign backgrounds (Figures 7.6 and 7.7). However, the way in which ethnicity has been measured by SCB has changed substantially since 1976, resulting in the use of only two categories when making comparisons over time: 'Swedish' (i.e. both parents born in Sweden) and 'Foreigner' (one or both parents born outside Sweden).

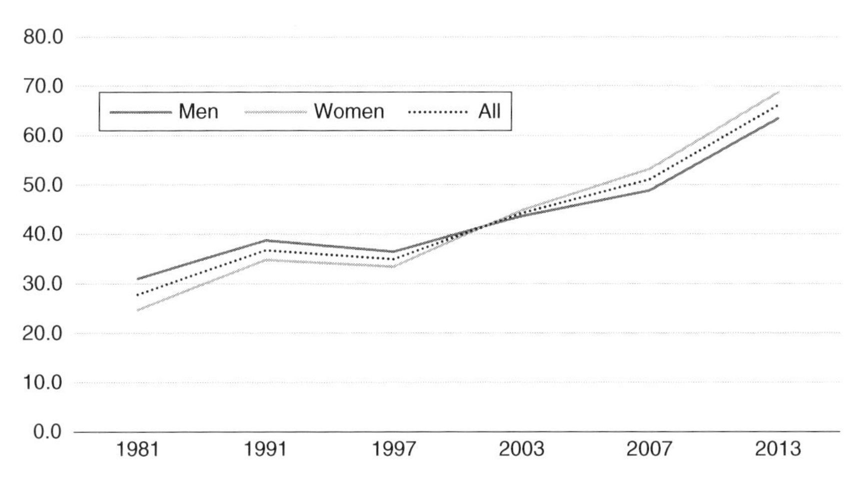

Figure 7.4 Proportion of men and women and all who exercise at least two times a week (SCB, n.d.).

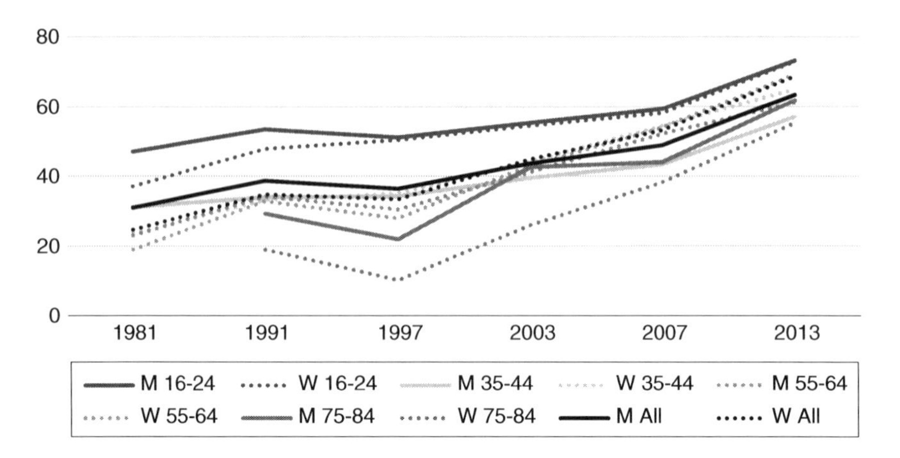

Figure 7.5 Proportion of men and women in different age groups who exercise at least two times a week (SCB, n.d.).

Changing interpretations of social class in the SCB surveys over the past 40 years or more make class comparisons over time difficult. However, in all surveys, questions have been asked about education level and this is used, therefore, as a rough indication or proxy measure of class. It should be noted, however, that although the classification of education has stayed the same over time, the meaning of education has altered. For example, in 2015 most Swedish citizens entered and completed upper secondary education. This was not the case during the 1970s, thereby negating comparisons. Nowadays, elementary

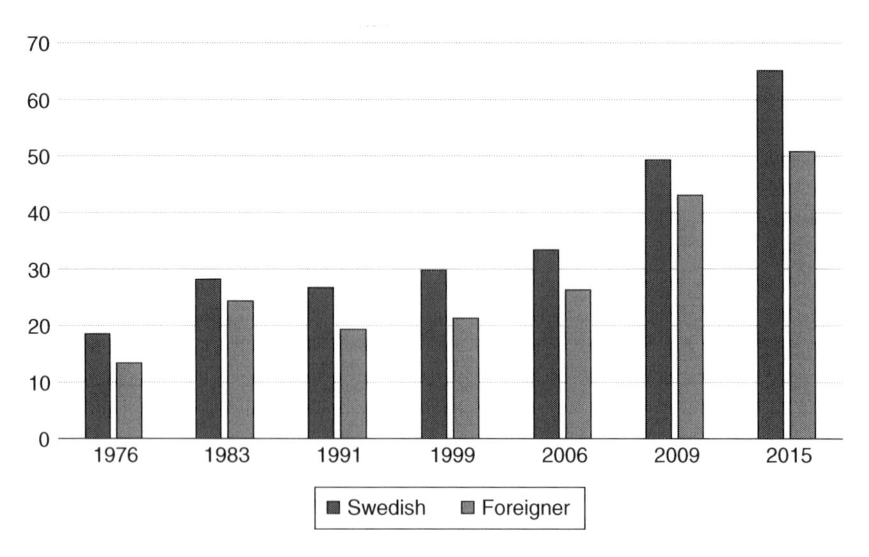

Figure 7.6 Often exercising in sport and exercise *outdoors*, proportion of the population (SCB, n.d.).

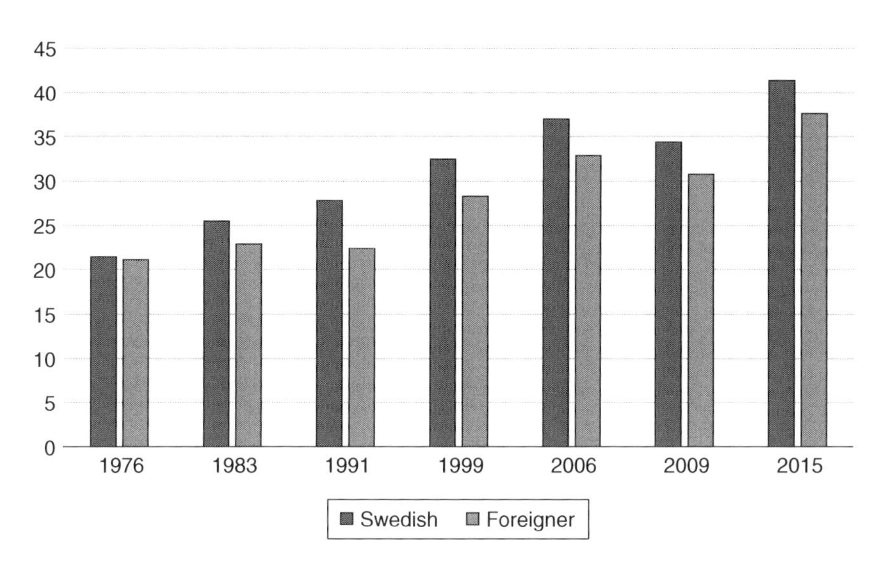

Figure 7.7 Often exercising in sport and exercise *indoors*, proportion of the population (SCB, n.d.).

education (*grundskola*) involves nine years of mandatory education (age 7–16), whereas upper secondary education (*gymnasieskola*) (age 17–19) and post-upper secondary education (*högskola och universitet*) are both optional.

These results show that participation rates in sport or exercise in Sweden increase with the level of education (Figures 7.8 and 7.9), with the highest

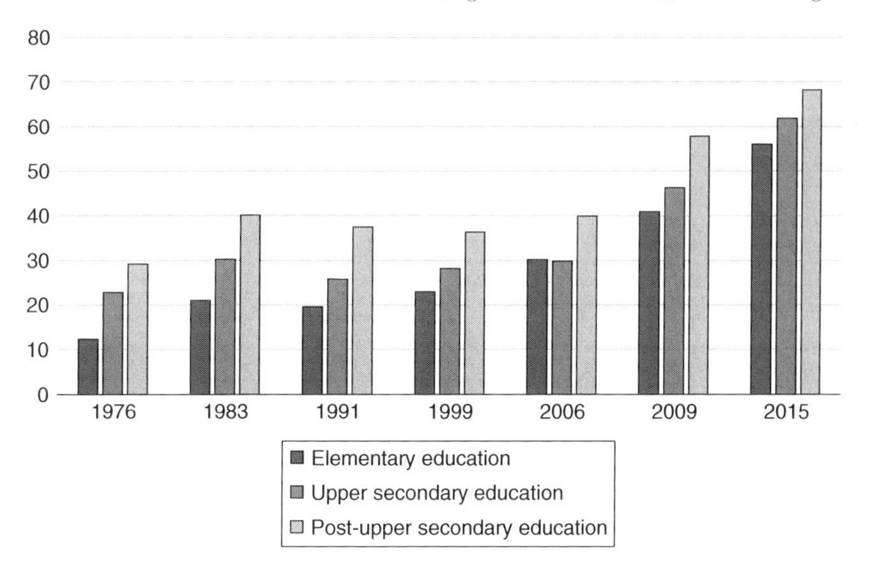

Figure 7.8 Often exercising in sport and exercise *outdoors*, proportion of the population (SCB, n.d.).

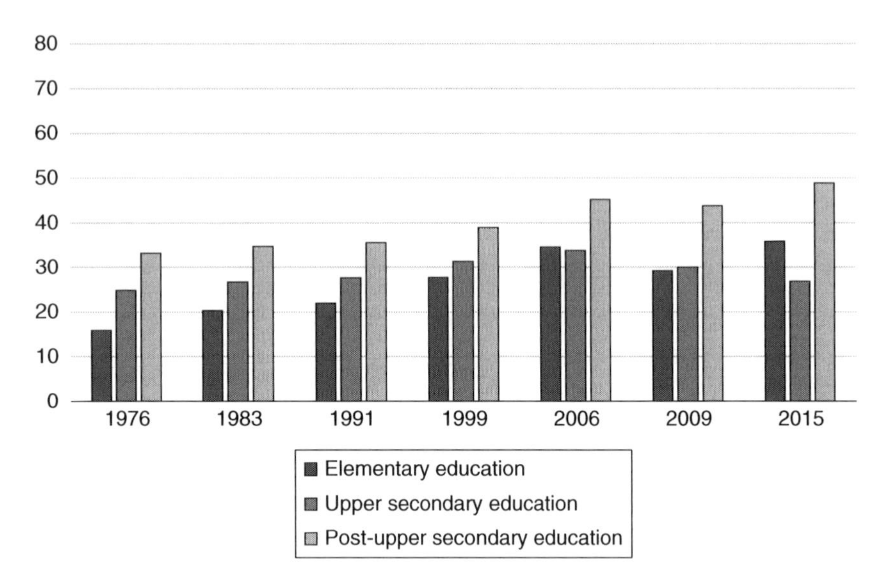

Figure 7.9 Often exercising in sport and exercise *indoors*, proportion of the population (SCB, n.d.).

participation rates to be found among those with post-secondary education: 68% and 49%, respectively, having participated often in an outdoor or indoor activity in 2015.

Settings and venues for sports participation among adults

According to membership statistics, the total number of members in Swedish sports clubs decreased between 1999 and 2012 (CIF, 2010, 2016). More than 60% of all boys and girls in Sweden aged 7–19 years were members of a sports club in 2012, compared with less than 40% of those aged 20–39 or 40–70. These figures are deceptive, however, for when it comes to 'active' membership (i.e. actually participating in sport rather than merely being a club member), results reveal increasing participation rates (Figure 7.10). The largest proportion of active participants was found among those aged 7–19, wherein 60% were active members of a sports club compared with less than 30% among other age groups.

Since the SCB survey in 1982–1983, questions have been asked about activities at particular venues. Recurring venues, allowing comparisons over time, are outdoor sports facilities – such as running trails (*motionsspår*) and football pitches (*fotbollsplan/idrottsplats*) – and indoor sport facilities – such as sports centres (*idrottshall/gymnastiksal*). The results revealed that exercising at least five times during the previous year declined with age at all venues (Figure 7.11, 7.12 and 7.13). Furthermore, between 1983 and 2007, a higher proportion of the population used football pitches and running trails while a lower proportion exercised

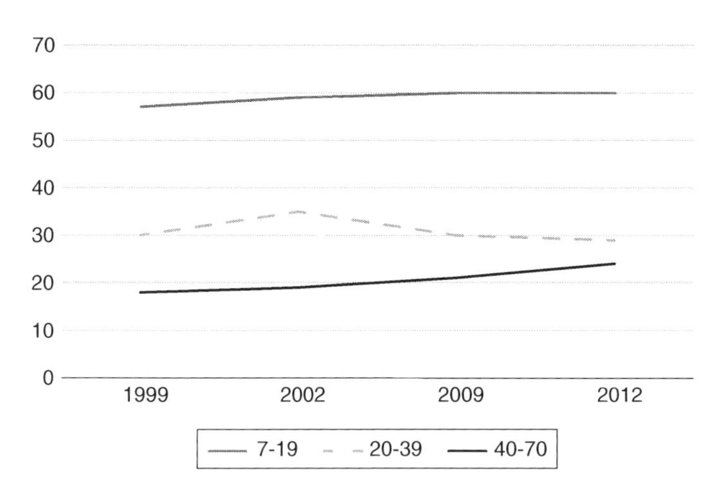

Figure 7.10 Active members of sports clubs, proportion of the population (CIF, 2010; 2013).

at sports centres. Comparing the different venues, the highest proportion of participants (in 2006–2007) used running trails and the lowest proportion football pitches.

At all venues, a larger proportion of men compared with women exercised at least five times during the last year. In relation to age, these differences existed among all age groups and venues except for sport centres, where a slightly larger proportion of older women exercised more than men.

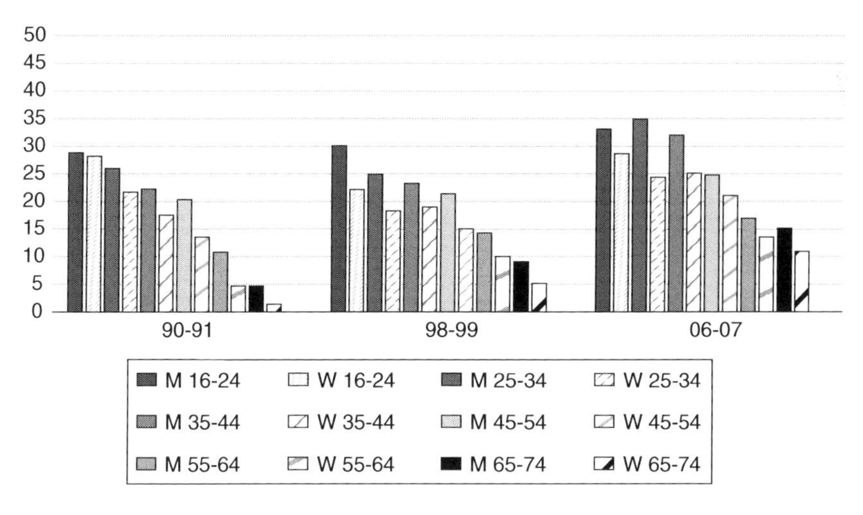

Figure 7.11 Proportion of the population exercising on a running trail at least five times in the previous year (SCB, n.d.).

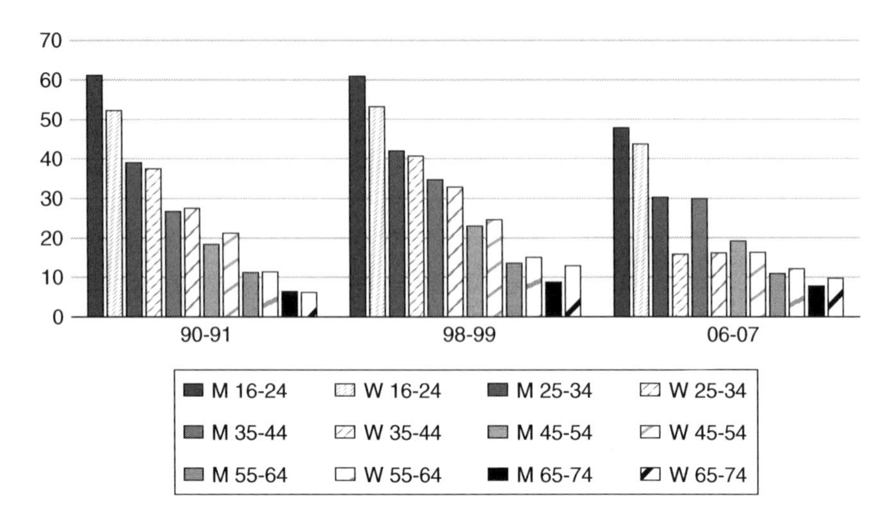

Figure 7.12 Proportion of the population exercising at a sport centre at least five times in the previous year (SCB, n.d.).

In relation to ethnicity, a larger proportion of men and women with a Swedish background exercised at all venues compared with their 'foreign' counterparts – the highest proportions being Swedish men and the lowest foreign women (Figure 7.14). However, the largest proportion exercising at football pitches in 2007 was foreign men (20%), followed by Swedish men (16%), Swedish women (6%) and foreign women (3%).

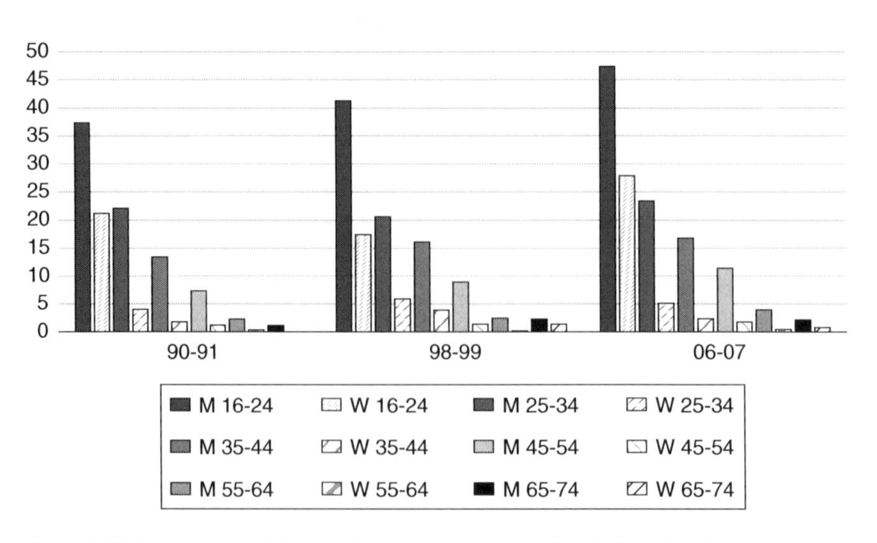

Figure 7.13 Proportion of the population exercising at a football pitch at least five times in the previous year (SCB, n.d.).

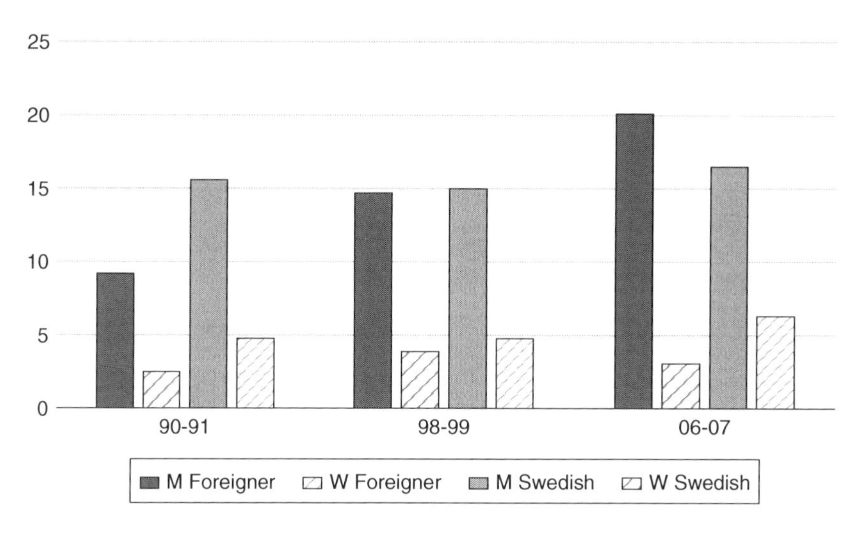

Figure 7.14 Exercising at a football pitch at least five times in the previous year, proportion of each group (SCB, n.d.).

With regard to the relationship between education level and exercise, large changes at the different venues were observable (Figures 7.15, 7.16 and 7.17). For example, the largest proportions using running trails were men and women with post-upper secondary education, and these differences increased between 1990 and 1991 and between 2006 and 2007. In 2006–2007, 38% of all men and 27% of all women with post-upper secondary education had exercised at least five times during the previous 12 months. By comparison, 23% and 18% of all men

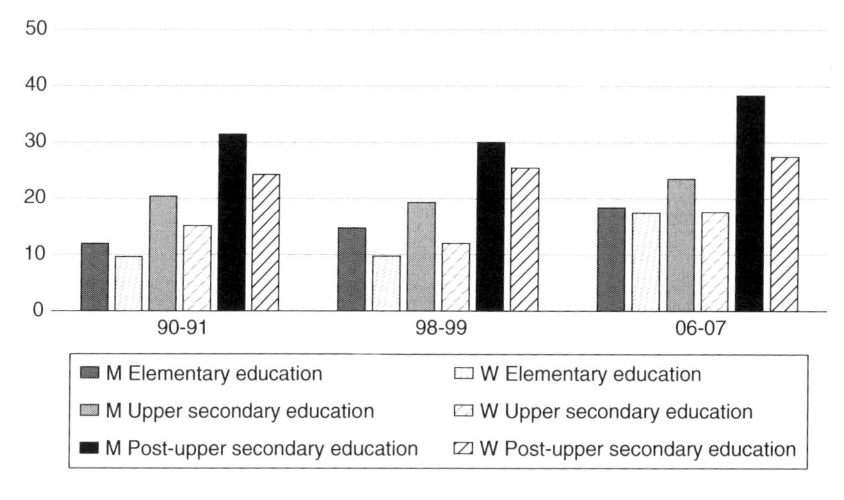

Figure 7.15 Exercising on a running trail at least five times during the previous year, proportion of each group (SCB, n.d.).

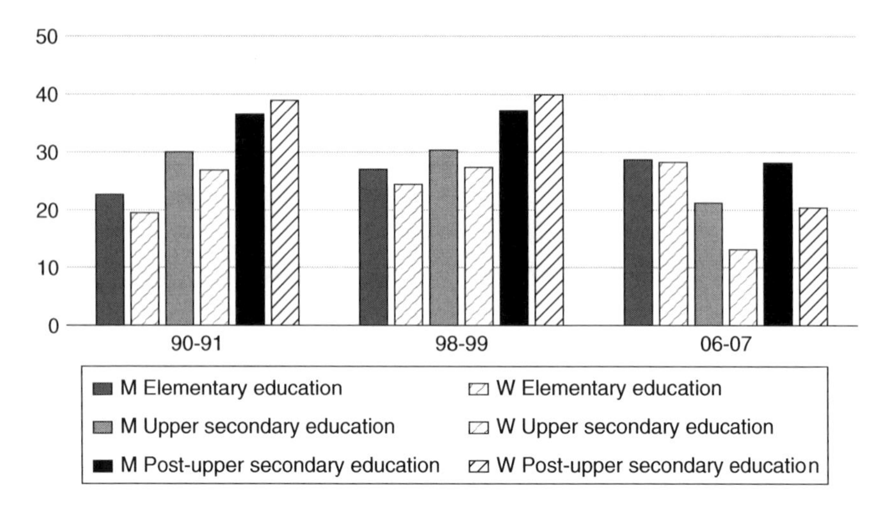

Figure 7.16 Exercising at a sports centre at least five times during the previous year, proportion of each group (SCB, n.d.).

and 18% and 17% of all women with upper secondary education and elementary education, respectively, exercised at least five times on a running trail.

By focussing on three selected activities, it is possible to further scrutinise participation in certain venues.

Table 7.1 displays sex differences in three selected activities (swimming in a swimming pool, golfing and skating at an ice-rink), with a larger proportion of men golfing and skating at an ice-rink. For swimming at a swimming pool, the

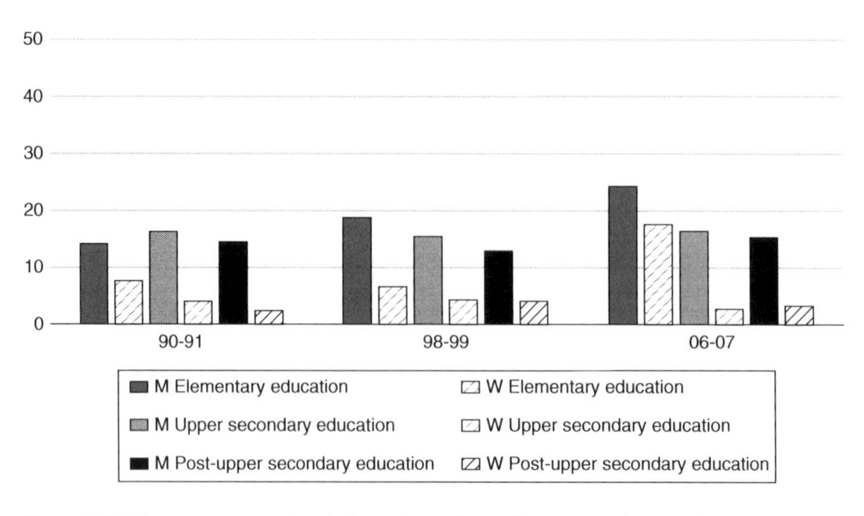

Figure 7.17 Exercising at a football pitch at least five times during the previous year, proportion of each group (SCB, n.d.).

Table 7.1 Proportion of women and men in each age group who have participated at least five times during the previous year (SCB, n.d.)

Activity	*Sex*	*Year*	*16–24*	*25–34*	*35–44*	*45–54*	*55–64*	*65–74*	*All*
Swimming in a swimming pool	Men	1990–1991	25	20	15	11	6	4	14
		1998–1999	22	17	24	12	7	6	15
		2006–2007	21	15	18	14	7	10	14
	Women	1990–1991	36	26	16	14	10	5	18
		1998–1999	27	25	24	13	12	10	19
		2006–2007	26	19	22	19	16	14	19
Golfing	Men	1998–1999	13	11	9	9	10	5	10
		2006–2007	11	9	12	11	10	7	10
	Women	1998–1999	3	4	4	5	4	2	4
		2006–2007	2	2	4	5	5	3	3
Skating at an ice-rink	Men	1990–1991	14	10	7	3	1	0	6
		1998–1999	14	8	10	3	1	0	6
		2006–2007	13	7	11	6	1	1	7
	Women	1990–1991	5	2	3	1	0	0	2
		1998–1999	2	3	3	2	0	0	2
		2006–2007	4	3	4	2	1	0	2

pattern was reversed, with women forming the highest proportion. For all activities, the overall pattern was one of participation in these particular activities decreasing with age.

In relation to ethnicity, for all groups except Swedish men, the proportion swimming in a swimming pool at least five times during the past year had increased slightly (Table 7.2). Golf was most popular among Swedish men, where 11% had played at least five times.

In terms of the level of education, there was a higher proportion of women swimming than men at all educational levels. In addition, the proportions increased with education level, with the highest proportion among women with post-secondary education (23%) in 2006–2007 and the lowest proportion among men with elementary education (13%). Golf was more popular among men, regardless of education level, with the highest proportion among men with post-secondary education (15%) (Table 7.3).

Physical recreation

One recurring question in the SCB survey relates specifically to the area of physical recreation, namely: 'Have you been wandering in the forest (*Strövat i skog och mark*) during the last year?'. Measured in terms of wandering in the forest often (at least 20 times during the past year), the proportion of citizens engaging

Table 7.2 Proportion of Swedish and foreign men and women who have participated at least five times during the previous year (SCB, n.d.)

Activity	*Sex*	*Year*	*Foreigner*	*Swedish*
Swimming in a swimming pool	Men	1990–1991	15	14
		1998–1999	16	15
		2006–2007	21	13
	Women	1990–1991	16	18
		1998–1999	16	18
		2006–2007	19	19
Golfing	Men	1998–1999	2	11
		2006–2007	4	11
	Women	1998–1999	2	4
		2006–2007	1	4
Skating on an ice-rink	Men	1990–1991	2	7
		1998–1999	3	6
		2006–2007	2	8
	Women	1990–1991	1	2
		1998–1999	2	2
		2006–2007	3	2

Table 7.3 Proportion of men and women at different education levels who have participated at least five times in the previous year (SCB, n.d.)

Activity	*Sex*	*Year*	*Elementary education*	*Upper secondary education*	*Post-upper secondary education*
Swimming in a swimming pool	Men	1990–1991	11	14	20
		1998–1999	12	14	20
		2006–2007	13	13	18
	Women	1990–1991	15	18	25
		1998–1999	12	18	25
		2006–2007	15	19	23
Golfing	Men	1998–1999	7	8	14
		2006–2007	7	9	15
	Women	1998–1999	2	3	6
		2006–2007	2	2	6
Skating on an ice-rink	Men	1990–1991	6	7	6
		1998–1999	7	6	7
		2006–2007	7	7	6
	Women	1990–1991	2	1	3
		1998–1999	1	1	3
		2006–2007	3	2	3

in physical recreation increased with age (disregarding those aged 75–84). In total, the proportion of the Swedish population engaged in physical recreation-has increased slightly over the last 40 years. During 2015, the largest proportion engaged in physical recreation was found among those aged 65–74 years (41%), followed by 45–64 (38%) and 25–44 (26%) and, finally, those aged 16–24 (18%).

In total, a higher proportion of women 'wandered' often in the forest, except for the oldest age groups (65–74 and 75–84). Physical recreation, in the form of wandering, was most popular among women aged 35–64 (Figure 7.18).

In terms of ethnicity, more people with Swedish backgrounds 'wandered' in the forest compared with those with foreign backgrounds. This has remained the case over time (Figure 7.19).

For wandering in the forest 'often', the highest proportions were found among those with post-secondary education and the lowest among those with elementary education (Figure 7.20).

Exercise in outdoor activities

In relation to participation in outdoor activities (*friluftsliv*) beyond 'wandering', recent SCB-surveys have included questions about specific activities, including alpine wandering (*fjällvandrssat*), hunting and fishing.

As indicated in Figure 7.21, fishing at least once in the previous year (approximately 30%) was the most common outdoor activity between 1982 and 1983 and in 2006–2007. An additional 5–10% had undertaken alpine wandering or hunting at least once. There were no major changes in these patterns during the period. In relation to age, the proportions of the population taking part in alpine wandering tended to decrease with age.

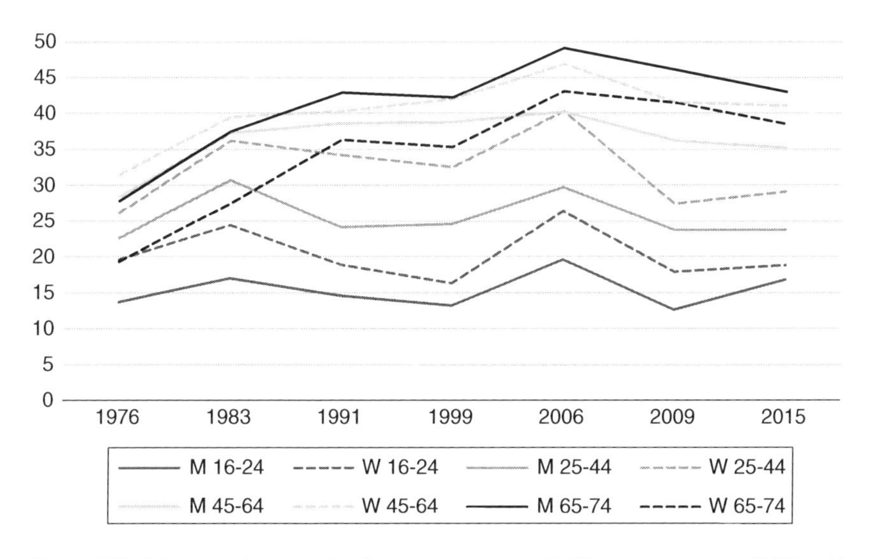

Figure 7.18 Often wandering in the forest, proportion of different age groups (SCB, n.d.).

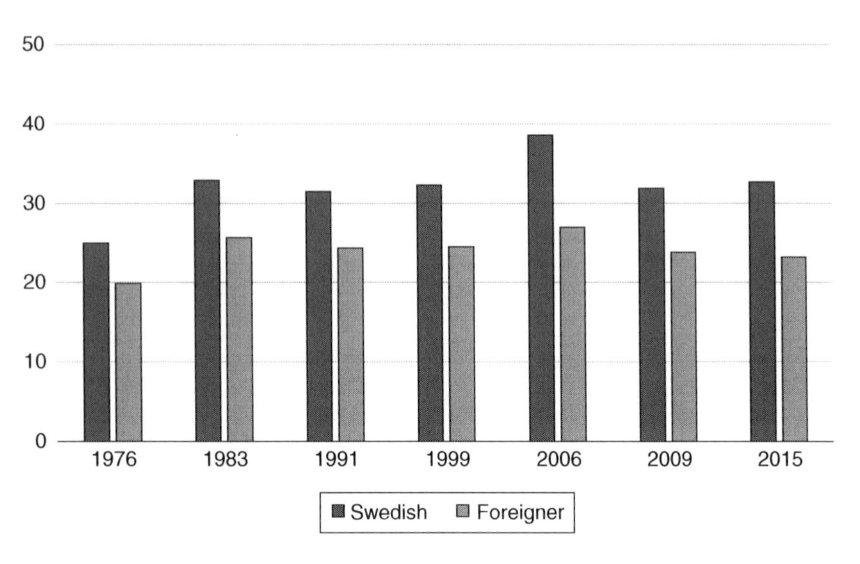

Figure 7.19 Often wandering in the forest, proportion of total groups (SCB, n.d.).

Clear sex patterns for the specified outdoor activities can be observed (Figures 7.22, 7.23 and 7.24). A larger proportion of men compared with women had been hunting or fishing, with the same pattern in all age groups. For hunting, these differences also increased with age, with the largest proportions among men aged 65–74 (16%) and lowest among women aged 65–74 (1%). In general terms, a higher proportion of men also engaged in alpine wandering. These differences

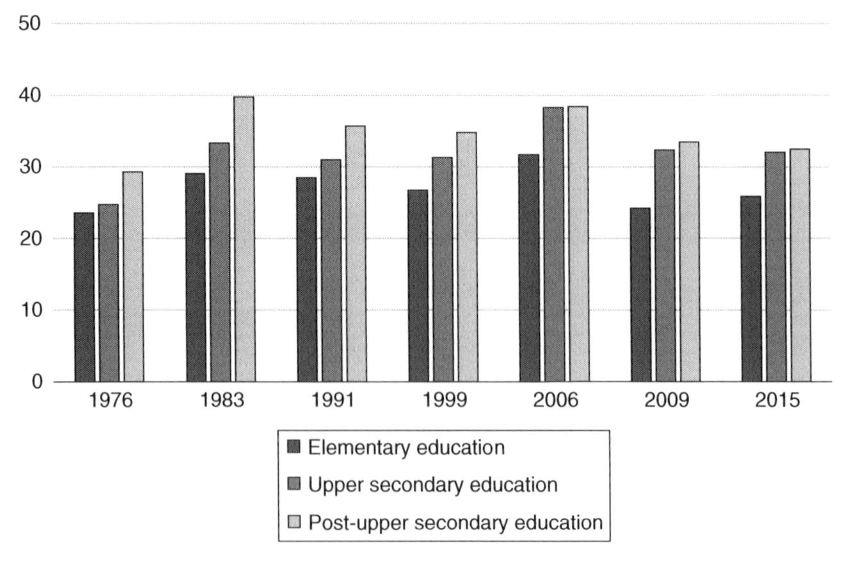

Figure 7.20 Often wandering in the forest, proportion of different education levels (SCB, n.d.).

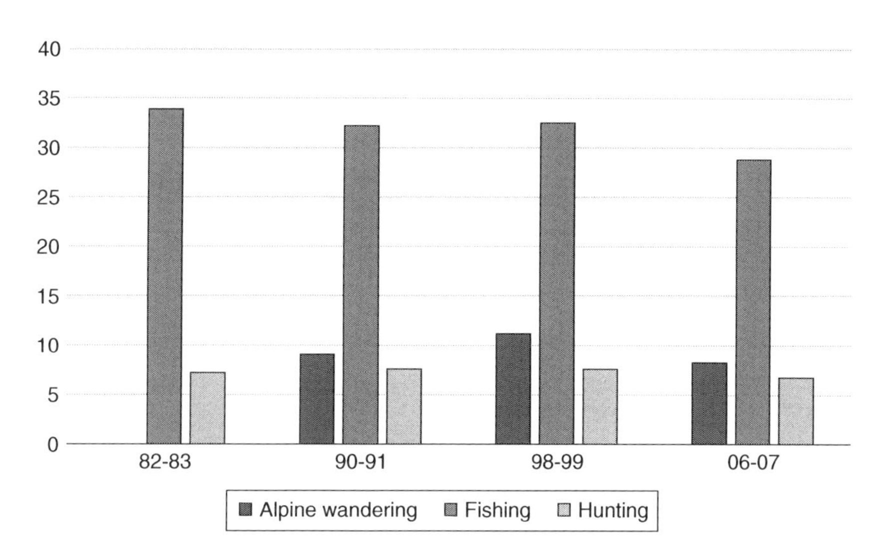

Figure 7.21 Proportion of the population who have performed different outdoor activities at least once in the previous year (SCB, n.d.).

were smaller, however, for those aged 55–64. In 2006–2007, a slightly larger proportion of women (9%) compared with men (7%) had been alpine wandering at least once.

In terms of ethnicity, there were no major differences between groups participating in alpine wandering while a higher proportion of men – both Swedish (21%)

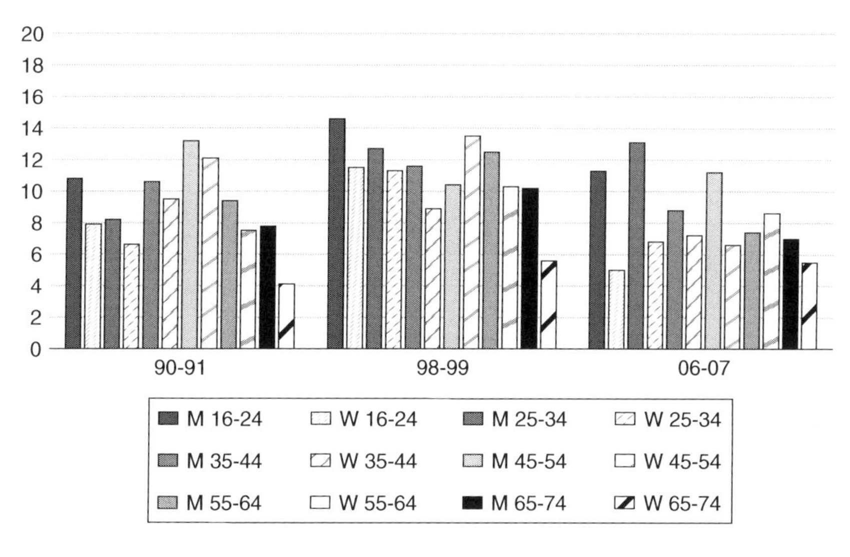

Figure 7.22 Proportion of men and women in different age groups who have been alpine wandering at least once in the previous year (SCB, n.d.).

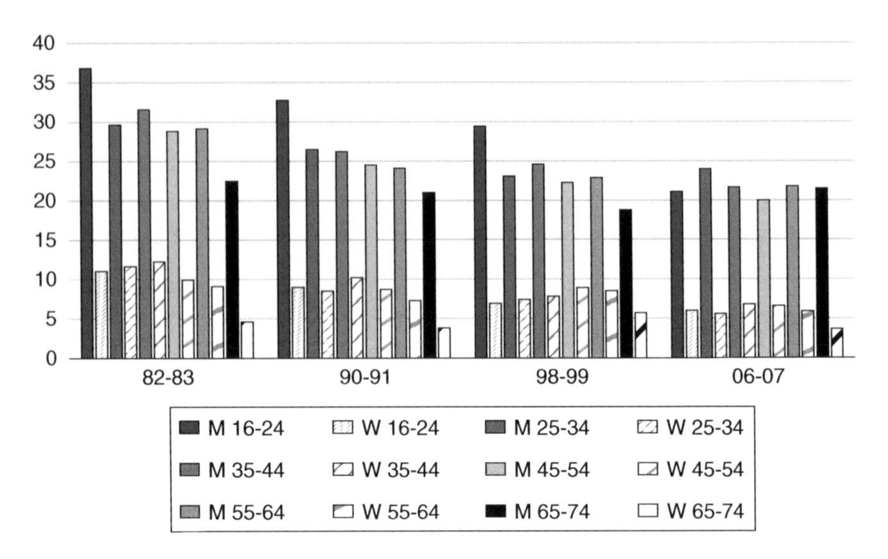

Figure 7.23 Proportion of men and women in different age groups who have been fishing at least five times in the previous year (SCB, n.d.).

and foreign (18%) – had been fishing compared with Swedish (6%) and foreign (4%) women. For hunting, there were larger differences between the groups, with a larger proportion of Swedish men (13%) compared with foreign men (7%) having been hunting at least once during the previous year. For both Swedish and foreign women, the proportions were below 2% (Figures 7.25, 7.26 and 7.27).

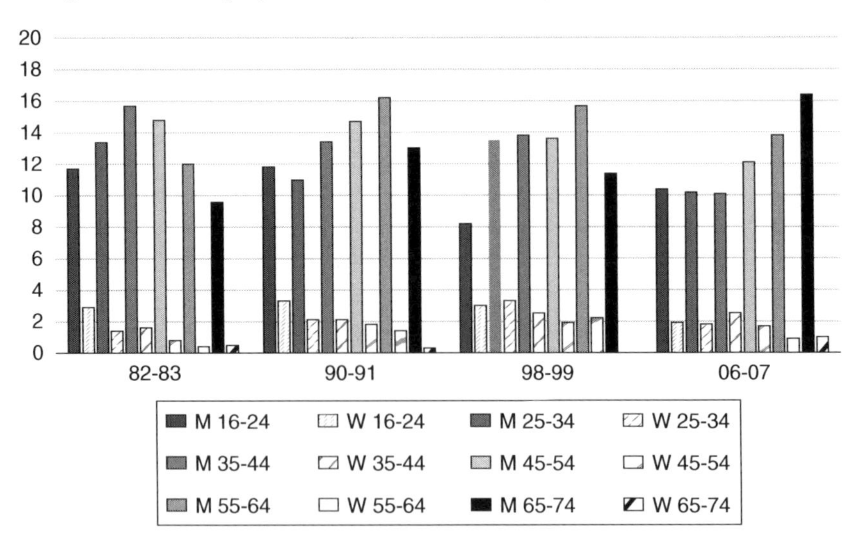

Figure 7.24 Proportion of men and women in different age groups who have been hunting at least once in the previous year (SCB, n.d.).

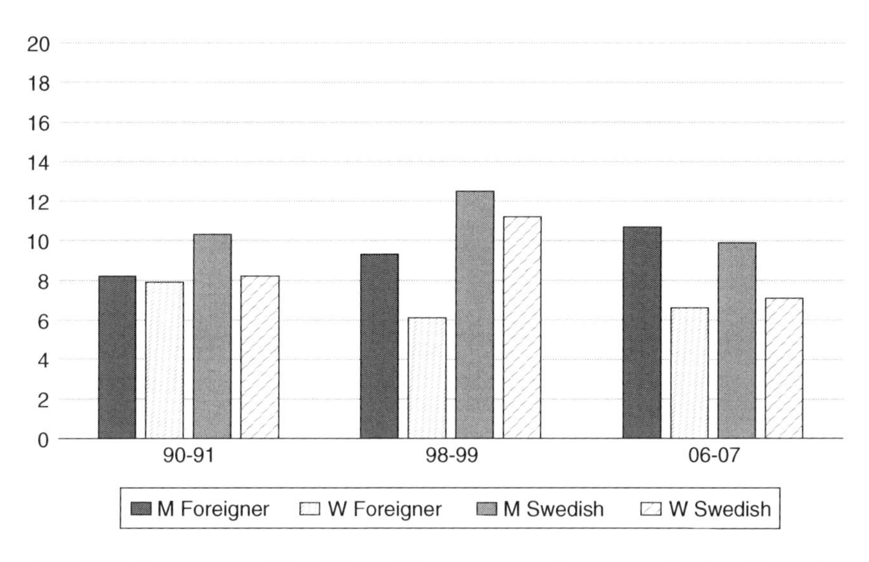

Figure 7.25 Proportion of Swedish and foreign men and women who have been alpine wandering at least once in the previous year (SCB, n.d.).

With regard to education, the proportion of men and women who had been alpine wandering increased with level of education (Figure 7.28). The largest proportion could be observed for 2006–2007 among men (13%) and women (10%) with post-upper secondary education, and the smallest among men (8%) and women (4%) with elementary education. For men,

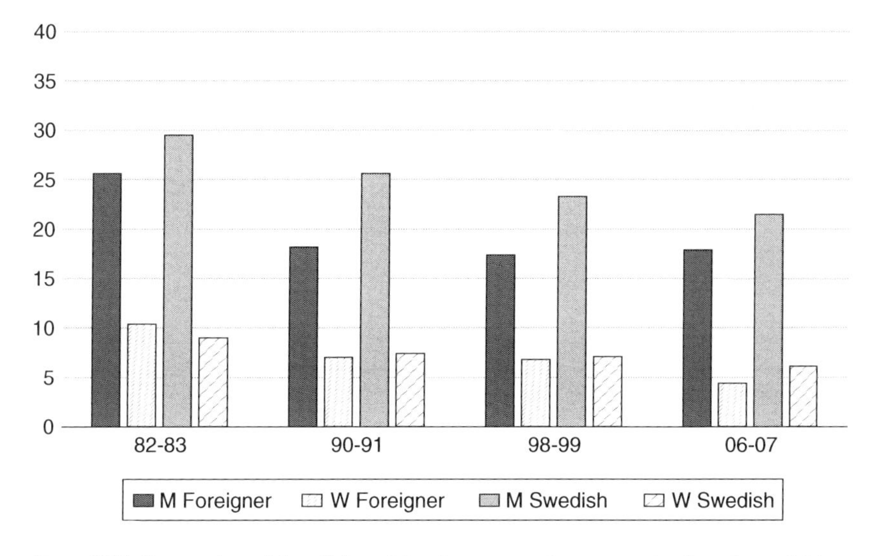

Figure 7.26 Proportion of Swedish and foreign men and women who have been fishing at least five times in the previous year (SCB, n.d.).

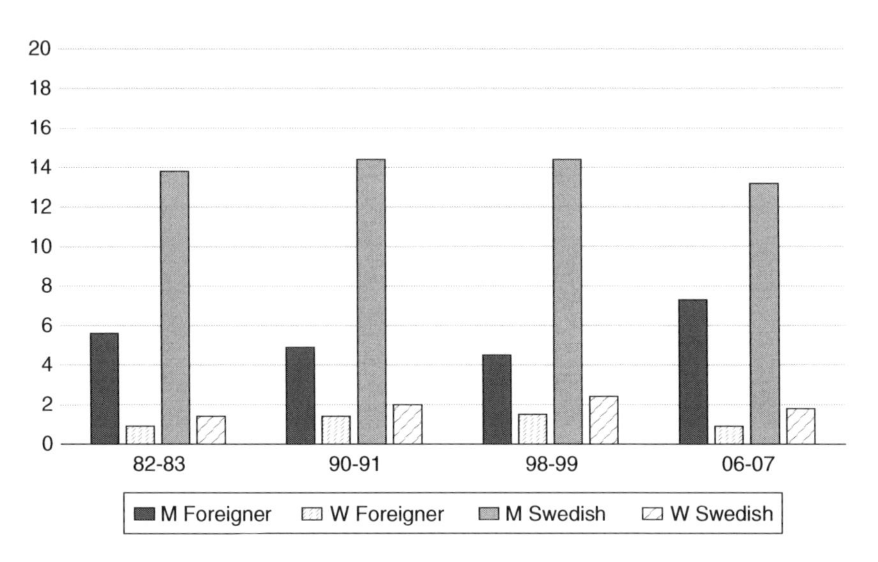

Figure 7.27 Proportion of Swedish and foreign men and women who have been hunting at least once in the previous year (SCB, n.d.).

the patterns were reversed for both fishing and hunting, with the smallest proportions among those with the highest levels of education, suggesting that these are predominantly working-class pursuits (Figures 7.29 and 7.30). In 2006–2007, 16% of those with post-upper secondary education and 23% of those with elementary education had been fishing at least five times during

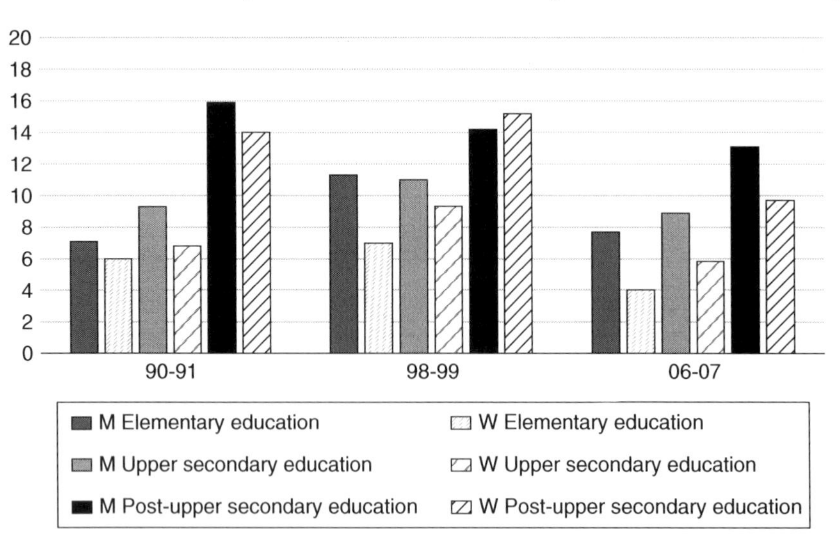

Figure 7.28 Proportion of men and women with different education levels who have been alpine wandering at least once in the previous year (SCB, n.d.).

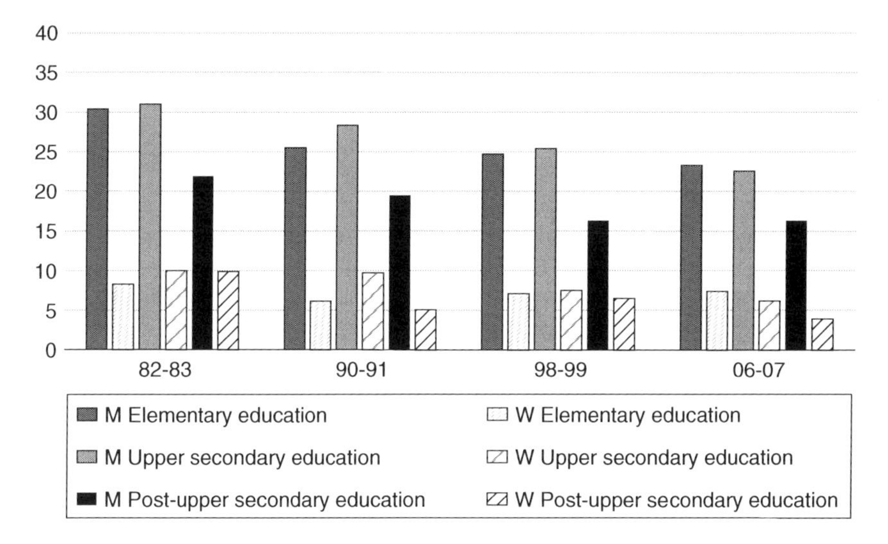

Figure 7.29 Proportion of men and women with different education levels who have been fishing at least five times in the previous year (SCB, n.d.).

the previous year while 9% of those with post-upper secondary education and 14% of those with elementary education had hunted. For women, there were only minor differences between the education levels in relation to fishing and hunting, reinforcing the impression that these are quintessentially male activities.

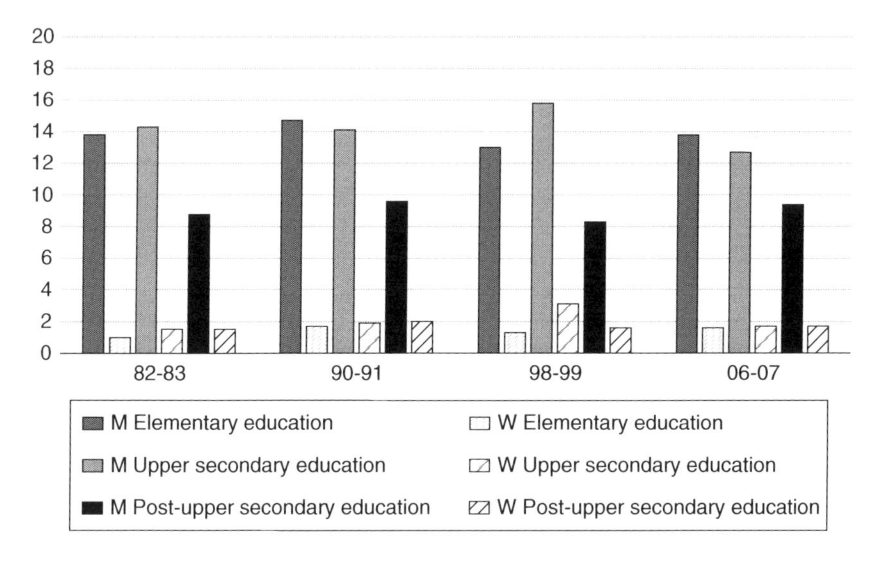

Figure 7.30 Proportion of men and women with different education levels who have been hunting at least once in the previous year (SCB, n.d.).

Sports participation among children and young people

The data presented above demonstrate that a large proportion of the youngest group of men and women participate regularly, in general, in different sports and physical activities. By drawing on the specific SCB reports (2005, 2009) on young people's living conditions (the CIF and RF reports), it is possible to describe participation patterns among younger boys and girls in greater detail.

Unlike the results for the whole population, the results for those aged 7–19 reveal that participation in sport and physical activity decreased between 2009 and 2015. Results from the CIF reports also show that the proportion of those aged 16–19 with a Swedish background who reached the goal of 30 minutes of physical exercise each day had decreased over time to 62% for boys and 54% for girls in 2015 (Figure 7.31). Unfortunately, no information on foreign boys and girls is available. The SCB reports (2005, 2009) also revealed that, among 12–18-year-olds, 91% of all boys and 86% of all girls participated in intensive exercise on a weekly basis. Viewed in relation to some background variables, a larger proportion of those who had parents with post-secondary education (90%) than upper-secondary education (86%), and a larger proportion of those with a Swedish background (90%) compared with a foreign background (82%), participated in intensive exercise on a weekly basis.

Settings and venues for sports participation among children and young people

The RF report revealed that most children aged 6–12 practiced sports in a sports-club setting. This proportion declined with age, nevertheless, as participating beyond the sports-club setting increased with age (Figure 7.32).

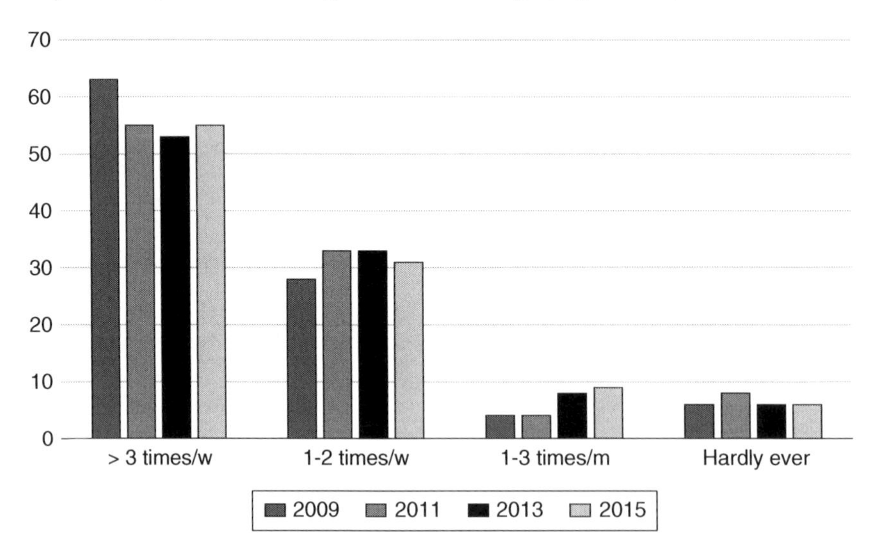

Figure 7.31 Participation in sport and physical exercise, proportion of the population aged 7–19 (CIF, 2010; 2012; 2014; 2016).

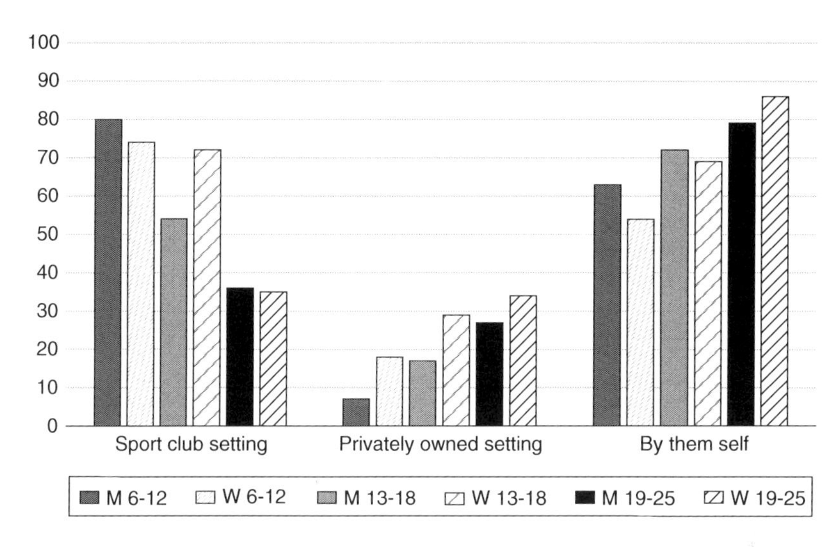

Figure 7.32 Sport practice in different settings, proportion of all participants in 2015 (RF, 2015).

During the period 2007–2015, young males exercised slightly more than young females (Figure 7.33). This appears to be changing, however. In 2014–2015, girls aged 13–15 exercised slightly more than boys. In relation to age, the youngest boys and girls exercised slightly more than the older ones.

In all age groups, females accounted for a smaller proportion of the total sports participation in sports-club settings (Figure 7.34). These differences have

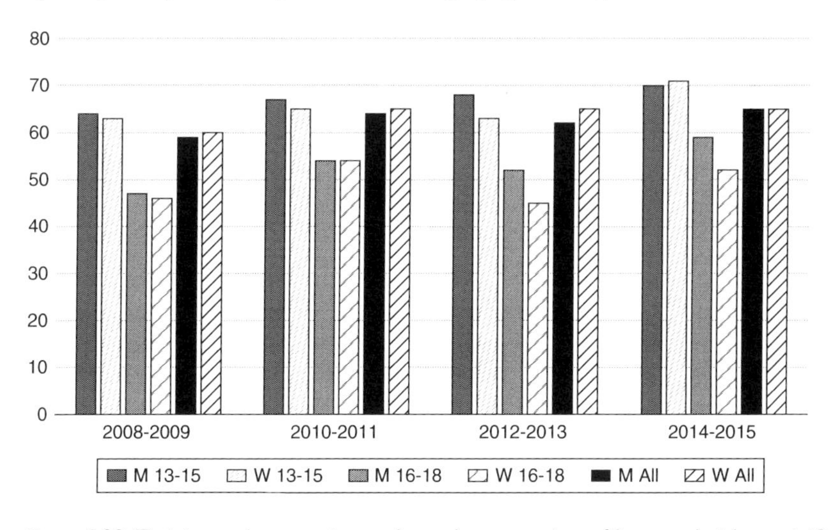

Figure 7.33 Training and competing each week, proportion of boys and girls aged 13–18 (SCB, n.d.).

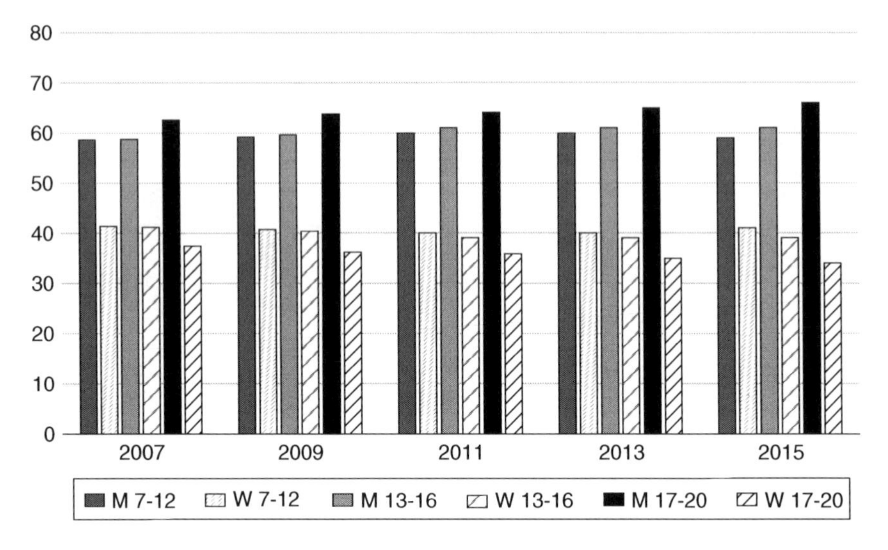

Figure 7.34 Proportion of all sports participation in sport clubs among boys and girls aged 7–20 (RF, 2008; 2010a; 2012; 2014; 2016).

increased recently. In relation to age, the differences were largest among the oldest age group. During 2015, young females made up 34% of those aged 17–20 and 41% of those aged 7–12 participating in a sports club.

In relation to family situation, a higher proportion of youngsters aged 13–18 who lived with cohabiting parents (compared with single parents) trained or competed weekly, with differences increasing over the years. When comparing ethnic backgrounds, young Swedish females were the highest participants in 2014–2015. In 2012–2013, the proportion of young males with a foreign background training or competing was larger than that of young foreign females. Similar to the whole population, participation in sport among young people tends to be related to parental education level, with higher proportions among the children of parents with post-secondary education (Figure 7.35).

Data on the numbers of participants and training sessions in different sports affords the possibility of further scrutinising children's participation patterns. Tables 7.4, 7.5 and 7.6 show that the number of youngsters participating in sports-club activities and the number of training sessions decreased between 2009 and 2015. Even allowing for a smaller population in 2015, this represents a real decrease in participation (CIF, 2016).

The same sports occur in both lists with only minor changes in their rankings over the years. Team sports are, in general, more popular among youngsters than individual sports. The most popular sport was football for both young males and females, both in relation to the number of participants and training sessions.

The largest proportion of participants in Swedish sports clubs was children 7–12 years old. This was also the group in which sex distribution was most equal.

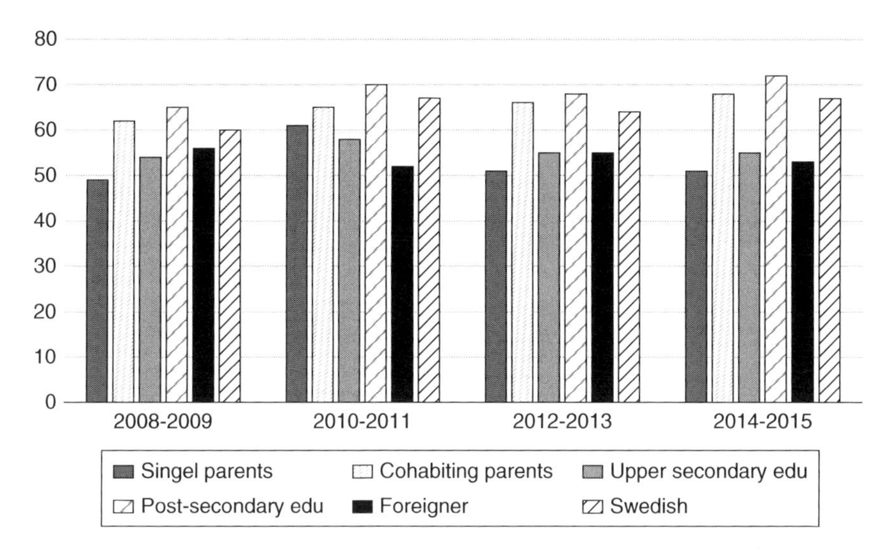

Figure 7.35 Training or competing weekly, proportion of the population aged 13–18 (SCB, n.d.).

Current levels of participation in different activities

In the SCB survey of 2015, questions were asked about participation in four specific activities. In this context, participation was defined as having undertaken the specified activity at least once during the previous year. On this basis, the most common activity was running, followed by cross-country skiing and golf. Least common was horse-riding. For all activities, the proportions participating generally declined with age. With regard to more frequent participation (i.e. at least 20 times/year) (see Table 7.7), running continued to be the most popular activity, decreasing with age but as popular among young females as males. Cross-country skiing was also equally popular among women and men across all age groups. For golf, participation rates declined with age. Golf was more popular among males for most age groups.

In terms of ethnicity, running, cross-country skiing and playing golf were more popular among Swedish males and females than their 'foreign' counterparts, while horse-riding was most popular among Swedish females in comparison with all other groups.

Participation in these selected activities was also related to education. For running and cross-country skiing, the proportion increased with level of education. In golf, a slightly larger proportion of participants was observed among those with post-secondary education in comparison with other education levels. For horse-riding, no major differences in relation to education level were visible.

In addition, a question was asked in the 2015 survey about exercising at a training centre (gym, *träningscenter*) (see Table 7.8).

Table 7.4 Sports with the highest numbers of participants in 2009–2015, including leaders aged 13–20 (CIF, 2010; 2011; 2012; 2013; 2014; 2015; 2016)

	2009	*2010*	*2011*	*2012*	*2013*	*2014*	*2015*	*Change (%)*
Football	19,446,576	18,982,349	18,169,413	18,499,021	18,266,198	18,491,127	18,859,329	−1
Floorball	5,237,187	5,345,565	5,197,650	5,183,675	5,019,067	4,990,899	5,030,827	−6
Ice hockey	4,301,080	4,307,327	4,165,460	4,212,395	4,010,567	3,956,659	3,966,722	−8
Gymnastics	2,166,774	2,226,624	2,059,619	2,283,395	2,456,067	2,622,609	2,931,049	32
Handball	3,141,812	3,045,070	2,876,571	3,014,933	2,862,092	2,750,477	2,737,107	−10
Equestrian	3,627,493	3,413,880	2,990,538	2,766,539	2,609,922	2,516,933	2,288,721	−33
Basketball	2,862,021	2,848,200	2,580,338	2,643,338	2,359,459	2,206,677	2,255,312	−21
Swimming	2,087,930	2,194,417	1,997,009	2,166,685	2,145,067	2,189,950	2,191,935	5
Athletics	1,712,204	1,675,783	1,626,320	1,473,485	1,338,812	1,329,580	1,442,256	−14
Tennis	1,693,752	1,754,264	1,532,428	1,710,182	1,543,629	1,474,595	1,228,573	−30

Table 7.5 Number of training sessions in the largest sports 2009–2015 (CIF, 2010; 2011; 2012; 2013; 2014; 2015; 2016)

	2009	*2010*	*2011*	*2012*	*2013*	*2014*	*2015*	*Change (%)*
Football	1,779,904	1,690,645	1,675,160	1,636,209	1,611,991	1,638,646	1,656,504	−7
Equestrian	518,020	472,722	438,337	424,842	422,974	424,973	424,046	−18
Floorball	449,823	431,360	424,888	414,059	405,971	412,757	423,011	−6
Tennis	337,574	338,992	340,230	340,641	331,658	324,487	316,232	−6
Swimming	297,452	292,360	298,374	307,284	309,075	309,127	307,423	3
Ice hockey	350,924	321,751	316,645	300,307	289,195	289,760	294,159	−16
Gymnastics	228,777	224,943	225,729	234,472	247,529	264,399	285,730	25
Handball	284,546	265,096	269,084	261,302	248,810	244,840	244,404	−14
Basketball	297,948	276,406	270,654	264,498	256,245	232,616	228,036	−23
Athletics	219,985	207,986	194,399	184,617	175,605	200,305	193,645	−12

Table 7.6 Participants 7–20 years old, 2011–2014, proportion of girls (RF, 2012; 2013; 2014; 2015)

	2011	*2012*	*2013*	*2014*
7–12	24,348,351 (46)	25,420,490 (48)	25,916,777 (50)	26,433,915 (51)
13–16	17,883,279 (34)	17,402,284 (33)	17,097,447 (33)	17,017,972 (33)
17–20	10,189,906 (19)	9,608,081 (18)	8,890,649 (17)	8,017,942 (16)
Total	52,421,536 (39)	52,430,855 (39)	51,904,873 (39)	51,469,82 (39)

Table 7.7 Participation in exercise activities (often) by gender, ethnicity and education level (SCB, n.d.)

	Running		*Cross-country skiing*		*Golf*		*Horseback riding*	
	Men	*Women*	*Men*	*Women*	*Men*	*Women*	*Men*	*Women*
16–19	76	71	23	24	26	19	5	22
20–29	62	58	13	13	21	9	9	21
30–49	54	45	20	19	15	6	5	14
50–64	26	19	18	15	13	6	4	7
65–79	9	4	16	9	9	6	1	2
80+	3	0	6	2	1	3	0	0
Swedish	42	34	19	17	16	8	4	12
Foreigner	34	24	10	6	5	4	4	4
Elementary education	35	28	13	9	12	7	3	9
Upper secondary education	36	27	14	11	15	6	5	11
Post-upper secondary education	51	41	27	22	16	8	4	12
All	40	32	17	15	14	7	4	11

The proportion of those who exercised often (more than 20 times each year) at a training centre decreased with age, being most popular among males 16–24 years and more popular among females beyond the age of 35 than males. In relation to ethnicity, more women than men with a Swedish background exercised at a training centre. Among young foreign males and females, the pattern was reversed. The proportion of people who often exercised at a training centre increased with level of education.

The organisation of sport in Sweden

Voluntary and membership-based club sport is characteristic of the Nordic region (Bairner, 2010) as well as an integral part of Swedish society (Fahlén, 2015). Testament to this are the 3.1 million club members out of a population of 9.9 million

Table 7.8 Exercise at a training centre (often and never) by gender, ethnicity and education level, proportion of the population (SCB, n.d.)

	Often			*Never*		
	Men	*Women*	*All*	*Men*	*Women*	*All*
16–24	45	35	40	39	44	41
25–34	34	31	32	51	51	51
35–44	21	28	24	68	60	63
45–54	16	24	20	76	68	72
55–64	11	14	13	83	80	81
65–74	6	8	7	93	89	91
75–84	2	2	2	98	97	98
Swedish background	20	22	21	71	68	69
Foreign background	22	19	21	72	72	72
Elementary education	20	16	18	73	75	74
Upper secondary education	18	20	19	74	70	72
Post-upper secondary education	29	29	29	59	58	58
Total	21	22	21	70	68	69

Swedes, forming 20,164 sports clubs (Centrum för idrottsforskning, 2015). These clubs are affiliated to some 1,000 district sports federations (DSFs), 21 regional sports federations (RSFs) and 71 national sports federations (NSFs), and federated to the Swedish Sports Confederation (SSC) (Riksidrottsförbundet, 2010b). The SSC is responsible for (i) representing club sport in communication with the authorities and surrounding society, (ii) servicing and distributing government funds to affiliated organisations, (iii) stimulating sports development and research and (iv) coordinating social and ethical issues. The SSC is also in charge of coordinating anti-doping work and international cooperation, and for acting as government authority for 51 upper-secondary elite sports schools with some 1,200 students from 30 NSFs. Responsibility for Olympic preparation and participation is delegated to the Swedish Olympic Committee (SOC), which incorporates 36 of the 71 NSFs. Responsibility for overarching educational issues is delegated to SISU (Svenska idrottsrörelsens studieförbund) Sport Education – a non-profit support organisation aiding clubs and federations in training coaches and leaders, organisational development, conferences and project management (Riksidrottsförbundet, 2010b).

The defining characteristic of, and main organising principle for, contemporary club sport in Sweden is that of individuals forming and/or taking part as voluntary members of sports clubs. Individual sports-club members can be elected to represent their clubs at regional and national levels. This representative democracy is often described as the cornerstone of Swedish club sport as well as a significant contributory factor in the civic education of Swedish citizens.

This structure relies on extensive funding. One-third of sports clubs' revenues are generated from membership and training fees, one-third from commercial activities and the remaining third from public funds (Riksidrottsförbundet, 2012). The latter amounts to some €200 million from the national government (Prop. 2016-2017: 1) and is part of the national budget monitored annually by the Swedish parliament (local government funding to sport and culture amounts to some €2,925 billion; Sveriges kommuner och landsting, 2013). Parliament and the government decide on the extent and purpose of the funding while the recipient, the SSC, determines the details of its distribution. The responsibility for the government's sports policy is located within the Ministry of Health and Social Affairs. Government sports policy is also part of its broader civil society policy for which the Department of Culture has the main responsibility (Dir. 2014).

Although enjoying close to a monopolistic position in the landscape of Swedish sport, the SSC has over the years been challenged by other actors – as illustrated by early antagonism with the Swedish Gymnastics Federation about the very idea of sport (or gymnastics) to later skirmishes with the Swedish Federation for Company Sports and the Swedish Outdoor Association over access to government funding (Lindroth, 1988). Today, the main challengers have their base in the commercial sector (SOU, 2008: 59). Gyms and fitness clubs are seen as both drivers of and responses to commercialisation and individualisation trends, as well as answers to a changed population structure and 'new' needs, views and wishes, thereby questioning the hitherto almost taken-for-granted position of the SSC as the sole provider of leisure-time physical exercise. As indicated earlier, we can see how memberships in club sports have levelled out or even decreased while other forms of physical recreation have increased. However, more research is needed to uncover the mechanisms and processes. Also lacking are facts regarding the size and numbers of private actors and how many individuals are doing what, when and where.

The SSC's monopoly has also recently been challenged by the Swedish Sámi Sport Federation (SSIF) (Fahlén & Skille, 2017), questioning the government's unilateral support for sport organised under the SSC umbrella. This questioning rests on the fact that Sámi sport organisations refuse to affiliate themselves with the SSC since that would compromise the independence of the Sámi as an indigenous people (Fahlén & Skille, 2017). Even so, the SSIF is a small organisation, federating only 24 clubs (no information on the number of individual members exists (Skille & Fahlén, 2016)). However, despite their small numbers, the conflict still highlights fundamental frictions in the Swedish sports system regarding allocation of resources and mandate to decide which organisations should be eligible for government support.

Sports policy and politics in Sweden

Public policy for sport has a long tradition in Sweden, dating back to the first annual national government grant in 1913 (Lindroth, 1974). However, while growing almost exponentially in size in every decade since, the grant has never been undisputed or unscrutinised. So although sport was included early on in what would later would be conceived as the Scandinavian 'take' on welfare (i.e. not limited to health care and schools but also including citizen's access to recreation and leisure activities), several public inquiries were initiated in order to investigate the legitimacy of government funding for sport. The third of these (SOU 1969), and its subsequent government bill (Prop 1970), is viewed as a formative event in Swedish sports politics and, as a policy, still influences the contemporary context – in the sense that it expresses the government's far-reaching ambition to enable citizens to access recreation and meaningful leisure, along with the aim of doing so via organised sport (Bergsgard & Norberg, 2010). As in 1969, the main argument nowadays concerns sport's alleged ability to cost-effectively decrease health-care costs, promote social integration and challenge norm-breaking behaviour (Österlind & Fahlén, 2015).

While still cherishing the legacy from the late 1960s and early 1970s, the sports policy landscape of today is also significantly impacted by the financial crises at the beginning of the 1990s and in 2008. These developments have resulted in rapid processes of liberalisation, deregulation and privatisation (The Heritage Foundation, 2012) transforming Sweden from a typical social democratic regime, in Esping-Andersen's typology (1990), to a Scandinavian country increasingly known for its deregulated schools, railway, pension systems, television and radio broadcasting, postal service, telecom and pharmacy markets (Bergh & Erlingsson, 2009).

Subsequently, sport has occupied a more salient position on the government agenda, with more instrumental goals being accompanied by increased resources to aid their attainment. Testament to this has been the government's growing concern with diminishing sports-club membership expressed in four large government interventions. Since much of the legitimacy of supporting sport with taxpayers' money rests on organised sport's ability to engage large parts of the population, it has become vital for organised sport and the government alike to account for high membership numbers (Fahlén, 2015). The most recent of these (*The Lift for Sport*, 2007–2011) is ongoing, albeit in a more-or-less permanent form, adding €50 million annually to the regular government funding for sport. This supplementary financial support for sport is, however, about more than simply additional funding. It is also about the political programming of sport. While the lion's share of government funds is still distributed through block funding, the main funding trend has become one of contracting out sports' external goals in temporary and time-limited projects (Fahlén & Karp, 2010). As such, governmental support is subject to accountability and evidence and 'numbers' are the Swedish government's preferred means of 'keeping score'. In that way, recipients of government funding are made responsible for the appropriate use of resources and monitoring. So-called 'KPIs' (key performance indicators) are the means for making sure that responsibility is shouldered by sport (Fahlén, Eliasson & Wickman, 2015). Thus, evidence on the efficient use of taxpayers' money is a key feature in current government policy towards sport.

Sámi sport has also arrived on the government agenda in an alternative form and with different consequences. Even though Swedish sport was the subject of five public inquiries between 1922 and 2008, Sámi sport is considered in the latest one alone, and then only briefly and implicitly (Fahlén & Skille, 2017). The inquiry (SOU, 2008: 59) reports problems associated with the fact that organisations outside the SSC cannot receive government support for sport. This requirement prevents organisations that arrange sporting activities but do not wish to be members of the SSC, such as the SSIF, from receiving government support. It is readily apparent, therefore, that the current system is constructed with 'mainstream sport' in mind. It is not, however, favourable for organisations such as the SSIF in their struggle for acknowledgement and public funding.

Explaining sports participation in Sweden

As noted in several recent texts on Swedish sport (e.g. Fahlén, 2015, 2016; Fahlén & Stenling, 2016), and elsewhere in this chapter, understanding participation in sport and physical activity in Sweden requires attention to the institutional arrangements of which Swedish sport is part. The first point worthy of note is that overall levels of participation in sport and exercise appear to be increasing while participation in sports-club activities per se seem to be decreasing. As demonstrated in the above data, this seemingly paradoxical development is partly explained by the fact that Swedes, in general, have tended increasingly to participate in physical exercise and sport beyond the sports-club setting; that is to say, in self-organised and/or commercial as well as outdoor settings. Reinforcing this tendency has been the increasing involvement over time of girls and women in sport and exercise and the fact that these groups in particular appear to favour the self-organised and/or commercial settings. It is also apparent that self-organisation and the use of commercial alternatives is connected to educational level. The higher the level of education, the more likely Swedes are to be physically active by themselves or, at least, beyond the sports club. Contributing further to these trends has been the increasing involvement in physical activity among older age groups (i.e. adults) – in short, the older the participants, the more likely they are to exercise in self-organised and/or commercial forms. Taken together, these results provide part of the explanation for the fact that overall participation levels increase while participation in sports-club activities decreases – that is to say, smaller age groups (i.e. fewer children born each year) entering voluntary club sport, alongside a levelling-out or even decrease in club participation while, simultaneously, adults (and more of them) prefer other alternatives to sports clubs (and, by extension, competitive sport).

It is important to note, however, that these observations represent not so much explanations – at least in terms of answering questions such as, 'Why do Swedish girls and women (for example) choose self-organised and/or commercial settings and forms over activities arranged by sports clubs?' – as mere co-variations. In terms of the gender dimension to participation, Sutter and Glätzle-Rützler (2014) have shown how the will and propensity to compete, one of the cornerstones of organised club sport (Stenling & Fahlén, 2009), is more prominent among boys than girls already in the pre-school ages and that the differences persist into adulthood. They argue that such differences are not biological but are a result of socialisation: parents' direct and indirect influence supporting a more competitive orientation in boys than girls. Used as an explanation for the findings in this chapter, this would imply that the competitive focus of organised club sport is less suited to girls' tastes and dispositions. When organised club sport activities are oriented more around play and less around competition, as regulated by the Swedish Sports Confederation (Riksidrottsförbundet, 2018), participation is more evenly distributed between girls and boys. But as the focus on performance, results, competition and ranking increases, participation in more conventional club sport activities diminishes among girls. However, it is important to recognise that it is not girls' interest in physical activities that diminishes; rather it is interest in physical activities arranged by sport clubs that decreases. Fahlén (2015) points to the format and design of activities as a significant explanatory factor in why sports activities attract different individuals and groups.

Another general observation relates to the characteristics of the current situation in Swedish voluntary, club-organised and membership-based sport in understanding diminishing levels of participation among children and adolescents. First, being able to take part in club sport requires economic capital. In Sweden, the costs of membership fees, training fees, equipment and travel have risen to levels not affordable for all families (Hertting, 2010). Second, many Swedish sports clubs have trouble in recruiting the leaders, coaches and officials they need to be able to welcome all children aspiring to take part in their activities (Fahlén, 2015). Using data from CIF (2014), Fahlén shows how 71% of Swedish sports clubs rank this phenomenon as the most serious threat to their activities. Compared with competition from private sector alternatives (18%) and reaching sporting goals and ambitions (29%), the problem of recruiting leaders is experienced as the main problem in increasing (or keeping) sports club participation among children and youth. Third, and drawing on the same data, Fahlén (2015) shows how retaining youth poses the second most challenging task for Swedish sport clubs, with 58% of all clubs experiencing this as very challenging.

Taken together, these two features (namely, the increasing levels of participation in sport and exercise while participation in sports club activities *per se* seems to be decreasing alongside the characteristics of the current situation in Swedish voluntary, club-organised and membership-based sport) may provide some explanation for the decreasing participation rates (including club membership) presented in this chapter. One explanation hinges on the way we measure participation. In their study of sports participation in four Swedish municipalities, Ferry, Fahlén and Lindgren (2016) demonstrated that – while data charting a trend towards participation declining with age was in accordance with national trends – the very definition of participation in the national statistics from CIF and RF obscures actual participatory patterns. Since statistics are based on participation in voluntary, club-organised and membership-based sport only, they fail to take into account participation in other equally organised and also membership-based (albeit in other forms) activities such as aerobics, spinning and yoga. By including data on such activities in their measures of activities in one of the municipalities, Ferry *et al.* (2016) demonstrated how participation had actually increased. In all of the studied municipalities, participation at a general level declined steadily from the age of ten, becoming further accentuated at age 18. But by singling out girls/women in one of the municipalities, they revealed how participation among girls/women increased significantly from the age of 18. They explained this phenomenon by pointing to the exercise carried out extensively at commercial gyms, fitness centres and other facilities not affiliated to the Swedish sports movement; in other words, lifestyle sports. This highlights not only the importance of defining sports participation inclusively, but also, the need for healthy scepticism towards the numerous moral panics surrounding the allegedly decreasing levels of sports participation and physical activity all over the world. This finding is by no means counter-evidence against such reports, but calls for further scrutiny of the definitions and approaches used to create national statistics and international comparisons.

Conclusion

To conclude this chapter, we summarise several key points indicating some of the main issues surrounding sports participation in Sweden and end with a brief prognosis for the future. The first issue is that of volunteering in Sweden and other Nordic countries. If the main challenge for Swedish sports clubs is recruiting enough leaders, the Swedish sports movement needs to address the way in which leaders are recruited and the conditions for being a leader. But since one of the most common motives for becoming a volunteer leader is having children in sports club activities, the issue is as much a question for the parents of those children taking part in club-organised activities. This is an issue for the Swedish sports movement as much as it is for the Swedish government funding its operations (thereby providing legitimacy to its activities), since taking current membership rates and extrapolating from these results in a gloomy prognosis for those advocating the value of voluntary, club-organised and membership-based sport.

The second issue relates to the decreasing membership rates in club sport. As demonstrated earlier, Swedes born abroad or with immigrant parents are under-represented in club sport participation (as in physical exercise more broadly). This is an obvious challenge for the sports movement, both in terms of adhering to the long-standing agreement with the government to offer 'sport for all' and in maintaining present membership rates (or even increasing them). Equally challenging is the fact that the domestic ethnic minority – the Sámi – has restricted access to public support for voluntary, club-organised and membership-based sport and thereby inclusion in 'sport for all'. This is an issue because no measures have been taken to make the Sámi more included, compared with ventures launched to include other underrepresented groups (e.g. girls, socially vulnerable children, refugees and immigrants). In relation to decreasing membership rates, this should be a problem for the sports movement and the government alike. However, more worrying when prognosticating future sports participation is the fact that individuals wanting to participate in voluntary, club-organised and membership-based sport are in practice kept from public subsidies for political reasons.

Note

1 That is to say, incorporating the various forms of physically active recreation and 'lifestyle sports' referred to in the editors' Introduction to the text.

References

Bairner, A. (2010). What's Scandinavian about Scandinavian sport? *Sport in Society*, *13*(4): 734–743.

Bergh, A. and Erlingsson, G.Ó. (2009). Liberalization without retrenchment: understanding the consensus on Swedish welfare state reforms. *Scandinavian Political Studies*, *32*(1): 71–93.

Bergsgard, N.A. and Norberg, J.R. (2010). Sports policy and politics – the Scandinavia Way. *Sport in Society*, *13*(4): 567–582.

Centrum för idrottsforskning (2010). *Statens stöd till idrotten – uppföljning 2009* [Government support to sport – follow up 2010]. Stockholm: Centrum för idrottsforskning.

Centrum för idrottsforskning (2011). *Statens stöd till idrotten – uppföljning 2010* [Government support to sport – follow up 2010]. Stockholm: Centrum för idrottsforskning.

Centrum för idrottsforskning (2012). *Statens stöd till idrotten – uppföljning 2011* [Government support to sport – follow up 2011]. Stockholm: Centrum för idrottsforskning.

Centrum för idrottsforskning (2013). *Statens stöd till idrotten – uppföljning 2012* [Government support to sport – follow up 2012]. Stockholm: Centrum för idrottsforskning.

Centrum för idrottsforskning (2014). *Statens stöd till idrotten – uppföljning 2013* [Government support to sport – follow up 2013]. Stockholm: Centrum för idrottsforskning.

Centrum för idrottsforskning (2015). *Statens stöd till idrotten – uppföljning 2014* [Government support to sport – follow up 2014]. Stockholm: Centrum för idrottsforskning.

Centrum för idrottsforskning (2016). *Statens stöd till idrotten – uppföljning 2015* [Government support to sport – follow up 2015]. Stockholm: Centrum för idrottsforskning.

Dir. 2014:40. Ett stärkt och självständigt civilsamhälle [Committee directive. A consolidated and independent civil society].

Esping-Andersen, G. (1990). *The Three Worlds of Welfare Capitalism*. Cambridge: Polity Press.

Fahlén, J. (2016). Elitidrott i ett svenskt perspektiv [Elite sport in a Swedish perspective]. In S. Hedenborg (ed.) *Idrottsvetenskap – En Introduktion*. (pp. 233–258). Lund, Sweden: Studentlitteratur.

Fahlén, J. (2015). Sport clubs in Sweden. In H. van der Werff, C. Breuer, S. Nagel and R. Hoekman (eds.). *Sport Clubs in Europe – A Cross-National Perspective*. (pp. 396–429). New York: Springer.

Fahlén, J. and Karp, S. (2010). Access denied: the new sports for all – programme in Sweden and the reinforcement of the sports performance logic, *Sport & EU Review*, *2*(1): 3–22.

Fahlén, J. and Skille, E. (2017). State sport policy for indigenous sport: inclusive ambitions and exclusive coalitions. *International Journal of Sport Policy and Politics*, 9(1): 173–187.
Fahlén, J. and Stenling, C. (2016). Sport policy in Sweden. *International Journal of Sport Policy and Politics*, 8(3): 515–531.
Fahlén, J., Eliasson, I. and Wickman, K. (2015). Resisting self-regulation: an analysis of sport policy programme making and implementation in Sweden. *International Journal of Sport Policy and Politics*, 7(3): 391–406.
Ferry, M., Fahlén, J. and Lindgren, J. (2016). *Aktivitetskort på nätet: barn och ungdomars deltagande i föreningsledda idrottsaktiviteter* [Activity cards online: Children and Young People's Participation in Sport Clubs Activities]. Umeå, Sweden: Umeå universitet.
Hertting, K. (2010). *Valuta för pengarna: Om föräldrars kostnader för barnens deltagande i tävlingsidrott* [Value for money: On parents' costs for children's participation in sport]. Stockholm: Riksidrottsförbundet.
The Heritage Foundation (2012). *Index of economic freedom: graph the data – Sweden* [online]. Available from: http://www.heritage.org/index/visualize. [Accessed 5 November 2012].
Lindroth, J. (1988). *Från 'sportfåneri' till massidrott. Den svenska idrottsrörelsens utveckling 1869–1939* [From 'sport-heads' to mass-sport. The development of the Swedish sports movement 1869–1939]. Stockholm: Stockholm universitet.
Lindroth, J. (1974) *Idrottens väg till folkrörelse: studier i svensk idrottsrörelse till 1915* [Sport's way to popular movement: studies of the Swedish sports movement until 1915]. Uppsala, Sweden: Acta Universitatis Upsaliensis.
Lindroth, J. and Norberg, J.R. (eds.) (2002). *Riksidrottsförbundet 1903–2003* [The Swedish Sports Confederation 1903–2003]. Stockholm: Informationsförlaget.
Norberg, J.R. (2002). Idrottsrörelsen och staten [The sports movement and the state]. In J.R. Norberg (ed.) *Riksidrottsförbundet 1903–2003*. (pp. 551–552). Stockholm: Informationsförlaget.
Österlind, M. and Fahlén, J. (2015). Reconsidering the epistemology of the Swedish sports model through the lens of governmentality: notes on the state-civil society relationship, government, power and social change. *Idrott, Historia & Samhälle*, 35: 146–168.
Prop. 1970:79. *Förslag angående stöd till idrotten* [Propositions regarding state support].
Prop. 2008/09:126. *Statens stöd till idrotten* [Government's proposition. State support to sport].
Prop. 2016/17:1. *Budgetpropositionen för 2017* [The budget proposition for 2017].
Riksidrottsförbundet (2008). *Idrotten i siffror* [Sport in numbers]. Stockholm: Riksidrottsförbundet.
Riksidrottsförbundet (2010a). *Idrotten i siffror* [Sport in numbers]. Stockholm: Riksidrottsförbundet.
Riksidrottsförbundet (2010b). *Idrotts-Sverige: En presentation av Riksidrottsförbundet* [Sports Sweden: a presentation of the Swedish Sports Confederation]. Stockholm: Riksidrottsförbundet.
Riksidrottsförbundet (2012). *Idrotten i siffror* [Sport in numbers]. Stockholm: Riksidrottsförbundet.
Riksidrottsförbundet (2013). *Idrotten i siffror* [Sport in numbers]. Stockholm: Riksidrottsförbundet.
Riksidrottsförbundet (2014). *Idrotten i siffror* [Sport in numbers]. Stockholm: Riksidrottsförbundet.
Riksidrottsförbundet (2015). *Idrotten i siffror* [Sport in numbers]. Stockholm: Riksidrottsförbundet.

Riksidrottsförbundet (2016). *Idrotten i siffror* [Sport in numbers]. Stockholm: Riksidrottsförbundet.

Riksidrottsförbundet (2018). Riktlinjer för barn- och ungdomsidrotten [Guidelines for youth sport]. Available from http://www.svenskidrott.se/Barnochungdomsidrott/Riktlinjerforbarn-ochungdomsidrotten/. [Accessed 22 January 2018].

Schön, L. (2012). *En modern svensk ekonomisk historia: tillväxt och omvandling under två sekel* [A modern Swedish economic history: growth and transformation during two centuries]. Stockholm: SNS Förlag.

Sjöblom, P. (2006). *Den institutionaliserade tävlingsidrotten. Kommuner, idrott och politik i Sverige under 1900-talet* [Institutionalised competitive sport. Municipalities, sport and politics in Sweden during the 20th century]. Stockholm: Stockholms universitet.

Skille, E. and Fahlén, J. (2016). Sámi sk idrett og statlig politikk i Sverige og Norge. In H. Pedersen & E. Skille (eds.). *Utafor sporet? Idrett, identiteter og regionalisme i nord.* (pp. 135–169). Vallset: Oplandske bokforlag.

SOU 1969:29 *Idrott åt alla. Betänkande avgivet av Idrottsutredningen* [Sport for all. Commission report given by the sports commission]. Stockholm: Handelsdepartmentet.

SOU 2008:59 *Föreningsfostran och tävlingsfostran En utvärdering av statens stöd till idrotten* [Democratic fostering and competition fostering. An evaluation of the government support to sport]. Stockholm: Fritzes.

Statistiska Centralbyrån (2005). *Barns villkor* [Children's conditions]. Stockholm: Statistiska centralbyrån.

Statistiska Centralbyrån (2009). *Barns fritid* [Children's leisure time]. Available from: http://www.scb.se/statistik/_publikationer/LE0106_2006I07_BR_LE116BR0901.pdf [Accessed 31 May 2017].

Statistiska Centralbyrån (n.d.). Statistikdatabasen. Available from: http://www.statistik databasen.scb.se. [Accessed 31 May 2017].

Sutter, M., & Glätzle-Rützler, D. (2014). Gender differences in the willingness to compete emerge early in life and persist. *Management Science*, *61*(10), 2339–2354.

Stenling, C., & Fahlén, J. (2009). The order of logics in Swedish sport–feeding the hungry beast of result orientation and commercialization. *European journal for sport and society*, 6(2): 121–134.

Sveriges kommuner och landsting (2013). *Elitidrottens anläggningar – finaniering, kostnader och dialog med idrotten* [Elite sport facilities- funding, costs and dialogue with sport]. Stockholm: Sveriges kommuner och landsting.

Conclusion

Ken Green, Thorsteinn Sigurjónsson and Eivind Åsrum Skille

This edited collection set out to explore sports participation in Scandinavia and the Nordic countries. As indicated in the Introduction, the book is entitled *Sport in Scandinavia and the Nordic Countries* due to the currency of the term 'Scandinavia' in relation to sport in the popular imagination. Having noted this, we will now revert to the more accurate over-arching collective noun 'Nordic', only referring to 'Scandinavia' if and when we wish to make a specific point about Denmark, Norway and Sweden collectively.

In this final chapter, we tease out the main patterns in sports participation, including similarities and differences between the countries, in order to answer the question 'What is Scandinavian or Nordic about Scandinavian and Nordic sport?' (Bairner, 2010). Contributors to the collection were asked to focus, in the first instance, on trends in sports participation in their respective countries, including forms of participation, settings and venues, and social divisions. In addition, authors have commented on the organization of sporting provision and policies towards sport in their respective countries, before offering a brief explanation of the story of sports participation.

The differing methods employed by the many and various sources that underpin each of the country-specific chapters, as well as the different points in time when the relevant data were collected, mean that any comparisons need to be tentative. Given that, on the whole, what we have to say appears a 'good news' story it will also be important to bear in mind the well-documented methodological issues associated with all surveys that involve self-reported data. These issues are outlined in more detail in the Introduction. The relative weaknesses of self-reported data were exacerbated by the fact that almost all the surveys (with the exception of Denmark and Greenland) that provided the foundation for the various country profiles utilised quite different survey methods, including a tendency to interpret what counted as sport/exercise and regularity differently. Potential shortcomings notwithstanding, the collection has a significant strength: much of the underpinning data were generated by representative samples of known populations, thereby enabling authors to make general statements about the wider populations from which the samples were drawn, among other things.

Describing sports participation in the Nordic countries

Trends in sports participation in the Nordic countries

Trends are interesting because they focus our attention on directions of change rather than merely profiling existing participation. As indicated in the Introduction, it has long been recognised that the highest proportion of adult sports participation in Europe occurs in the Nordic countries, followed by the western and central European countries, with far lower levels of sports participation in southern Europe (van Bottenburg, Rijnen & van Sterkenburg, 2005; van Tuyckom, 2016). As with many Western nations, leisure sports participation increased significantly in the 1970s and 1980s in all of the Nordic countries and the chapters in this collection confirm the impression of sustained high levels of participation in the region. The continued growth in sports participation into the new millennium marks many of the Nordic countries out by comparison with other western nations, such as the United Kingdom, where participation plateaued in the 1990s and has remained more-or-less stagnant ever since. Country-by-country differences notwithstanding, more people are doing a good deal more sport, exercise and physical recreation more often in the Nordic region than half a century earlier.

Trends are, nevertheless, a matter of degree and it is important to acknowledge that the Nordic countries do not have equally high levels of sports participation nor identical upward tendencies. While sports participation is thriving in Iceland and Norway, there are Nordic countries where the story of sports participation is not so rosy. 'Normal' or current activity in Greenland, for example, appears relatively low, with well below half of the adult population 'normally active' in 2015 and a figure approaching half not participating at all. The relatively high proportion of 'currently inactive' youngsters in Greenland – over one-third – stands in marked contrast to elsewhere in the Nordic region. In Denmark, Iceland, Norway and Sweden, for instance, participation (including regular participation) has continued to grow steadily over the last 50 years.

The upward trends across much of the region over the past half-century notwithstanding, the most recent data may indicate that 'saturation' (Denmark) or 'stagnation' (Finland) have been reached in levels of participation among both children and adults, and in those below middle age in particular. In some Nordic countries, there is concern regarding the possibility of a 'generational effect' whereby younger generations may be establishing weaker attachments to sport.

As Roberts (2016a) observes, sport in the West tends to be different from most other leisure activities in terms of the small size of its core of dedicated or regular players relative to the larger number of lower-key or occasional participants – 'dabblers', as he refers to them. In the Nordic region, the picture is noticeably different. In Nordic countries, the 'normal distribution' (the archetypal 'bell-shaped curve') has, on the whole, become a (negatively) skewed distribution: i.e. it has moved to the right, the more active or regular pole. Among young and old alike, the proportion of those who never participate or do so rarely has diminished in size while the proportions participating regularly have increased. Indeed, the most marked increases over time have been among those who exercise 'a lot'. Approximately nine out of 10 adults in Finland, for example, have reported participating in sport at least two to three times each week. Although the numbers of 'hardcore' regular participants may have plateaued in recent years (in Denmark and Sweden, for example), they have done so at levels considerably higher than in very many countries beyond the Nordic region and, for that matter, the countries themselves several generations previously.

Fifty years ago, sport around the world was a pastime for young males. Nowadays sport is populated by all age groups and both sexes. Increasing proportions of all the Nordic populations have been taking part in sport from younger and younger ages through to later in life, while a marked feature of the general democratisation of sport has been a convergence between the sexes. Fifty years ago, sport consisted of physically vigorous, competitive and organised activities (predominantly games). Nowadays we need to refer to 'sport' in inverted commas to reflect the fact that conventional sports have been supplemented by a broad and diverse range of so-called 'lifestyle sports' (see Introduction) in the participatory repertoires of Nordic people.

Trends in physical activity (PA) in the Nordic lands are similar to those elsewhere in the West. As counter-intuitive as it might seem, increasing sports participation and decreasing overall levels of PA appear to be two sides of the same coin, even in Nordic nations. Although very few young people and adults are completely sedentary, more appear to be participating in sport and exercise during leisure while, at the same time, becoming more sedentary in everyday life. Finland, Norway and Sweden are illustrative of this tendency. Nonetheless, the spread of home-centred, privatised lifestyles does not appear to have impacted on sports participation in the Nordic countries as much as elsewhere. Indeed, even in Greenland – where relatively high numbers of young and old are reported to be relatively inactive in sporting terms – it is noteworthy that a large section of the population is active in relation to internationally recognised health-related PA thresholds, despite increased sedentariness.

Alongside the cultural traction of sport (see below), relatively high levels of active transport (30% of Danes cycle daily (Celis-Morales & Gill, 2017)) result in fewer people being completely sedentary. Less than one in seven of the adult population in Denmark is completely sedentary, while nine in every ten youngsters in Iceland report engaging in strenuous exercise on a weekly basis and around three-quarters of 'senior citizens' take part in sport or exercise once a week or more. It is clear that on the whole there is a trend towards increased physical inactivity (in relation to World Health Organisation recommendations) in everyday life in Nordic countries. Nevertheless, PA remains more commonplace generally in the Nordic region than in very many countries.

Forms of participation

Nordic people and the young, in particular, are also engaged in broader and more diverse forms of sport, including lifestyle and adventure sports. As many of the chapters demonstrate, there has been an overall shift towards individual and small group participation in lifestyle activities (e.g. running and cycling) and commercial settings (e.g. private gyms) and away from team games and formal settings (e.g. sports clubs). In this respect, trends in the region are similar (but not identical) to trends elsewhere in the Western world: participation in individual sports has grown over the past three decades while participation in team sports has declined (see, e.g., Harris, Nichols & Taylor, 2017). There are notable exceptions, nonetheless: participation in club-based sports has not declined in Finland.

This shift reflects the growing appeal of lifestyle sports (including alternative and adventure sports) and activities among young and old alike in the region. Among adult and older age groups, the most popular lifestyle activities tend to be health and fitness gym-based activities, walking, cycling, spinning, running and swimming (e.g. Denmark). Among youth, these are more likely to be strength training/gym activities as well as alternative 'sports' (such as parkour) and more adventurous activities (such as mountain biking, climbing and alpine skiing). Among children, the more popular activities remain predominantly club-based games, increasingly supplemented by lifestyle activities such as the various forms of boarding and blading. It is noticeable that the drivers for increased participation among adults in Norway over the past 50 years have been physical recreation and exercise rather than (competitive, institutionalised and physically vigorous) sport as such. More recently, these have been supplemented by strength training and other fitness-centre activities. Similarly, the driver for growth among Swedish citizens appears to have been physical recreation in particular rather than sport, especially among adults.

Although lifestyle sports have been growing in appeal and games losing popularity, this has not occurred to the same degree in the Nordic countries (if at all in some) as elsewhere in the world. In the Nordic region, it is important to recognise that any downturn in participation in games has not signalled the demise of conventional or 'traditional' sports. Some games have waxed while others have waned. Games remain popular sports throughout the region, especially among the young, whose sporting and exercise portfolios tend to consist of a mix of typically club-organised sports and informal activities (e.g. Greenland and Iceland). All-in-all, there has been a good deal of change alongside the undoubted continuities in the forms of sports participation in the Nordic countries, similar to those found across the developed world.

While 'dabbling' is likely to be as commonplace in the Nordic nations as elsewhere, regular, committed participation in sport and physical recreation has become normative. Nonetheless, dabbling appears equally likely to be a feature of regular participants' leisure-sports styles, whether young or old. It seems that adults in Denmark, for example, intersperse their sporting repertoires with new activities during the adult years as they experiment with new types and forms of activity and change their mix of sports in a manner reminiscent of the young people who were on a trajectory towards lifelong participation in sport and exercise in

Flanders, Belgium (Scheerder *et al.*, 2005, 2006; Vanreusel *et al.*, 1997), Sweden (Engstrom, 2008), and the UK (Roberts and Brodie, 1992).

Overall, trends in forms of sports participation in the Nordic countries reflect a broadening and diversification of participation rather than a wholesale rejection of sport *per se* and traditional sporting styles. While the shift toward more individualistic, informal, recreational, lifestyle activities globally might not signal the end of sport in its more competitive, institutionalised forms, it is, at the very least, signalling a "redrawing of the traditional boundaries and meaning of sport" (Coalter, 1999, 37).

The particular case of friluftsliv

Friluftsliv is an especially interesting example of change alongside continuity in sporting trends in the Nordic region. In those countries where *friluftsliv* is considered part of the cultural fabric (e.g. Finland, Norway and Sweden), recent decades have brought a significant decline in the proportion of youth (mid-teens to mid-20s) taking part in traditional *friluftsliv* activities (e.g. being in nature). Instead, young Nordics are more likely to get involved in adventurous outdoor activities (such as mountain biking, skiing, climbing and kayaking). Hunting and fishing remain quintessentially (lower-educated) male activities, while foraging for berries and mushrooms and short walks in the woods are increasingly the preserve of older adults and older females in particular. These changes may well reflect a shift among Nordic youth towards lifestyle sports that offer alternative forms, as well as types, of participation to conventional sports (albeit still outdoors): put simply, more outdoor adventure less outdoor life.

Social divisions: the 'big picture' and socio-demographic groups

Average levels of sports participation are an outcome of some groups doing more and others doing less. The 'big picture' provided by averages inevitably conceals differences within socio-demographic groups. Once again, however, these differences are a good deal less marked in the Nordic countries than elsewhere: the averages conceal relatively small deviations from the mean. In all walks of Nordic life, there was a narrowing of socio-economic differentials during the latter decades of the twentieth century. This corresponded with a weakening of the major social divisions, particularly in relation to age and gender, in sports participation. Things are said to have changed somewhat since the 1990s, however, and we will return to this issue below.

Age

While more people of all ages have been taking part in sport and exercise internationally over the past 50 years or so it has become something of a truism to note that sports participation has a strong tendency to decline with age – markedly so at the end of formal schooling, in the middle-age years and on retirement. Ageing and retirement have a history of reducing overall levels of leisure activity and spending – older people spend less on leisure and participate in fewer out-of-home leisure activities than those of working age (Roberts, 2016b). This age-related fact does not apply so readily to the Nordic countries, however. In the Nordic lands of Denmark, Finland, Greenland, Iceland, Norway and Sweden, age differences in sports participation have significantly diminished over time. Three things stand out: (i) the trend towards increased participation in leisure-sport reported in the Nordic countries has occurred across all age groups; (ii) levels of participation have risen, in particular, among older age groups; and (iii) many whose participation diminishes during their 30s and 40s return to sport in later life. This latter point is worth dwelling on.

In countries such as Finland, Norway and Sweden, any drop-off in regular participation occurs in the main years of career and family responsibilities (roughly around 30–45 years). While more in the retired/nearly retired age groups (67+) 'never' participate, many Nordic countries witness a 'bounce back' in regular participation – after the main work and child-rearing years – to levels associated with the mid-20s (e.g. Finland and Norway), and these renewed levels of participation tend to be sustained into old age. Thus, the dip in participation during the middle years is relatively shallow and middle age is more likely to be associated with drop-off in sports participation than drop-out. This is likely to be due not only to socio-economic conditions in the Nordic countries but also the cultural traction of sport. The trend towards 'active ageing' will almost certainly have something to do with the sporting predispositions and capitals developed during childhood and youth in the Nordic nations.

Regular participation has been markedly increasing among young Nordics in particular. The percentage of young Icelanders, for example, who took part on a regular basis more than doubled in the quarter century following 1992. In several countries across the region, sports participation has tended to begin earlier and earlier (e.g. 3–4 years of age in Denmark and Iceland, and 6 in Finland). At the same time, peak participation occurs considerably later in youth (among the 16–19 age group in Norway) than it tends to elsewhere in the West while drop-off and drop-out occur later also. Drop-out from sports clubs does not become marked until at least age 15 in Finland, where roughly one-third of 15–19-year-olds still participate in club sport on a weekly basis.

All-in-all, many Nordic youngsters are the quintessential sporting omnivores in at least two senses: first, they engage with a wide range of sport (and leisure) forms, and second, they are inclined to dabble in and experiment with a breadth of activities. While young people are found in increasing numbers in strength training and gyms, they remain prominent in conventional sports and sports clubs. That said, as with their Western counterparts, disengaging from organised competitive sport (particularly in sports clubs) is a feature of the developing leisure-sport profiles of Nordic youngsters – albeit usually at a later point in the teenage years than elsewhere in the world. Overall, participation rates in 'formal' (i.e. club-based) sports tend to slowly decline from the early teenage years as youngsters shift their blends of participation towards lifestyle sports and informal settings. In this regard, it appears a taken-for-granted assumption that Nordic youngsters would remain engaged with sport and sports clubs if the clubs did not increasingly focus on sporting competition as youngsters grow older. It is noteworthy, however, that in Iceland participation has continued to grow despite sports clubs' tendencies to emphasise competition and achievement from an early age.

Alongside the competitive nature of much club-based sport, a preference for engaging with more recreational, informal activities in mixed-sex rather than single-sex groups is also likely to be part of the explanation for the shift away from sports clubs in the Nordic region, as elsewhere in the world. In effect, disengaging from sport during the life stage is part of a lifestyle strategy for growing up as youth negotiate and develop their own adult-oriented and adult-like leisure profiles and trajectories (Roberts, 2016a). There may be evidence of this in Denmark, where active engagement in sport and exercise is often put 'on hold' during youth. The fact that sports participation is described in this way tells us not only that Danish youngsters (as with middle-aged Nordics, more generally) are likely to return to sport eventually but also that sports participation is not seen in the Nordic countries as simply the province of childhood – far from it, as sport and exercise have become normative for young and old alike.

Social class and education

Being a regular sports participant – especially over the longer-term – is demanding, not only in terms of time but also money. The financial costs can be significant. Money makes it possible for people to do more during leisure of the things they already do or that those around them (or that they aspire to be among) do. Money, in particular, facilitates sport, in the form of transport, equipment, coaching, club memberships and so on. It saves time and enables individual sovereignty. Economic capital is one reason that the sporting lives of players from lower socio-economic groups tend to be fragile. However, social-class differences are relatively narrow in the Nordic countries vis-à-vis the rest of Europe and, over time, the gaps between social-class fractions have been closing, most notably among the young. Growing evidence of a recent widening of relative inequalities in all countries in the Nordic region notwithstanding, Strandbu *et al.*'s (2017) review of sports participation in Norway revealed that despite major differences in sports participation by occupation and educational level in the 1950s, no obvious inequalities were apparent in the 1980s, 1990s or even the early 2000s.

The various chapters in this collection seem to confirm that the more significant impact of social class (using educational level as proxy) is not so much on whether Nordic people are doing sport in the first place but rather what they do, where and with whom. The lengthier-educated groups are generally more involved in informal and commercially organised sport and exercise than those with truncated educational careers. The correlation between particular sports and level of education across the Nordic region is especially significant in some countries, such as Greenland. What the relationship between the level of education and involvement in commercial 'sports' provision is telling us is not that more- or less-educated citizens are becoming included and excluded groups, respectively, in terms of sports participation. Rather, it is indicative of a 'tiering' of sports participation in terms of facilities being used (e.g. public or private) (Roberts, 2017).

Company Sport is a particular feature of the Nordic sporting landscape (see Introduction), originally intended to provide opportunities for the working classes in the second half of the twentieth century. Nowadays, however, in countries such as Denmark, Company Sport appears far more likely to be offered to and populated by middle-class professionals than by those in working-class occupations. Thus, in Denmark, those population groups generally less likely to take up leisure-time sport and exercise are also the ones less likely to benefit from opportunities for exercise through the work setting: i.e. the working classes and early school-leavers.

Sex/gender

There are two main take-home messages regarding the sexes and sports participation in the Nordic region. The first is increased rates of participation among females such that levels of female participation tend to be higher in the Nordic countries than almost anywhere else in the world. The increases in sports participation among girls and women have fuelled the general increases in participation since the 1970s and continue to do so. The second message is one of convergence in levels of participation if not, as yet, forms of participation. Rates of sports participation among girls and women have been moving towards the previously considerably higher rates of participation among boys and men since the 1970s. In some countries (e.g. Greenland, Norway and Sweden), some aspects of participation have converged. Indeed, against some measures, females have surpassed males (e.g. in Denmark, Finland, Norway and Sweden). Males, for instance, are more likely on the whole to be inactive or sedentary than females. Boys are more often found at either end of the spectrum of frequency of participation: boys 6–15 years are most likely to be inactive, but at the same time they are most likely to be active 'almost daily'. Although 'active boys' were typically active more often (three times a week or more) than 'active girls' in Greenland, for example, there was a convergence between the sexes at the level of two to three bouts of participation per week.

The clear convergence between females and males in sports participation notwithstanding, a number of gender-stereotypical features remain relatively intact. Men and women, and girls and boys, still tend to be found disproportionately in gender-stereotypical male/female sporting domains. Men not only spend more time on sport on the whole, they tend to be involved in competitive sport more than women, who are more likely to be found in such lifestyle activities as gym/fitness, Pilates, spinning, running and Nordic walking (e.g. Denmark). Young Nordic males and females still tend to take part in traditionally masculine and feminine leisure-time sports (boys are a good deal more likely to play football). Nevertheless, there is increasing overlap, with a number of historically masculine and feminine sports increasingly populated by the opposite sex. In some instances, the tables have turned. In handball, for instance, more young women than men now take part on a regular basis in countries such as Norway and female participation in football – high up on girls' list of most popular activities – has been growing in recent decades across all the Nordic countries, as it has around the world.

Lifestyle sports have been a significant driver for the increases in participation among females (Coalter, 2013). Thus, the significant increases in the proportions of girls and young women participating in sport worldwide appear intertwined with the increased centrality of lifestyle sports and, in particular, the growing demand for more exercise-oriented and body-management activities (Fridberg, 2010). This is especially true of the Nordic region.

Ethnicity

Sport and leisure differences between ethnic groups can be complex. Within countries, sporting practices can vary between different ethnic minorities as well as between the minorities and majority populations. All the Nordic countries exhibit differences of one form or another in sports participation between host and immigrant populations. Participation rates are relatively equal in Norway, for example, with the exception of immigrant girls and girls in Sámi areas. In general, nevertheless, native speakers in the Nordic region are considerably more likely to engage in sport.

Ethnicity tends to be a source of difference in forms as well as levels of participation. People born in Denmark, Finland, Norway, Sweden or other European/western countries are more likely to participate in sport (and club-based, competitive games in particular) than people born elsewhere. The largest differences between ethnic groups in the Nordic countries tend to be found, perhaps unsurprisingly, in outdoor activities. It is noteworthy, however, that as elsewhere in the world the biggest differences in levels of participation tend to be between the sexes within ethnic groups than between the groups themselves – reminding us that accounts of sports participation framed exclusively in terms of social class, ethnicity or gender are likely to be inadequate.

Finland, Norway and Sweden experience a particularly acute issue in relation to the indigenous Sámi people. It is important to keep in mind, nevertheless, that while the sporting marginalisation of the Sámi may tell us something about sporting ethnocentrism in the Nordic nations, it is also likely to reflect ethnic minorities' cultural backgrounds. Western sports are not part of indigenous people's cultural heritage (Fahlen & Skille, 2017), where the 'field' sports of hunting, fishing and shooting tend to be valued far more. Nor do Sámi sports appear to be organised in such a way that they might fit neatly into the national sporting systems of many Nordic countries (Skille, 2012). There are Sámi sports associations in Norway and Sweden but the Finnish equivalent no longer exists.

Western sports tend not to have strong cultural roots among the growing numbers of Muslim immigrants in Nordic countries such as Denmark, Norway and Sweden. Notwithstanding the fact that South Asian-heritage youngsters tend to be substantially less physically active than their Western counterparts – with Asian girls especially sedentary – Islamic cultures emphasise PA (as long as it does not take precedence over faith) rather than sports *per se*. This is one substantial reason why Muslim youth are significantly underrepresented in sport in Europe. In addition, some aspects of Islam serve to hinder sports participation among Muslim youth, and among girls in particular: e.g. Islamic norms for gender-segregation and gendered items of clothing (such as the hijab [headscarf] worn by Muslim females) (Walseth, 2016). That said, the situation may be different in Nordic countries, such as Norway, where religiosity seems to have relatively little influence on Muslim girls' enjoyment of many sporting activities in school, and their orientations towards PE and sport are not inevitably determined by faith and religiosity (Walseth, 2015).

Beyond the vexed question of sports participation among the physically and mentally impaired, the main social divisions in sport in the Nordic countries are now found in relation to levels of education, and immigration in particular. People born in the Nordic countries are significantly more likely to participate in sport overall, and the same can be said for those who remain in education beyond the statutory minimum. All-in-all, the differences in participation according to age, class (education) and sex have been relatively small in Nordic countries when compared with many other countries beyond the region. The negative consequences – independently and as they intersect – of class and ethnicity, among other social dynamics, impact females more than males. So far, so typical of all Western countries. What appears different about the Nordic countries is, once again, the differentials between top and bottom. In other words, the children of immigrant families (and Muslims, in particular) and those who leave school at the earliest opportunity appear more likely to play sport and undertake exercise than similar groups beyond the region.

Sport does not create social divisions but it is affected by them and can, and does, sharpen, deepen or diminish such divisions and become characteristic of particular groups (Roberts, 2016d). While democratisation in sports participation has occurred over time in the Nordic countries, particularly in relation to age and gender, social stratification in sport persists in relation to levels of education and ethnicity.

Explaining sports participation in the Nordic countries

In all attempts to explain social phenomena such as sports participation, we need to keep in mind the tentative status of all social science explanations. Thus, the account we provide here needs to be considered as nothing more or less than a plausible explanation of sports participation in the Nordic countries.

In making sense (seeking 'causes') of the patterns and trends in sports participation in the Nordic countries, we take as our starting point Coalter's (2013, 18) observation that sport should be considered largely epiphenomenal: "a secondary set of social practices dependent on and reflecting more fundamental structures, values and processes". The structures are socio-economic and political. The values lie in the cultural traction of active lifestyles in general and sport in particular in the Nordic region. The processes involve, among other things, the cultivation of children's sporting and active leisure dispositions, habits and capital in families, sports clubs and schools, and among friends and peers.

We begin with the role of the economy and politics and policy in explaining trends in sports participation in the Nordic countries.

The significance of the economies of the Nordic countries

Patterns and trends in sports participation in the region are partly explicable in terms of the relative levels of economic development in Nordic countries over the past half century or more. Increases in participation, as well as the popularity of particular settings (e.g. commercial fitness gyms), have corresponded with the substantial improvements in the economic conditions of Nordic societies and individuals since the 1960s. Steady, incremental and cumulative growth in sports participation can at least partly be attributed to a growing middle class and the increased discretionary expenditure associated with upward trends in incomes. Fridberg (2010) has highlighted the manner in which participation rates in Denmark and other Scandinavian countries have correlated with GDP (gross domestic product), insofar as higher GDP has resulted in higher proportions of sports-involved inhabitants. As the Nordic countries have become more prosperous and standards of living correspondingly higher, the proportions of income devoted to leisure in general and sport in particular have tended to rise along with rates of sports participation (Fridberg, 2010). It is important to remember, however, that higher standards of living are not evenly spread across all regions of any particular country. Greenland provides an illustration of how small towns and settlements have been left out of much of the economic development, with the result that Greenland has lower levels of sports participation.

But the economic motor for sports participation is not limited to how 'well-off' countries and their inhabitants are. What also matters is the distribution of income and wealth. It is well established that the more equally income is distributed in a country, the more favourable tend to be a range of social and health indicators, including life expectancy, obesity, mental illness, educational performance (Wilkinson & Pickett, 2009) *and* sport: "more equal countries have more leisure time and higher levels of participation in cultural and sporting activities" (Veal, 2015, 1).

In this context, the marked trend towards increased participation (in exercise, in particular) among older age groups in the Nordic countries may not be so counter-intuitive. The cohorts currently retiring across Europe are the so-called 'baby boomers'[1] who are in better health and have more wealth than any of their predecessors. In the Nordic region, they are doing so in countries with strong social welfare systems that underpin and augment their relatively prosperous and active lifestyles. Many older people in the Nordic countries do not need to cut back dramatically on leisure expenditure and participation.

Relatively high levels of cross-generational mobility and widespread improvements in standards of living since the 1970s have resulted in level of education becoming the favoured proxy measure for social class in the Nordic countries. Education has become an effective indicator of disposition towards participation in sport and exercise. In all of the Nordic countries, the longer individuals remained in education and the higher the educational level achieved, the higher the proportions reporting participating in leisure-time sport or exercise. As well as how much, level of education impacts what Nordic people do and where. In Denmark and Sweden, for example, self-organised and commercial activities tend to be more prevalent among those who remained in education the longest and, although club-organised sport attracts members from all backgrounds, it tends to be disproportionately from those who have remained longer in education.

Around the world, the main sporting divide nowadays is not straightforwardly between the middle and working classes (nor, for that matter, class fractions). Rather it is between an omnivorous and voracious middle class and the rest (Roberts, 2016b). While this will also be true of the Nordic countries, the contributions to this collection suggest that Nordic sporting omnivores tend, in particular, to come from the 'professional' occupational groups normally entered via higher education. All-in-all, while class (largely in the form of levels of education) effects are still to be found in Nordic countries, the correlations between length of education and sports participation underscore the point that sports participation is class (education)-*related* rather than class (education)-*based*.

The effects of recession

Given the seeming importance of socio-economic circumstances for sports participation, it is necessary to reflect on the impact of economic downturns, such as that associated with the 2008 banking crisis and subsequent recession or 'crash' – not least because relative inequalities in income and wealth have widened in all Nordic countries since 2008. Sport, and leisure more generally, cannot remain beyond – in effect, ring-fenced from – the kinds of cutbacks in consumer and public (government) spending associated with austerity. Nor can income differentials and changes in these fail to impact on leisure and sport. Inevitably, households tend to rein in their spending and discretionary expenditure in particular (Roberts, 2016b). Nevertheless, the advantaged classes remain able to spend and do more while the disadvantaged are forced to cut back as austerity hits the less well-off and less-educated most harshly.

Despite this, the impact of the post-2008 recession appears less dramatic than one might have expected in the Nordic countries. Social-class differences in sports participation in much of the Nordic region have shown little sign of undermining sports participation (see, e.g., Strandbu *et al.*, 2017). Indeed, in a number of Nordic countries (e.g. Iceland and Norway), sports participation rates continued their upward trend after 2008 rather than flat-lining, let alone declining. This, we suggest, is for two broad reasons: the first economic and the second sport-specific.

With their relatively large welfare states and high levels of personal taxation, the Nordic social democracies might have been expected to struggle more than the low-tax, low-welfare countries, such as the UK and USA – from the 'liberal' category in Esping-Andersen's 'welfare capitalism' typology. But the opposite appears to have happened. They have coped, relatively successfully (Fouché, 2015). How to explain this? In the first place, countries such as Denmark, Norway and Sweden had very sound public finances to begin with. These sound public finances were rooted in long-term planning, most obviously illustrated by Norway's $1 trillion sovereign-wealth fund and low budget deficits since the 1990s[2]. Consequently, most, if not all, of the Nordic countries had budget surpluses when the crisis occurred. Thus, even though Nordic countries have not remained apart from the widening income inequalities that have been recorded in most parts of the world during the last 30 years, they have been able to respond post-2008 by stimulating their economies without (until relatively recently, at least) having to cut public budgets or increase taxes (Fouché, 2015). In this regard, it is worth noting that the effects of prolonged austerity post-2008 have tended to be (west) Europe-specific (Roberts, 2017) as a consequence of government policy in countries such as the UK. The Nordic countries have not adopted similar policies. Second, despite the fact that the Nordic governments, on the whole, intervened to stimulate their economies and unemployment rose overall, these 'high-tax, high-benefit' welfare systems have served as stabilisers against the vagaries of markets; not least because loss of employment has not meant major loss of income (Fouché, 2015). Coupled with the size of the public-sector workforce (roughly one in three of the overall workforce in the Nordic countries) and the job security of those employed therein, the upshot has been continued spending in relatively vibrant economies (Fouché, 2015). Third, and as well as having introduced tighter regulation of their banking sectors in the 1990s, the Nordic countries have very competitive economies based around exports. All of this has meant that national lottery funding has continued to be available to fund 'sport for all' and municipalities have been able to sustain some degree of support for public sporting facilities.

In addition, it seems that fluctuations in incomes do not necessarily lead to the well-off doing more or the poor doing less (Roberts, 2016b). There tends, for example, to be a limit to how much time the well-off can devote to leisure and sport. Instead, being better-off tends to impact where sport is undertaken – at private gyms, for example. Individuals have, to varying degrees, maintained their spending on and involvement in leisure, sport and exercise. The general tendency among sports players in times of economic downturn is to reduce spending on sporting goods rather than sporting services, and otherwise to do things less frequently or more cheaply rather than to lapse completely. It is possible to engage in most activities at scaled-down or scaled-up levels of spending (Roberts, 2016b).

This stability in sports participation over time also highlights a sport-specific explanation: where people are deeply attached to the pleasures and satisfaction and social bonds that sport can involve, sports careers tend to develop their own structures and momentum, remaining relatively unaffected by wider social changes (Roberts, 2016b). Sport is normative in Nordic countries and serves as a source of continuity in Nordic people's lives. Hence, sports participation rates can be resistant to damage where sport, exercise and physical recreation are deeply embedded in national cultures and, as a consequence, 'part and parcel' of many people's lives from an early age: i.e. where sport has 'cultural traction' (see below). In short, appropriate sports socialisation (from an early age) in the family enables participation to endure and withstand later socio-economic constraints (Birchwood, Roberts & Pollock, 2008). It may be unsurprising, therefore, to find that none of the Nordic participation rates display any clear response to the economic trough post-2008, let alone any earlier recessions, and the adult populations of Nordic countries such as Norway (Strandbu *et al.*, 2017) have maintained their sporting practices.

The tendency for sports participation to be a largely secular trend notwithstanding, in the near future it will be necessary to keep an eye on the implications for sports participation of wider economic inequalities within the Nordic countries. It is feasible that the current stagnation and even downturn in participation in countries such as Denmark and Sweden is partly explicable in terms of the effects of recession on widening inequalities. Nevertheless, the aforementioned stability of sports participation among those committed to it – especially among populations who are relatively better-off in countries where sport has deep cultural roots – means that there are grounds for optimism regarding continued high levels of participation among Nordic citizens.

Politics and policy

The election of more conservative coalition governments in countries such as Finland, Norway and Sweden in recent times notwithstanding, Nordic governments have long demonstrated a willingness (alongside an ability) to intervene economically and socially in an effort to create optimal conditions for individual and social wellbeing. This has had implications for sports participation. The willingness to intervene is best illustrated by Nordic governments' commitment, since the second half of the twentieth century, to the development of social democratic welfare states with a strong focus on equity and inclusiveness (including 'sport for all') as aspects of citizenship and welfare.

The Nordic welfare states

Nordic countries take pride in their welfare states. In recent decades, many have extended the basic rights of citizenship, treating leisure as a branch of the welfare system rather than as merely an industry. In the process, Nordic governments have sought to make sporting opportunities available to all citizens via 'sport for all', thereby extending the notion of social welfare upwards to incorporate leisure and sport. The Nordic model of relatively high expenditure on welfare and large state involvement in the health and general welfare of the population is typified by Sweden, where "the governing of good and healthy citizens has been part of the sport political project for a long time" (Osterlind, 2016, 349–350). In Finland it is considered a social right of citizenship to be afforded sporting possibilities and, since the 1970s, governments have been subsidising sports gyms in even the smallest towns. In Denmark, support for the voluntary sports-club sector is deeply rooted in arguments about the reproduction of democratic values, such as voluntary engagement and binding communities. Consistent with the notion of leisure and sport as an aspect of citizens' welfare, municipalities in Iceland often subsidise participation fees for youngsters from less well-off families. Indeed, those who are less well-off can apply for full funding of participation fees.

The future of sport as part of welfare policy

As Roberts (2016a, 22) observes, around the world, "sport has a multitude of vocal supporters and hardly any opposition". This is especially true in the Nordic countries, where there is little or no opposition to encouraging children and young people into sport: "The value of sport is endorsed by virtually all parents, teachers and other public authority figures" (Roberts, 2016a, 19). Given their commitment to welfare, spending tax-payers' money and lottery funds (the source of much of the funding for sport) on sport has, until recently at least, been relatively uncontentious in the countries featured in this text.

Since the 1970s, however, Western governments have struggled to curb growth in state spending (Roberts, 2016c) and the current age of austerity in government expenditure on public 'goods' is likely to bring with it greater political reluctance to fund universal social services, including sport, out of taxation. In a number of Nordic countries, there is "declining support for the unconditional Nordic welfare state" (Raphael, 2014, 7) and the principle of universalism. What Raphael (2014) calls "welfare state fatigue" may well translate into reduced public and political support for the Nordic model and, as a corollary, a rolling-back of public provision, including sports provision, unless sport is geared towards measurable outcomes. This political shift is manifest in recent policy developments towards sport in Nordic countries.

Sports policy

Despite the Nordic countries' commitment to 'sport for all', the extent of their involvement in sports policy varies quite markedly. Toftegaard Støckel *et al.* (2010, 625) observe that, in Scandinavia, "traditions regarding the voluntary sport organizations have been much more diverse and ranged from heavy interference in Norway to almost no interference in Denmark". In Greenland, for example, the state has been a heavy investor but limited legislator in the field of sport. Denmark does not have a formal, national strategy for sport and exercise, relying heavily on the civil sector in the form of the voluntary sports clubs and their national federations to develop policy and practice. By contrast, Sweden has a century-long tradition of public sports policy aimed at enabling Swedish citizens' access to recreation and meaningful leisure as well, more recently, as sport. Similarly, the Ministry of Education and Culture in Finland makes the vast majority of decisions related to state subsidies for sport. This variability is especially notable in policy terms vis-a-vis one of the central pillars of sport in Nordic countries – the voluntary sports clubs.

Whether the Nordic countries have formal national strategies for sport or not, they have all, historically, signalled their preference for the voluntary sector to take the lead in providing 'sport for all'. More recently, however, the relationship between the state and sport has altered somewhat and it is a feature of recent Nordic history that governments have become increasingly interested in the sports sector's 'wider social role' (Coalter, 2007). In Norway, for example, there has been a trend towards more explicit sports policies than ever before and a more complex system of funding for sports. Most Nordic countries now expect publicly funded bodies to achieve measurable outcomes, usually related to public health and social integration. With pressures on the public purse, the voluntary sports club sector is increasingly expected to impact general levels of PA and health via participation in sport and exercise. Greenland is a notable exception to the tendency to make formal demands of those (typically voluntary sports associations) to whom they provide public subsidies. Unusually, in Greenland the club-organised voluntary sports sector stays largely off the public agenda and public subsidies have not historically been formally tied to any conditions, let alone to a political agenda.

In all discussions of public policy, it is worth bearing in mind that while governments can provide for sport and exercise (through provision of sports halls and public footpaths and cycleways, for example, as well as by funding the voluntary sports-club sector) and, by degrees, constrain those they support financially (e.g. sports clubs), they cannot force participation. This is a cultural matter. As we have already noted in relation to economic fluctuations, those committed to sport tend to maintain constant involvement almost irrespective of government policy initiatives – the considerable benefits of facility provision by municipalities notwithstanding. This may not be what those concerned with sports policy want to hear. Nonetheless, those whose focus is mere participation are likely to be reassured by the realization that the sports-playing public can be quite indifferent to politicians' efforts to shape not only their uses of leisure in general but their involvement in sport in particular (Roberts, 2016b). The marked shift towards commercial provision in the form of gyms is a case in point. Perhaps more important than policies specifically targeting sport are those broader policies that have shaped the more general socio-economic conditions of Nordic people.

The wider policy context

The relatively narrow class and gender differences in sports participation reflect the Nordic region's relatively narrow class and gender differences in the labour market and wider society. All of the contributions to this collection note, for example, that the growth in female sports participation has occurred alongside, and largely as a consequence of, the strengthening position of females in Nordic societies and the corresponding strategic political shifts in favour of women, as well as the growing influence of feminist movements. As indicated in the Introduction, many of the Nordic countries are at the top of the world's most gender-equal countries. The correlation between increased sports participation among Nordic females and their improved position in socio-economic terms is striking. In the Nordic region, especially, second-wave feminism has opened up girls' and women's options in all walks of life, including sport, and they are taking advantage of these. The female parental role-model for children (and girls especially) in the Nordic countries is increasingly likely to be a (paid) working, sporty mother. In terms of ongoing sports participation, the crucial issue is whether young females develop sporting habituses in their early lives and, in the Nordic countries, they appear to do so. The upshot is that young women are no more likely to be forced out of sport by marriage and parenthood and other such life events in young adulthood than young males (Birchwood *et al.*, 2008).

All-in-all, evidence of potentially significant political and ideological changes (alongside the undoubted cultural continuities) notwithstanding, the Nordics cluster at the top of league tables of everything from economic competitiveness through public health, guaranteed income, provision of nursery places and parental leave, to sports participation and happiness – including a well-developed work-life balance in the Nordic countries which, among other things, makes it possible for Nordic citizens to both work and play, i.e. to pursue a career and have ample time for family and leisure activities as well.

The organisation and provision of sport

The Nordic way of playing and organising sport may not be as unique or as homogeneous as sometimes assumed (Veal, 2015). At the same time, however, it has some distinctive features. One of these is the continuing centrality of sports clubs (and volunteer members) to overall sports participation. While elsewhere in the world they may appear under threat, voluntary sports clubs remain a pillar of sporting provision and participation in the Nordic countries, recent trends notwithstanding.

Voluntary sports clubs

Voluntary sports clubs came into being (for men, by men, in the first instance) towards the end of the nineteenth century – well before the emergence and development of the Nordic welfare states. Clubs for activities such as hunting and skiing predate the arrival of modern sports,[3] but the sports-club sector took off as the Nordic countries increasingly imported English sports from the late nineteenth- through to the mid-twentieth century. Consequently, as elsewhere in the Western world, it has been the voluntary sector – joined by the public sector in the latter half of the twentieth century – that has facilitated much sports participation. As Roberts (2016c) observes, public provision alongside voluntary organisation of sports teams and leagues has proved to be the most favourable circumstances for sports participation across the Western world for more than a century.

A feature of Nordic countries that has reinforced the pre-eminent position of voluntary sports clubs is the normative character of civic engagement. Sport in general and sports clubs in particular evidently benefit from – and neatly illustrate – the expectation that adults (especially parents) will become involved in civil organisations, particularly when they have children attending institutions such as schools and sports clubs. Involvement in sports clubs often appears a rite of passage for many Nordic citizens whether as sports participants or, of equal importance, volunteers. Characteristic of sports clubs in the Nordic countries is the assumption that membership involves duties – that members not only pay dues but also play a full and active part in the day-to-day activities of the club (for example, parents adopting voluntary positions as managers and coaches). Many Nordic parents – particularly fathers – are centrally involved in the team-based sports-club scene and spend a large amount of time facilitating their children's involvement in sport as well as coaching, organising and administrating activities (Toftegaard Støckel *et al.*, 2010). Consequently, sports clubs remain important social institutions in Nordic civil society, not least in the popular imagination. Although times are evidently changing as much of the growth in sports participation occurs increasingly beyond sports clubs, they remain a prominent feature of many children's as well as their parents' lives. Participation in the voluntary sports-club sector has never been higher in Iceland, for instance, where clubs remain at the heart of the sporting scene, and the sports club is the primary arena for youth leisure-time sport in Norway, among boys in particular.

The centrality of the voluntary sports-club system to sports participation in the Nordic countries notwithstanding, and the fact that participation in sport via sports clubs remains more popular in the region than elsewhere, it is necessary to keep in mind Coalter's (2013) observation that while sports clubs are important social institutions, high levels of sports participation have not been achieved via organised sport. This is especially so in relation to females, who are less likely to take part in competitive and organised sport. The upshot is that the popularity of clubs has diminished across the region over the past decade or so as a growing number have found their way to commercial provision, such as fitness gyms. At the same time, self-organised activities have gained ground among youth to become by far the most popular organisational form of participation – often in combination with commercial provision and/or voluntary clubs when young. This has resulted in an apparent paradox in countries such as Sweden, where sports participation has been increasing while sports-club membership has been decreasing.

The trend towards youngsters leaving the voluntary sports-club scene earlier is international, as is the shift towards lifestyle sports and informal means of participating. Nonetheless, in Greenland, participation in sports clubs does not differ much between age groups and the voluntary sector has managed to retain a good proportion of adult members in countries such as Denmark. Nor is the move away from clubs as marked in Finland before age 15 – almost 90% of Finnish youth participated in sports-club activities during their youth, albeit boys more than girls. Interestingly, in Norway, increases in participation rates among young people are partly explained by the increased rates of children aged 6–12 becoming members of sports clubs (while for older age groups the memberships rates are stable). In Iceland, sports clubs have maintained their central position despite the emergence and increasing popularity of lifestyle sports. Indeed, lifestyle sports have supplemented rather than displaced the traditional sports and formal sports-club scene in Iceland.

It is worth bearing in mind that part of the explanation for downward trends in sports club membership with age is that sports-club participation rates are relatively high among children and youth in the Nordic countries in the first place. Across the Nordic region, very many children experience sport through sports clubs in their early years. It is evidently the sports clubs that play a part in the development of young Nordics emerging and developing sporting abilities, habits and predispositions.

Fifty years ago, participation took place in voluntary clubs for the most part. Nowadays, the voluntary sports-club sector has been joined by public facilities, commercial venues and the natural environment – a shift towards self-organised sports participation and private/commercial settings. All-in-all, even though sports-club memberships have been declining over the past decade or more in the Nordic countries as a whole – by roughly a quarter in the three decades between 1985 and 2015 in Norway, for example – the voluntary sector in sport has not reduced significantly in terms of numbers of clubs since the public sector and commerce became involved with participatory sport in the mid- and late-twentieth century, respectively. In part, this is likely to be due to the fact that the Nordic welfare states have never sought to utilise public provision to duplicate let alone replace the voluntary sector. Rather, they have supplemented sports club provision with public facilities while making improved outdoor and indoor sports facilities and amenities available to voluntary clubs. The rapid growth of public and commercial provision notwithstanding, voluntary sports clubs have continued to offer something unique in participatory terms, not least because voluntary sports clubs and societies provide the kinds of experience that cannot easily be replicated by the public sector or commerce. However, in these 'post-crash' times it remains an open question whether Nordic governments are doing enough to protect the voluntary sports-club sector, let alone enabling it to flourish, and whether the 'implicit contract' (Fahlén and Stenling, 2015) between national and local governments and voluntary, non-profit and membership-based club sport is sustainable. It certainly remains intact at present.

The issue of political support is also pertinent for the public sector because, while commercial and voluntary sports provision can be relied on to be driven by the profit motive and sheer enthusiasm, respectively, the public sector is at the mercy of politicians and their policy-makers.

Public provision

The rapid growth of local authority (municipal)-funded and -managed public sporting facilities was a feature of increasing levels of sports participation in the West in the 1970s and 1980s. The emergence of multi-sport, indoor facilities heavily subsidised for the user is generally accepted to have been a key driver in the significant upsurge in sports participation around that time. Making facilities available to the general public and voluntary sports clubs has characterised municipal policy towards sport in the Nordic countries. The vast majority of sport facilities in the Nordic region continue to be owned by the municipalities and sports clubs.

As well as building more specialist sports facilities in recent years to supplement the multi-sport halls, the municipalities play a major role in ensuring that amenities – including the natural environment – are available, maintained and accessible. This includes outdoor spaces, playing fields, sports centres and swimming pools and, more recently, facilities responsive to the growing appeal of lifestyle activities. Running and walking trails, outdoor fitness stations, skateboard parks, parkour venues, and public (ball) pitches are examples of the increased opportunities for lifestyle sports provided in local neighbourhoods by the Danish municipalities, for example. In countries such as Greenland and Iceland, sports clubs also function as community centres for a wide range of communal activities and in regions relatively remote from the main population centres they often serve as the focal point or 'heart' of the local community. This is likely to be an additional reason for municipalities to continue subsidising such facilities. Nonetheless, the intensification of the squeeze on the public purse, evident in Nordic countries as well as across the world, provides an additional challenge for public facilities that depend on municipal/state funding.

Public provision of sports facilities as an aspect of leisure as a social service is gradually being supplemented in Nordic people's leisure-sport lifestyles by leisure as a commercial enterprise (Roberts, 2016d).

Commercial provision

Commercialisation has always been a feature of leisure, and one of the defining features of sports participation in the Nordic countries in recent decades, as elsewhere, has been the growing popularity of health and fitness gyms and commercial provision more generally. The commercial sector is now bigger than the voluntary sports-club sector in both Finland and Norway. As well as being particularly popular among females – while more males are to be found in sports clubs, more females use private gyms – commercialisation has spread into the leisure lives of the young and old alike. This is a key element of a wider trend: all countries display a movement in organizational terms from traditional club-organised participation towards more self- and commercially organised sport and exercise, resulting in a broader and more diverse participatory 'market' that appeals more readily to all ages and both sexes. It is worth noting, nevertheless, that the Nordic countries established strong voluntary sectors and public provision before leisure and sport became so commercial. Nowadays, public facilities (made available for general public use, on a pay-as-you-go basis) and commercial settings (often involving monthly subscription) appear more congruent with the preferred lifestyles of both young and old than the types of commitment involved in club membership.

It is important to remember that commerce adds to rather than eliminates the existing 'offer' – together, the public sector, voluntary associations and commercial providers have become the triple pillars of sports provision. The rapid development of commercial gyms has not, for example, impacted on the provision of opportunities to play football or handball in the Nordic nations. Commercial sports provision (largely in the form of gyms) has simply enabled sports consumers to develop individualised sporting lifestyles including and/or based around lifestyle sports. This commercial provision does tend, nevertheless, to reinforce social divisions, especially those based on social class/education. In all Nordic countries, it tends to be the middle classes (particularly the highly educated) who are more likely to take advantage of commercial provision.

Commerce caters for demands that can generate a profit and, in the process, can be incredibly innovative (Roberts, 2016d). The indoor variants on skydiving, surfing, skiing and climbing (see Salome & van Bottenburg, 2016) exemplify the transformation of some recreational (adventure) activities into sporting enterprises. Most participatory sports cannot, however, be transformed in this way. Commercialization cannot eliminate the voluntary sector as long as it meets a need and there are members with sufficient enthusiasm for their particular sports (Roberts, 2016d). Like public facilities, commercial provision simply supplements existing provision. One challenge for any sport and exercise provider, whether voluntary sports club, public facility or commercial venue, is how to tune into the demand for more lifestyle sports while retaining the informal, individualised and self-determined elements that characterises these types of activities in the kind of institutionalised setting that almost inevitably undermines their original appeal (Rowe, 2012). The commercial sporting offer needs to be enjoyable and involve identity-conferring or confirming experiences if it is to attract customers (Roberts, 2016d).

Settings and venues

The natural environment

The significance of socio-economic conditions notwithstanding, some aspects of sports participation are at least partially explained in terms of geography and climate as well as national histories and cultures. For example, sports and activities with cultural ties to the Arctic are especially popular among the Inuit (the majority ethnic group in Greenland) and the Sámi (a significant minority in Finland, Norway and Sweden).

Natural capital in the form of natural environments is a gift of nature and the Nordic countries have a wealth of natural resources. Some of the region, for example, is semi-arctic, thereby facilitating a range of winter as well as summer sports. Unsurprisingly, all forms of skiing are popular in Norway and Sweden. Similarly, outdoor activities associated with woodland and fells (e.g. mountain-biking, orienteering and running) are especially popular in Finland, Norway and Sweden. While adults are the main participants in outdoor settings and Nordic youngsters tend to be the main users of sports halls, it is commonplace for children to play outdoors from an early age. It is likely to be no accident, therefore, that the proportion of youth engaging in sport or PA in a park or outdoors is particularly high in the Nordic countries (van Tuyckom, 2016). While the semi-arctic character of parts of the region can facilitate involvement in a range of seasonal sports, it can also hinder. Sports participation in some countries (e.g. Greenland) and regions (the northern arctic areas) often becomes 'the art of the possible'. Over the course of a year, the cold, snow- and ice-bound and dark conditions can impact significantly on many popular activities such as football, running and walking and this may be part of the explanation for the relatively depressed levels of sports participation in Greenland.

The omnipresence of nature (coasts, fjords, rivers, mountains, fields and forests) in sparsely populated countries has necessitated a closeness to nature, not least in terms of the use of natural resources for survival (hunting, fishing, forestry, agriculture) but also for physical recreation and sport. Very many towns and even cities in the Nordic countries have relatively easy access to the natural environment and this is enhanced by good transport infrastructure. In such circumstances, it is hardly surprising that outdoor family recreation is a leisure norm.

The built environment

Publicly funded sports centres and commercial gyms are especially popular venues in all Nordic countries. As elsewhere, the initial sharp rise in sports participation in the Nordic region coincided with the new sport and leisure centres opened since the 1970s as public provision took off. Public leisure facilities are plentiful across the Nordic region. Urbanization, however, seems to influence the organisational pattern of provision, with a higher private-sector share and lower voluntary sports club share in municipalities around big cities in Denmark, for example.

Nowadays, the built environment incorporates the 'indoorization' (Salome & van Bottenburg, 2016) of some adventure activities – the increasing indoor variants on skydiving, surfing, bouldering/rock-climbing and skiing (Salome & van Bottenburg, 2016), for example. In some cases, these indoor adventure facilities have lowered the thresholds of skill required and risk involved as well as the cost of participation, thereby making some 'adventure' sports more tempting, more accessible and easier, particularly for new participants; in other words, more democratised. While commerce may weaken the challenging element associated with 'peak experiences' or 'flow' (Csikzentmihalyi, 1990) in adventure sports – more likely to be encountered in the 'real thing', outdoors – this is not true for all commercial sporting ventures. Indoor rock-climbing and skiing, while safer, are in themselves demanding and potentially flow-generating.

Technological developments

The benefits of landscapes notwithstanding, major changes in rates and forms of sports participation tend to be driven by and partly explainable in terms of new provision (indoor sports halls in the 1970s and 1980s being a prime example) in conjunction with new technologies (e.g. mountain bikes, gym equipment and indoor climbing walls) and new uses of existing technologies (e.g. resistance machines in gyms, camming devices for climbing, fat tyres and suspension on mountain bikes, wingsuits for skydiving and waxless cross-country skis), as well as these uses becoming more widely available than hitherto (e.g. mountain-biking trails, health-and-fitness gyms).

Technological developments (e.g. skateboards and BMX bikes) and facility provision (e.g. skate parks and BMX tracks) are often commercial and public developments that result from sporting innovations driven by participants. This has been the case with many of the lifestyle sports that have been a feature of the explosion in sports participation in the West since the 1970s. The ingenuity of players has been aided considerably by technological developments often driven by commercial interest exploiting the technology behind revolutions in biking, boarding, blading and the like.

The cultural traction of sport

Their undoubted significance notwithstanding, it is important to recognise that sports participation in the Nordic region is not simply an epiphenomenon of the socio-economic conditions and policies of the last half-century or, for that matter, the geography of the region or the rapid growth of commercial provision. In other words, the likely significance for sports participation of far greater levels of economic and gender parity in the Nordic countries, as well as political commitment to continue to fund and treat leisure and sport as part of welfare provision and commercial innovation, is that it is unlikely that these will have been the only contributory factors to the high levels and increasingly varied forms of sports participation in the region. Sports participation is multi-dimensional and the 'causal' explanation is likely, therefore, to be multi-factorial. While money and opportunity are necessary for much sports participation, they are by no means sufficient: contact with ('sporty') people who can facilitate youngsters' access to particular sporting experiences (so-called 'social capital') and possession of the necessary skills and knowledge (so-called 'cultural' or 'sporting capital') tend to be additional pre-requisites for sports participation. It seems likely, therefore, that improvements in the general political, economic and social conditions of the Nordic population, and of females in particular, have augmented existing propensities towards active travel, outdoor recreation and sports participation – what amounts to the enormous cultural traction of sport (Roberts, 2016a).

As indicated in the Introduction, cultural traction refers to the rootedness of sport in what sociologists might call the 'group habitus' or 'natural attitude'; in other words, those aspects of physical culture deeply embedded in the everyday attitudes (or 'second nature') and practices of individuals and groups in particular societies and nations – the habits and dispositions acquired (via socialization) by Nordic peoples as a consequence of growing up and living in cultures within which sport is so common-place and so highly valued. The cultural traction of sport in the Nordic region needs to be set in historical context.

Physically active cultures in the Nordic countries have their historic roots in what might nowadays be termed 'active travel' (in other words, the various ways in which Nordic peoples travelled to and from work and home) – whether walking (including fell-walking), skiing (cross-country and ski-mountaineering), snow-shoeing, sledding and tobogganing, horse-riding, canoeing and kayaking, sailing, rowing and cycling. Alongside active travel was (and, of course, remains) outdoor life, in the form of the hunting and gathering cultures (that had their origins in subsistence among the agricultural communities that Nordic nations were and many regions remain) that have become associated with *friluftsliv* and are manifest in the hunting, fishing, shooting and 'berry and mushroom picking' categories found in some Nordic countries' participant surveys, such as Norway.

Throughout the twentieth century, modern sports were imported to the Nordic region and planted in the fertile soil of existing physically active outdoor lifestyles and cultures. The upshot is that in countries such as Finland, Norway and Sweden, citizens consider their national and regional cultural identities to be grounded in outdoor life and sport as much as social welfare democracies. Outdoor lifestyles were normative and sport became normative, hence the reason that many Nordic youths' and adults' leisure-sport lifestyles consist of a mix of conventional sports and outdoor activities.

The leisure-sport lifestyles of Nordic people tend also to reflect more recent developments. Some elements of sports participation are the outcomes of globalisation (the popularity of football and the growth of fitness gyms are prime examples). At the same time, however, sports participation in every country tends to consist of a mix of the global and the local – a process known as 'glocalisation'. The Nordic countries maintenance of traditional national (e.g. bandy and cross-country skiing), regional (e.g. handball), local (e.g. dog-sledding) and ethnic (e.g. reindeer racing) forms of sport and physical recreation illustrate this. While sport and physical recreation in the Nordic region bears the hallmark of both globalization and glocalization, this does not amount to homogenisation. In all Nordic countries, the sporting profiles of participants retain features of traditional physical activities and recreational cultures. The increased variety of global sports available notwithstanding, much sport and physical recreation across the Nordic region continues to exhibit distinct local and regional characteristics alongside international influences. It is, indeed, glocal. In each of the Nordic countries, modern sports have taken their meanings from the local, regional and national cultural contexts and the powerful impressions these have left. Particular uses of leisure – and especially those involving physical exercise in the form of sport or active outdoor recreation – become part of what it means to be a Dane, Finn, Greenlander, Icelander, Norwegian or Swede; indeed, Scandinavian and Nordic.

The growth of lifestyle and adventure sports in the Nordic countries and around the developed world and the associated splintering of tastes and lifestyles available to young people in the twenty-first century (Roberts, 2016c) reflect processes which collectively have come to be known as 'youth's new condition'. The new circumstances that youth find themselves in involve the extension, destandardization and individualisation of the life stage of youth (Roberts, 2016d) – including the individualisation of educational, employment, family and housing biographies (see Green, Smith & Roberts, 2005). The upshot is that although sports-club activities retain a central position among the young, adults nowadays tend to prefer to exercise in unorganised or informal settings (of the kinds associated with lifestyle sports and activities) alone or small groups (of friends, for example). The relatively low proportion of youth (16–19 years) normally sports-active in Greenland, for instance, might have something to do with youth transitions (e.g. from education to employment) pushing sport/exercise off youngsters' immediate agendas.

The popularity of lifestyle sports (worldwide as well as in the Nordic nations) also points up the general weakening of traditions, including deference towards adults and traditional constraints and authority more generally, such as the voluntary sports sector, associated with a process of informalisation. Youngsters negotiate their engagement with traditional constraints, such as expectations regarding *friluftsliv*. They display a growing desire to 'do it for themselves'. This trend is strongest among young people and especially those in the middle classes – the pre-eminent class grouping in the Nordic countries. These young people are likely to want (indeed, expect) to negotiate their own leisure and sporting profiles and trajectories, and they display a growing appetite for consumer goods and services. For the reasons previously mentioned, none of this has necessarily meant a weakening of the voluntary and public sectors.

Cultural traction and public health

Alongside the cultural traction of sport, it is worth briefly mentioning the heightened awareness of physical and mental health globally but in the Nordic countries especially. Participation in exercise rose among older people across the developed world in the latter decades of the twentieth century, "becoming understood as a more 'normal' part of the ageing process in Western countries" (Gard & Dionigi, 2016, 738). This is particularly true in the Nordic region. Senior or 'masters' sports events are growing and 'active ageing' has become the watchword for public health bodies. It is manifest in the upward trends in such activities as health and fitness, running, spinning, cycling and walking.

Cultural traction, socialisation and the family

Although some young Nordics nowadays see themselves in relation to sports participation as simply 'born this way', in reality they grow up with sport (in the broadest sense of the term) as a deep-seated aspect of Nordic culture such that it has become an established part of what sociologists would call the 'group habitus'. As all of the chapters indicate, socialisation into sport and physical recreation tends to begin early in the Nordic countries and tends to be all-pervasive. Attachments to sport that form the foundations of sporting habits typically begin in the family (Quarmby, 2016), and the Nordic countries have a long history of sport as a normal part of family life. Indeed, in the Nordic countries it is normal for parents and children to belong to and attend the same sports clubs and, as demonstrable in Greenland, children whose parents are sports-active are significantly more likely to be involved in sport.

Nordic parents take seriously the cultural requirements of 'good parenting' (Johansen & Green, 2017) as part of meeting their responsibilities in terms of socialising their youngsters into their country's culture, including sporting culture. Stefansen, Smette and Strandbu (2018) point to a marked generational change in Norway – that can plausibly be extrapolated to the rest of the Nordic region – since the 1970s and 1980s, when most parents were not involved in sport. Nowadays, they observe, parents in the middle classes, in particular, view involvement in sports not only as a means of enhancing their child's development but also as a way of connecting with the child emotionally. Stefansen *et al.* (2018) attribute this 'new role' of sport in the practice of parenthood to the increasing normalisation of youth involvement in sports from the 1970s alongside the new norms for greater involvement of parents.

As part of this 'concerted cultivation' (Lareau, 2003), parents employ a range of strategies (e.g. enrolling their children in sports clubs and sampling a variety of activities) and practices – both active (e.g. equipment, logistical, encouragement) and passive (e.g. modelling sporting behaviours and transmitting values (Quarmby, 2016)). Elsewhere in the West, mothers tend to perform much of the 'hidden work' of sports socialisation – planning and generally enabling participation and encouraging, while fathers are far more likely to participate directly with their sons (Quarmby, 2016). But this is not so true in Nordic countries where mothers are every bit as likely to participate with and provide role models for their sons and daughters and fathers are more likely to be involved with the 'hidden work'.

Youngsters do not, however, simply and straightforwardly adopt their parents' sporting tastes and behaviours unreflexively. While family transmission explains the stability of the rate for a social aggregate, young people will develop their own particular mixes of sporting habits. Sports clubs, as well as parents and friends, can be a catalyst for these (Johansen & Green, 2017). All-in-all, the family appears a significant variable in sports participation, not least because, as Birchwood *et al.* (2008) demonstrated, appropriate sports socialisation (from an early age) in the family may enable participation to endure and withstand later socio-economic constraints. Childhood appears the critical life stage for laying enduring foundations for long-term careers in sport (Roberts, 2016a), as with many other forms of leisure.

In this regard, one interesting aspect of sports participation in the Nordic countries is the likelihood of youngsters continuing in sport well into the youth life stage. Lifelong sports participants have usually not only developed sporting habits in the family as children but, crucially, have continued to practise and have maintained frequent participation in a wide range of sports throughout the youth life stage. "If", as Roberts (2016a, 23) notes, "these foundations are not built by this stage and sustained throughout youth, it is unlikely that individuals will play sport regularly into and then through adulthood". While the sporting repertoires that are often a precondition for lifelong participation are usually formed during childhood, often in sports-active families, they need to be sustained through youth. That is clearly happening in the Nordic region and helps to explain both the relatively high levels of sports participation during adulthood but also the 'bounce back' effect likely to occur beyond the main career and family years.

Childhood and sport appear "a natural couplet" (Roberts, 2016a, 20) in the Nordic countries and very many have sport built into their routines, quite often on a daily basis. The upshot appears to be that very many young Nordics enter youth with the foundations for sporting habituses in place. Hence, as they progress through the life stage of youth, their attachments to sport are less vulnerable than they might otherwise be. Even when the escape into their own (increasingly young adult-oriented) worlds and move from under the control and supervision of adults, they are more likely to remain favourably predisposed towards sports participation, despite the many other things they could be (and often are) doing as sports faces more competition from alternative leisure activities during youth.

Concluding remarks

Based upon existing research, we had anticipated that much of the evidence – presented here for the first time in the round – would simply confirm what we suspected: (i) that Nordic people on the whole do a lot of sport, many regularly; (ii) and do so in a wide variety of forms – including both conventional sports and so-called lifestyle and adventurous sports; (iii) the peak in sports participation would come significantly later during youth than the early years of secondary schooling typically found elsewhere; (iv) there would be 'bounce back' into relatively high levels of participation among older age groups in some countries; (v) as well as a high degree of convergence between the sexes, but less so between the social classes or 'host' populations and some minority ethnic groups; and last, but by no means least, (vi) that in one form or another there would be clear evidence of deliberate government intervention in creating favourable conditions for 'sport for all'. We already suspected, and the various chapters simply confirmed, these things.

At the same time, however, the country contributions have thrown up some surprises. We had not anticipated (i) the volatility in adults sporting lives in some countries, in the form of on-going movement into and out of activities – similar to the patterns evident in youngsters' sporting lives; (ii) examples of widespread regular participation alongside increasing levels of sedentariness; (iii) the possibility of a younger generation establishing weaker attachments to sport; and (iv) the extent of the shift away from sports clubs in some countries. In organizational terms, we had not quite anticipated the variability in terms of state involvement with regard to sports policies and strategies. In terms of provision, we had understood the significance of the public sector (the municipalities) with regard to public facilities. We had not, however, anticipated the extent and rapidity of growth of commercial provision and participation therein, not only at health-and-fitness gyms but also at dance studios and the like. In addition, while we had anticipated the significance of the outdoors (in nature but more especially within urban areas) for sports participation, we may have underestimated just how popular a setting it would be and, by extension, the significance of 'everyman's right' – the right of citizens to roam freely.

Is there anything Nordic about Nordic sport?

All-in-all, Nordic countries have unusually high rates of sports participation. But does this mean that there is something particular, not to say peculiar, about them that creates propitious circumstances for sports participation? The answer is 'yes and no'! Eurobarometer data serve to remind us that the Nordic countries are not truly exceptional in participatory terms. A handful of European countries have almost comparable (if somewhat lower) rates of sports participation, e.g. Luxembourg, the Netherlands, Belgium and Slovenia (van Tuyckom, 2016). What the Nordic countries reveal, nevertheless, is how favourable conditions for sports participation can be formed from the cultural traction of sport (populations who are sufficiently predisposed towards, and habitually involved in, sport – a group habitus) in conjunction with favourable socio-economic conditions (that result in relatively narrow differentials between socio-economic groups), all aided and abetted by a political commitment to resourcing sport and sports facilities (in pursuance of 'sport for all' as an aspect of citizenship) as well as a suitable (natural and human-made) environment. Each of these may be necessary. Together, they appear very likely to be sufficient. This is what Coalter (2013) was alluding to when he observed that sport should be considered as largely a secondary effect or by-product of more fundamental structures (socio-economic and political), values (the cultural traction of sport) and processes (widespread socialization into sport and exercise).

Current trends towards neo-liberal, post-industrial, increasingly globalised, ICT (information and communication technology)-dependent economies may well have consequences for Nordic societies – and sports participation therein – that are yet to become fully apparent. There may be grounds for optimism, however. While particular branches of sport may be threatened (e.g. some club-based team sports), sports participation as a whole is developing. Austerity in the West is not depressing sports participation (Roberts, 2017). We have yet to see if participation is stagnating in the Nordic region as a whole despite the continued growth into the noughties witnessed in Denmark, Iceland, Norway and Sweden. Indeed, membership of fitness gyms has continued to grow even where sports participation may have begun to flat-line and overall levels of PA and fitness have declined. The main trend in sports participation in the Nordic countries, as elsewhere, nevertheless, "is horizontal – out of competitive sports, especially competitive team sports, and into individualised forms of physically active recreation" (Roberts, 2017, 127). This is a trend that has been underway for several decades and has continued through recessions in the 1990s and 2000s and shows no signs of ending, economic downturn notwithstanding. All-in-all, the changes in sports participation in the Nordic countries post the 1970s/1980s boom have, for the most part, been steady and incremental. They look likely to continue this way. While there may be concerns in all of the Nordic countries regarding the direction of travel in sports participation, there is certainly no crisis as we write.

The Nordic countries are not true comparators for other countries. It is likely to be the greater socio-economic inequalities in countries beyond the Nordic countries that make the region unrealistic as a benchmark for sports participation – not least because socio-economic determinants of participation inevitably lie well beyond the control of sports policy (Coalter, 2013). Nevertheless, the Nordic lands offer evidence for everyone's preferred policy for boosting participation – the 'big society' (e.g. voluntarism), state support, greater equality and so on.[4] Nordic governments' pro-sport policies (and funding, in particular) work because they operate through and complement a strong voluntary sector and on a population with particularly strong sporting, exercise and physical recreation habituses in environments conducive to physically active and sporting lifestyles.

Notes

1 The term 'baby boomer' refers to those people born during the 20 or so years following the end of the Second World War who experienced conditions of increasing economic growth and relative prosperity following the years of scarcity and deprivation associated with the previous three decades.

2 For the first time since the mid-1990s, Norway ran a budget deficit in 2016 whereby state expenditure exceeded state revenues.
3 For example, in 2018 The Norwegian Trekking Association (DNT: Den Norske Turistforening) celebrates its 150-year anniversary.
4 We are grateful to Ken Roberts for this observation.

References

Bairner, A. (2010). What's Scandinavian about Scandinavian sport? *Sport in Society*, *13*(4), 734–743.

Birchwood, D., Roberts, K. and Pollock, G. (2008). Explaining differences in sport participation rates among young adults: evidence from the South Caucasus. *European Physical Education Review*, *14*(3), 283–300.

Celis-Morales, C. and Gill, J. (2017). Cycling to work: major new study suggests health benefits are staggering. *The Conversation*, 20 April 2017.Available from: https://theconversation.com/cycling-to-work-major-new-study-suggests-health-benefits-are-staggering-76292.

Coalter, F. (1999). Sport and recreation in the United Kingdom: flow with the flow or buck the trends? *Managing Leisure*, *4*(1), 24–39.

Coalter, F. (2007). *A Wider Social Role for Sport. Who's Keeping the Score?* London: Routledge.

Coalter, F. (2013). Game plan and the spirit level, the class ceiling and the limits of sports policy? *International Journal of Sport Policy and Politics*, *5*(1), 3–19.

Csikszentmihalyi, M. (1990). *Flow. The Psychology of Optimal Experience*. New York: Harper and Row.

Engstrom, L.-M. (2008). Who is physically active? Cultural capital and sports participation from adolescence to middle age – a 38-year follow-up study. *Physical Education and Sport Pedagogy*, *13*(4), 319–343.

Fahlén, J. and Skille, E. (2017). State sport policy for indigenous sport: inclusive ambitions and exclusive coalitions. *International Journal of Sport Policy and Politics*, *9*(1), 173–187.

Fahlén, J. and Stenling, C. (2015). Country profile: Sport policy in Sweden. *International Journal of Sport Policy and Politics*, *2*(1), 1–17.

Fouché, G. (2015). Why Scandinavia can teach us a thing or two about surviving a recession. Sweden, Denmark and Norway are coping better with the economic downturn than most countries, despite having an expensive welfare system. *The Guardian*. 5 August 2009.

Fridberg, T. (2010). Sport and exercise in Denmark, Scandinavia and Europe. *Sport in Society*, *13*(4), 583–592.

Gard, M. and Dionigi, R.A. (2016). The world turned upside down: sport, policy and ageing. *International Journal of Sport Policy and Politics*, *8*(4), 737–743.

Green, K., Smith, A. and Roberts, K. (2005). Social class, young people, sport and physical education. In K. Green and K. Hardman (eds.) *Physical Education: Essential Issues*. (pp. 180–196). London: Sage.

Harris, S., Nichols, G. and Taylor, M. (2017). Bowling even more alone: trends towards individual participation in sport. *European Sport Management Quarterly*, *17*(3), 290–311.

Lareau, A. (2003). *Unequal Childhoods: Class, Race, and Family Life*. Berkeley and Los Angeles, California: University of California Press.

Johansen, P.-F. and Green, K. (2017). 'It's alpha omega for succeeding and thriving': parents, children and sporting cultivation in Norway. *Sport, Education and Society*. DOI:10.1080/13573322.2017.1401991.

Osterlind, M. (2016). Sport policy evaluation and governing participation in sport: governmental problematics of democracy and health. *International Journal of Sport Policy and Politics*, 8(3), 347–362.

Quarmby, T. (2016). Parenting and youth sport. In K. Green and A. Smith (eds.) *Routledge Handbook of Youth Sport*. (pp. 209–217). London: Routledge.

Raphael, D. (2014). The case of the Nordic nations. *Scandinavian Journal of Public Health*, *42*, 7–17.

Roberts, K. (2016a). Youth leisure as the context for youth sport. In K. Green and A. Smith (eds.) *Routledge Handbook of Youth Sport*. (pp. 18–25). London: Routledge.

Roberts, K. (2016b). Social class and leisure during recent recessions in Britain. *Leisure Studies*, *34*(2), 131–149.

Roberts, K. (2016c). Young people and social change. In K. Green and A. Smith (eds.) *Routledge Handbook of Youth Sport*. (pp. 10–17). London: Routledge.

Roberts, K. (2016d). *The Business of Leisure: Tourism, Sport, Events and Other Leisure Industries*. London: Palgrave.

Roberts, K. (2017). Sport in Europe's era of austerity: crisis or adaptation? *International Journal of Sociology and Social Policy*, *37*(1/2), 123–130.

Roberts, K. and Brodie, D.A. (1992). *Inner-City Sport: Who Plays and What Are the Benefits?* Culemborg, The Netherlands: Giordano Bruno.

Rowe, N.F. (2012). *Review of the Research Evidence on Young People and Sport. What Does it Tell Us About Their Underlying Attitudes and Interest in Sport and the Ingredients For Successful Programme Design?* London: Sport England.

Salome, L. and van Bottenburg, M. (2016). Indoorising the outdoors. Tempting young people's interest in lifestyle sports. In K. Green and A. Smith (eds.) *Routledge Handbook of Youth Sport*. (pp. 175–185). London: Routledge.

Scheerder, J., Vanreusel, B., Taks, M. and Renson, R. (2005). Social stratification patterns in adolescents' active sports participation behaviour: a time trend analysis 1969–1999. *European Physical Education Review*, *11*(1), 5–27.

Scheerder, J., Thomis, M., Vanreusel, B., Lefevre, J., Renson, R., Vanden Eynde, B. and Beunen, G.P. (2006). Sports participation among females from adolescence to adulthood: a longitudinal study. *International Review for the Sociology of Sport*, *41*(3–4), 413–430.

Skille, E.Å. (2012). Ethno-politics and state sport policy – the case of how the Sámi Sport Association–Norway challenged the Norwegian confederation of sport's monopoly for state subsidies to sport. *Scandinavian Sport Studies Forum*, *3*, 143–165.

Stefansen, K., Smette, I. and Strandbu, Å. (2018). Understanding the increase in parents' involvement in organized youth sports. *Sport, Education and Society*, *23*(2), 162–172.

Strandbu, A., Gulløy, E., Andersen, P.L., Seippel, Ø. and Dalen, H.B. (2017). Ungdom, idrett og klasse: fortid, samtid og framtid [Youth, sport and class: past, present and future trends]. *Norsk Sociologisk Tidsskrift [Norwegian Journal of Sociology]*, *1*(2), 132–151.

Toftegaard Støckel, J., Strandbu, Å., Solenes, O., Jørgensen, P. and Fransson, K. (2010). Sport for children and youth in the Scandinavian countries. *Sport in Society, Cultures, Commerce, Media, Politics*. Special Issue, *Sport in Scandinavian Societies*, *13*(4), 625–642.

van Bottenburg, M. Rijnen, B. and van Sterkenburg, J. (2005). *Sport Participation in the European Union: Trends and Differences*. Utrecht: Mulier Institute.

van Tuyckom, C. (2016). Youth sport participation. A comparison among European member states. In K. Green and A. Smith (eds.) *Routledge Handbook of Youth Sport.* (pp. 61–71). London: Routledge.

Vanreusel, B., Renson, R., Beunen, G., Albrecht, L., Lefevre, J., Lysens, R. and Vanden Eynde, B. (1997). A longitudinal study of youth sports participation and adherence to sport in adulthood. *International Review for the Sociology of Sport*, *32*(4), 373–387.

Veal, A.J. (2015). Leisure, income inequality and the Veblen effect: cross-national analysis of leisure time and sport and cultural activity. *Leisure Studies*, *35*(2), 1–26.

Walseth, K. (2015). Muslim girls' experiences in physical education in Norway: what role does religiosity play? *Sport, Education and Society*, *20*(3), 304–322.

Walseth, K. (2016). Sport, religion and religiosity. In K. Green and A. Smith (eds.) *Routledge Handbook of Youth Sport.* (pp. 297–307). Oxford: Routledge.

Wilkinson, R. and Pickett, K. (2009). *The Spirit Level: Why More Equal Societies Almost Always Do Better*. London: Penguin.

Index

Page numbers in *italics* refer to figures. Page numbers in **bold** refer to tables.